The Dynamics of Japan's Relations with Africa

The Dynamics of Japan's Relations with Africa
South Africa, Tanzania and Nigeria

Kweku Ampiah

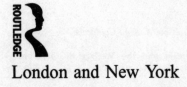

London and New York

First published 1997
by Routledge
11 New Fetter Lane, London EC4P 4EE

Simultaneously published in the USA and Canada
by Routledge
29 West 35th Street, New York, NY 10001

© 1997 Kweku Ampiah. The author has asserted his moral right.

Typeset in Times by LaserScript Limited, Mitcham, Surrey
Printed and bound in Great Britain by
Mackays of Chatham PLC, Chatham, Kent

British Library Cataloguing in Publication Data
A catalogue record for this book is available from the British Library

Library of Congress Cataloging in Publication Data
A catalogue record for this book has been requested

ISBN 0–415–14483–3

For
Ato
and in memory of my Grandmother
(Aunti) Ɛfua Mends

Contents

Series editor's preface

. . . we are a people whose glorious history will bear to be held up to the gaze of Western nations. We have learned a great many things from the West, but there are some instances of our having outstripped our tutors.

So wrote Count Okuma in *Fifty Years of New Japan*, published in 1910, some five years after Japan had emerged victorious in the Russo-Japanese war. Over the eighty-six years that have elapsed since those words were written, the history of Japan's relations with the rest of the world has passed through phases more turbulent than Okuma could probably have imagined. The tragic and terrible history of the 1930s and 1940s gave way, however, to decades in which the Japanese forged an amazing (and often deserved) reputation for economic development and efficiency. The idea of the Japanese outstripping their tutors is no longer as exotic as it must have sounded to an English-speaking readership in 1910, but its content has been radically changed with the passage of time. At the same time, Japan's performance and practice continues to attract withering skepticism from some Americans and others. In a recent message on the Internet, Chalmers Johnson attacks named 'Chrysanthemum Clubbers' and writes that one of his interlocutors 'seems not to know that Japan has basked in the favorable and exceptional treatment of the United States from John Foster Dulles's peace treaty to Mickey Kantor's last minute dive last summer in the auto talks.' How the Japanese seek to resolve the dilemma of how far they can preserve a distinctive Japanese identity and practice in an increasingly globalizing world is fascinating to watch.

The Nissan Institute/Routledge Japanese Studies Series is ten years old in 1996. The Series seeks to foster an informed and balanced, but not uncritical, understanding of Japan. One of its aims is to show the depth and variety of Japanese institutions, practices and ideas. Another is, by using comparison, to see what lessons, positive and negative, can be drawn for other countries. The tendency in commentary on Japan to resort to

outdated, ill-informed or sensational stereotypes still remains, and needs
to be combatted.

Relations between Japan and Africa have seldom attracted serious
scholarly attention. Africa has never been a major focus of Japanese
overseas development aid, investment or trade. Nevertheless, it would be
quite incorrect to say that Japan totally ignores Africa, and this book by Dr
Kweku Ampiah, a Ghanaian with extensive knowledge of Japan and an
impressive command of Japanese, follows Japanese policy in Africa down
some intriguing paths. Concentrating on Japan's presence in Tanzania,
Nigeria and South Africa, and on Japan's voting record at the United
Nations on issues relating to Africa, he has written a pioneering book on a
set of relationships likely to be of increasing importance in world affairs.

J.A.A. Stockwin

List of tables and figures

FIGURES

Preface

This book is an empirical analysis of the political, economic and diplomatic factors informing Japan's relations with sub-Saharan Africa from 1974 to the early part of the 1990s. Japan's relations with three African countries – South Africa, Nigeria and Tanzania – are examined in order to illustrate the dynamics of Japan's presence in the region. Specifically, these cases are used to ascertain the nature of the trade, investment and aid relations which Japan sustained with the region during the period under review. For example, by examining investments in, and divestments from, Nigeria, the case is dismissed that Japan had any significant resource interests amongst the Organization of African Unity (OAU) member states of the region. Not even the abundance of good-quality crude oil in Nigeria was seen as relevant to Japan's national security by the country's policy makers which underlines the fact that the popular conception of Japan as being 'obsessed' with Africa's raw materials was grossly exaggerated.

On the other hand, by looking at the case of Japan's aid to Tanzania, the idea is tested that Japan was keenly aware of, and ready to exploit, the political standing of President Nyerere amongst the sub-Saharan states in their opposition to minority rule in Southern Africa and to all those who supported the minority regimes in the region. Essentially, Japan's relation with South Africa was shaped by Japanese industry's need for raw materials, including certain 'strategic resources'. Hence, the three case studies also illustrate the subtle ties which existed between Japan's different economic and diplomatic interests in the region and how, by extension, Japan managed to set in motion coordinated responses which reflected its predominant interests in sub-Saharan Africa.

This is exemplified in Chapter 5 which examines Japan's diplomatic endeavors at the United Nations General Assembly in relation to South Africa's apartheid policy, and how that reflected Japan's economic interests in the country. Indeed, the central argument in the book is that

Japan's dependence on South Africa for these 'strategic resources' made it impossible for Tokyo, even as an Afro-Asian state within the UN framework, 'fully' to support the OAU states in their fight against the minority government. And it was indeed the lack of interest in the raw materials under the control of these countries that made it possible for Japan's policy makers to persist in their ambivalence on the apartheid debate at the UN. In other words, if the OAU sub-Saharan African states had been the custodians of the 'strategic resources' that South Africa controlled, the Japanese position on the apartheid question would have been markedly in favor of the position of the former.

Essentially, therefore, Japan's 'predominant' interests in sub-Saharan Africa revolved primarily around the country's relationship with South Africa. This amounted to what Morikawa Jun refers to as Japan's *nigen kōzō*, a 'double preoccupation' or dual structure policy of accommodating the interests of the minority regime in South Africa, on the one hand, and fulfilling certain diplomatic requirements pertinent to its relations with the other African states, on the other.

The inquiry uses the issue of the Japanese conception of national security as a framework for analysis, focusing in particular on the *sōgō anzen hoshō senryaku* or Comprehensive National Security (CNS) policy, within which the economic aspects of national security are paramount. The study suggests that it is within this perspective that Japan's primary interests in South Africa should be understood, not least because within the context of sub-Saharan Africa only South Africa had the type of economic assets that appealed to Japan's conception of national security. On the whole, the study concludes that the economic diplomacy employed by Japan in its relations with the region succeeded in reconciling its resource and other economic interests within South Africa, on the one hand, and its diplomatic efforts towards the OAU states, on the other.

Acknowledgements

In the years I spent working on this (originally a thesis submitted to the University of Oxford in 1993) I have become indebted to many individuals who have helped me at every stage of the research and writing-up process. Above all, I must thank my academic supervisor, Professor Arthur Stockwin, without whose immeasurable assistance, guidance and encouragement, not to mention patience, throughout my time at Oxford, this thesis would not have been written. I am also profoundly indebted to Dr Ann Waswo for all the moral support she gave me, and for prodding me on. I am particularly indebted to her for lending me a computer at a time when I needed one very badly. I also thank Dr Jenny Corbett for the invaluable advice she gave on one of my chapters. Gideon Ngwa and Dr Abdul Bello also need special mention here. Without their instructions and guidance on mathematics and statistics, respectively, my chapter on voting patterns would not have been written in the manner in which it exists. I should also thank Fukuda Nobutaka for being so generous with his time, Allan Lodge of Rhodes House Library and Izumi Tytler of the Bodleian (Japanese) Library. I am also grateful to David Hall (editor, International African Bibliography) and Roger Grosvenor of the Social Science Faculty Library, Oxford, for supplying me with the correct references. My sincerest gratitude goes to the Nissan Institute establishment for making the facilities in the institute's computer room easily accessible to me. And I thank Mrs Diana Dick, the Institute's secretary, for all the administrative help she provided, not to mention the moral support she gave me.

I owe a special debt of gratitude to Pembroke College for awarding me the Tokyo Electric Power Company (TEPCO) Senior Studentship for two years, and for providing further assistance towards my research in Tanzania and Nigeria. I must also thank Dr James McMullen, my college advisor, for showing interest in the progress of my work, and for supporting me. And I am very grateful to the Japan Foundation Endowment Fund Committee for the generous grant that made it possible for me, in the first instance, to concentrate on writing up and finishing the thesis; and secondly, for giving me a grant towards my research in South Africa in 1995. The Nuffield Foundation's grant towards my last period of research in Japan in 1996 is also greatly appreciated.

There are a number of people who made possible my research in Japan and in the African states I visited. I owe special thanks to Umahashi Noryō, of the United Nations Information Center, Tokyo, Takaoka Masato of the Ministry of Foreign Affairs, Hirasawa Eiji, and Takahashi Masakatsu. I am deeply indebted to Hayashi Kyoko for sending me, on a number of occasions, photocopies from the Diet Library. Luchibhikiye Lungu of the Ministry of Finance, Tanzania, and J.A. Oni of the Nigerian Institute of International Affairs both deserve mention for all the help they gave me in their respective capacities.

Certain tables in this book have previously been published by Macmillan Ltd, who I would like to thank for their permission to reproduce them.

Finally, a special note of thanks to Louise Haagh for her support and assistance in proofreading the manuscript and also for her insightful comments, and to Dr Vincent Wright for his invaluable advice. I am also thankful to Professor Joseph Moran for his unlimited support and encouragement, and to all my colleagues at the Scottish Centre for Japanese Studies. I also owe a great debt of gratitude to my son Ato who, in his own little way, and seemingly unknown to him, has served as a great source of inspiration to me.

Glossary of abbreviations and Japanese terms, and note on the text

ABBREVIATIONS USED IN THE TEXT AND FOOTNOTES

AA	Afro-Asian (Group)
AD	Average disagreement score
ANC	African National Congress
ASEAN	Association of South East Asian Nations
BHN	Basic human needs
CAM	Consolidated African Mines
CCM	Chama cha Mapinduzi (Party of the Revolution)
CENTO	Central Treaty Organization
CFAO	Compaigne Français D'LAfrique Occidental
CNS	Comprehensive National Security
DAC	Development Assistance Committee
Exim Bank	Export–Import Bank of Japan
FDI	Foreign direct investment
FLS	Frontline states of Southern Africa
GDP	Gross domestic product
GNP	Gross national product
IBRD	International Bank for Reconstruction and Development
IDA	International Development Agency
ISCOR	(South Africa) Iron and Steel Industrial Corporation
JETRO	Japan External Trade Organization
JICA	Japan International Cooperation Agency
JOCV	Japan Overseas Cooperation Volunteers
JSP	Japan Socialist Party
KADC	Kilimanjaro Agricultural Development Center
KIDC	Kilimanjaro Industrial Development Center
KADC	Kilimanjaro Agricultural Development Center
KMT	Kuomintang
KR	Kennedy Round

KRIDP	Kilimanjaro Regional Integrated Development Plan
LDP	Liberal Democratic Party (Jiyu minshutō or Jimintō)
LDC	Least-developed countries
MITI	Ministry of International Trade and Industry (Tsūshō sangyōshō or Tsūsanshō)
MOF	Ministry of Finance (Ōkurashō)
MOFA	Ministry of Foreign Affairs (Gaimushō)
NFI	New forms of investment
NICS	Newly industrializing countries
NNPC	Nigerian National Petroleum Company
OAPEC	Organization of Arab Petroleum Exporting Countries
OAU	Organization of African Unity
ODA	Official development assistance
OECD	Organization for Economic Co-operation and Development
OECF	Overseas Economic Cooperation Fund
PPRC	The Peace Problem Research Council (Heiwa mondai kenkyukai)
PRC	People's Republic of China
SAP	Structural adjustment programme
SDF	Self-Defense Forces
SPC	Special Political Committee
TCOA	Transvaal Coal Owners Association
UAC	United Africa Company
UNCN	United Nations Council for Namibia
UNGA	United Nations General Assembly
ZSA	'Z' score of agreement

JAPANESE TERMS USED REPEATEDLY IN THE TEXT AND FOOTNOTES

Keidanren	Japan Federation of Economic Organizations. In theory, this body represents virtually all branches of economic activity in Japan. The corporate members of the organization are leading Japanese enterprises and foreign companies operating in Japan.
zaikai	the Japanese business community – specifically those businessmen active in the peak economic organizations.
sōgō anzen hoshō (senrgaku)	comprehensive (national) security (policy)
seikei bunri	the separation of economics and politics

Nigen kōzō　　　'Dual Structure Policy' – a term used by Morikawa Jun to describe Japan's two-front diplomacy in sub-Saharan Africa.

A NOTE ON THE TEXT

In this book, the following stylistic conventions have been followed. All Japanese names are given in the Japanese order with family name first. This has been done consistently, even in those cases in which Japanese authors of English-language articles and books give their names in the English order. Titles of certain newspaper and magazine articles, where they are of significance to our analysis, are mentioned in the notes. The dollar sign ($) respresents the US dollar, (T/-) indicates the Tanzanian shilling, (R) is the South African rand, and (N) is a designation for the Nigerian naira. Macrons are used in the normal way to designate long vowels in Japanese words. The only exceptions to this rule are well-known place names such as Tokyo, Osaka and Kyoto, where macrons have been omitted. Names of organizations used in the text are in general the shortened versions by which they are commonly known.

1　Introduction

THE STUDY OF JAPAN'S RELATIONS WITH AFRICA: ISSUES AND PROBLEMS

The study of Japan's relations with sub-Saharan Africa[1] is virtually a new area of inquiry in the analysis of Japan's international relations. Those of us involved in it are therefore not, as yet, furnished with sufficiently complex and profound questions to explore and ultimately answer. The lack of appropriate 'tools of analysis' in relation to this discourse prompted one Japanese Africanist to note that 'there are no set ideas or methodological approaches' readily available for a critical analysis of any aspect of Japan's relations with Africa.[2] In short, we do not have a wealth of hypotheses to knock about. But, as Morikawa Jun points out in his review of a 1994 publication edited by Kawabata Masahisa, *Afurika to nihon*,[3] an intelligent management and application of theoretical issues and methodologies in relation to the study of this subject-matter has become increasingly important, not least because the debate needs to be licked into shape.

As social scientists and historians, we know that it is impossible to have the appropriate 'tools' of analysis ready, as it were, before considering the questions, and indeed the relevant answers. In other words, it is only after we have ascertained the usefulness of a certain approach that we may be able to fashion an answer for the relevant problem. Being aware of one's inadequacies is, however, far better than being ignorant of them. Needless to say, awareness – rather than complacency and lethargy – may stimulate the creative juices of those interested in the discourse to carry on with the search for the appropriate methodologies and ideas with which to approach, if not answer, the different ranges of questions and doubts that the subject may generate.

Almost by definition, one might say, the subject belongs to the next generation, or better still the generation after next. After all, there is hardly a mention of any of the African states in the social science and history publications on Japan. In a recent publication, *Japan's Foreign Policy After the Cold War: Coping with Change* (1993), edited by Gerald Curtis, for example, Africa is barely mentioned in what is otherwise a comprehensive conception and analysis of Japan's international relations. To be fair, the mention of Japan in any social science study on any aspect of Africa is a recent development. In that sense, Joanna Moss and John Ravenhill's *Emerging Japanese Economic Influence in Africa: Implications for the United States* (1985), a policy-oriented monograph of 152 pages, was a brave and useful attempt. So was S.O. Agbi's 1992 publication, *Japanese Relations with Africa 1868–1978*. This 153-page book is a good guide to the history and some of the major themes of Japan's relations with the African states.

Obviously, geographical and historical distance have served to create this gap in the analysis of Japan's place in the international scheme of things. Time and space are, therefore, of the essence here. And those involved in this exercise have no reasons to underrate the excitement that may be spawned by their attempts to permeate this historical and geographical distance that is gradually, if slowly, closing. Naturally, a new discipline of this sort always carries with it the allure of creativity and imagination. In essence, a serious and constructive study of the subject may unveil things both untrue and unwelcome and will, hopefully, include the exploding of myths and revealing of false premises.

What is interesting to note is that, almost as if pleading and at the same time agitating for more space and respect, the discourse is already showing the extent of its dynamism, by directing those involved in it away from a 'replication of uniformity' and stereotypes, towards an 'organization of diversity' in areas of analysis. Thus, rather than the quick bus trip on the 'Japan and Africa' bandwagon which at one point used to be the norm, especially in journalistic writings (my own included),[4] committed analysts have now started narrowing their focus to specific case studies and time frames. Some such analysts include Morikawa Jun, Kitagawa Katsuhiko and Kweku Ampiah.[5] And the chapters on Japanese economic assistance to Tanzania in Kawabata's edited volume are also examples of an attempt to narrow down the focus. Inukai Ichiro's 1993 article on Japanese aid to sub-Saharan Africa may also be classified as an attempt to look at a specific issue for study and analysis. Its appearance in *Japan's Foreign Aid: Power and Policy in a New Era* (1993), a book edited by Bruce M. Koppel and Robert M. Orr, Jr., is probably more important. It is fair to note, however, that despite the shortcomings of the section on 'Japan's relations with Africa' (by Oda Hideo and Aoki Kazuyoshi), Robert Ozaki and Walter Arnold's edited volume was a pioneer in this respect.[6] These publications show that a new set of observers of Japan's place in the global scheme of things are prepared to bring Africa into a discussion on Japanese foreign policy.

Kitagawa's works provide a 'healthy' historical, if descriptive, account of the development of Japan's economic interests in the region. Morikawa's writings, on the other hand, soundly 'problematize' the issue of Japan's relations with Africa. He approaches the discourse by raising questions in relation to the political nuances of the economic factors determining the relationship. In his 1985 article 'The Myth and Reality of Japan's Relations with Colonial Africa, 1885–1960', he makes the point that by taking advantage of the political constraints imposed on the African countries by European colonizers, Japan 'capitalized' on the economic weaknesses of the African people, without in the end being held responsible for anything.

The primary objective of this article, it seems, was to challenge the view, often bandied about by Japanese policy makers and bureaucrats, that on the question of Africa their country was protected from any form of 'historical guilt' (*te ga yogoreteinai*). The conclusive message of a sociopolitical debate of this sort, however, is bound to raise eyebrows (as it has managed to do especially among Japanese Africanists), if only because it embodies a certain kind of radical approach. However, one does not have to look hard to realize that Japan emerges almost with dignity (in a world that considered territorial aggression acceptable), as the best of a bad bunch, as far as the relations of the colonial powers with Africa are concerned. After all, ironic though this may seem, African intellectuals and political activists saw in Japan's militarism in the 1930s the signs of freedom for Africans from European domination. Yet Morikawa's attempts to 'demystify' Japan on the question of its relations with colonial Africa by reconstructing and contextualizing that aspect of Japan's historiography is justified, simply on the grounds of the need for historical awareness and intellectual objectivity. His work, as well as that of Kitagawa's, is good in letting us know, at least, that Africa as a political and an economic configuration is not purely a post-World War II phenomenon in the Japanese psyche.

The usefulness of Morikawa's 1988 publication (in Japanese), on the question of Japan's relations with South Africa, to the discourse is better captured in his identification of Japan's dual structure (*nigen kōzō*) policy in relation to sub-Saharan Africa. Several observers, no doubt, had commented extensively on Japan's attempts to enjoy the best of both worlds in its relationships with the OAU states, on the one hand, and Pretoria, on the other. Indeed, it was Kitazawa Yōko who, it seems, threw the first 'hand grenade' on this issue.[7] In fact, in November 1974,

Kitazawa testified before the United Nations General Assembly's Committee on Trust and Non-self-governing Territories, describing to the international community the growing network of Japanese industrial involvement in South Africa. Morikawa, however, provided a caption for Japan's pattern of behavior encapsulated in this "triangular discomfiture".

Embedded in this triangular set-up are a number of 'prickly' questions, some obvious, others subtle, but all needing attention sooner or later. Why does Africa remain, as S.O. Agbi put it, 'Japan's continent-sized blind spot'?[8] Writing in 1982 Ronald Dore also states, rather strikingly, that 'Africa (which at present provides six percent of Japan's metal raw material imports) could disappear from the globe with little lasting effect on Japan's resource position'.[9] This begs the question whether Japan would have been oblivious to a Cold War world without South Africa. On the contrary, the analyses in this book suggest that the 6 percent metal raw material imports from Africa (although small in quantity) were nevertheless crucial to Japan's economic security, in the sense that some of these were rare metals found (within the Western geo-political entity) only in South Africa. In other words, these conceptions of Japan as having its back to Africa need properly to be evaluated. Maybe, just maybe, there are certain spots on the continent that Japan cannot be oblivious to. Otherwise why, for example, did Tokyo send its Foreign Minister, Mr Kimura Toshio, on a trip to five African countries in 1974? It is pertinent that, although this event, from the perspective of Japan's policy makers, may conceivably be just another tangential phenomenon in the Japanese approach to their 'African problem', it has nevertheless become canonized in the debate on Japan's relations with the sub-Saharan Africa states. And why did Japanese policy makers go to such extraordinary lengths to appease the OAU states on the one hand, and, on the other hand, ignore the latter's diplomatic attempts to isolate the minority regime in South Africa from the international community? And what does it mean to say that Japanese policy makers were hypocritical on the issue of apartheid, for example? Furthermore, was Japan obsessed with Africa's raw materials, as some observers have claimed? This book is an attempt to turn the wheels in the right direction, as it were, by testing some of these questions and speculations both positively and empirically. Hopefully, as we turn our full attention to these issues, we will cover a wide range of 'answers'.

JAPAN'S 'DOUBLE PREOCCUPATION' WITH AFRICA

In view of the complexity of Japan's relations with the OAU member states, on the one hand, and South Africa, on the other, Japanese foreign policy towards sub-Saharan Africa during the period under review demonstrates a cross-current of conflicting requirements. As a member of the Afro-Asian group at the United Nations (UN), Japan, since the 1950s until the end of the period under review, 1991, professed solidarity with the OAU states in their fight against colonialism and the institution of racial discrimination in South Africa. Yet, Tokyo expanded its manufacturing concerns and its commercial interests in South Africa in a manner that qualifies as propping up the minority regime of Pretoria. Needless to say, Japan was often criticized by the African states for 'supporting' South Africa. In effect, Japan was faced with the *nigen kōzō* (double preoccupation) of accommodating specific interests of the minority regime in South Africa, on the one hand, and fulfilling certain diplomatic requirements pertinent to its relations with the other African states, on the other. This pattern of behavior could be said to be primarily dictated by Japan's economic and resource interests, which, from the perspective of Japan's policy makers, impinged directly on their conception of Japan's primary security interests.

The 1973 oil crisis, in particular, increased Japanese awareness of the politicization of economic issues, thus accentuating the Japanese perception of the indivisibility of economic and security matters, particularly in the realm of natural resource acquisition. In essence, the Arab states' oil embargo against the USA and its allies, including Japan, proved that the Japanese economy was potentially vulnerable to raw materials shortages. It was within this context that Japanese foreign policy towards the Middle East (Arab–Israeli) problem assumed a new dimension. Japan ostensibly deviated from the US policy position on the issue, towards a more autonomous foreign policy, and one that seemingly favored the Arab cause. And it was also within this context that, as part of its resource diplomacy, Japanese policy makers seemingly started to approach Africa with the objective of securing the steady supply of raw materials and energy resources necessary to keep its economy moving. In that respect, there were many parallels between how Japan approached the Arab–Israeli conflict, on the one hand, and the conflict between the OAU member states and the minority regime of South Africa, on the other.

The determining factor in how Japanese policy makers approached these two separate issues, and the critical difference between them, was with respect to where the resources (raw materials) were located in each of these regions. In the Middle East, the oil was firmly buried under the grounds of the Arab states (the morally strong), whereas in sub-Saharan Africa the minority regime of South Africa (the morally guilty) was the custodian of certain strategic resources (rare metals) that were crucial to some of Japan's major industries, if not to the national economy. Pretoria and the Arab states, irrespective of the role each played in the tension within their respective geographical spheres, can be seen, therefore, as being of great importance to Japan as far as its resource diplomacy in the two regions was concerned. In effect, it is being suggested in this study that, for Japan's policy makers, the essence of the 'game' in both regions was basically the same. What differed was where, in the political divide, the goal posts stood in the two areas in question.

Yet Japanese policy makers had to make sure that their policies towards the regions reflected the grievances and concerns also of Israel (the 'villain') in the Middle East and the OAU states (the 'offended party') in sub-Saharan Africa. That meant crafting their policies in a manner that would seem, at the same time, at least reasonable to both 'God' and 'Satan'. The reasons behind such accommodative policies towards the sub-Saharan African states, on the one hand, and Israel, on the other, as with the tensions within their respective regions, are very different. In the case of Israel Japan strove for a degree of neutrality, primarily because it could not afford to offend its most important ally, the USA.

However, it should be pointed out that Japan's big firms continued to trade extensively with South Africa in a way that they could not do with Israel in the advent of the 1973 oil embargo against Japan. It is tempting, therefore, to suggest that, if the resources of South Africa had been under the control of the OAU member states – that is, if the position of the goal posts in the region had been reversed – it is conceivable that, from the very start, Japan's attitude towards apartheid would have been markedly supportive of the OAU states. It may also be important to make the point that, given South Africa's dominance in the production of certain resources (examined in Chapter 3), Japanese dependence on it for these goods was inevitable. Needless to say, Japan was simply following the dictates of market forces, taking the liberal economic system to its logical conclusion. Yet, as has been argued here, the apartheid policies of the Nationalist Party and the international criticism against it made it impossible for Japan to take full advantage of South Africa's resources. This is confirmed by the ban imposed by the Japanese government on Japanese companies with regard to investments in the country. This was a factor that incidentally made apartheid rather unpopular to Japanese business executives and potential investors.

By the very nature of its national security initiatives, Japan's policy makers have, over the years, attempted to address their country's interests in Africa through the application of economic diplomacy. This research intends to answer the question of whether the economic diplomacy employed in relation to sub-Saharan Africa by Japan succeeded in reconciling Tokyo's resource and other economic interests in South Africa, on the one hand, and its diplomatic efforts towards the OAU states, on the other. The study is an empirical analysis of Japan's economic and political relations with sub-Saharan Africa, during the period from 1974 to 1991. The year 1974 is chosen as the beginning, because, by then, Japanese policymakers had realized the importance of making constructive responses to crisis situations abroad, as part of Japan's frantic attempts in the early part of that decade to offset what was essentially a potential threat to the economic welfare of the nation. This anxiety evolved largely as a result of the Nixon 'shocks' to the Japanese political economy in 1971,[10] the oil crisis of 1973 and an avalanche of other international crises. Crucial to these developments was the supposed decline of US hegemonic power and, most importantly, Japan's own rise to the status of economic superpower.

The new diplomacy included attempts by Japan's policy makers to initiate and implement coherent policies towards countries and regions to which Japan had paid scant attention in the past. This new approach to international politics was equally a reflection of, and in response to, growing global economic interdependence. Related to this, needless to say, was the increasing awareness among Japan's policy makers of the growing politicization of economic issues, which accentuated the Japanese perception of the indivisibility of economic and security issues.

In essence, Japan's new foreign policy initiative was an attempt to devise a new security policy that would stand up to the changes in the balance of power and nature of international relations itself. Consequently, with respect to sub-Saharan Africa, the then Foreign Minister Ōhira Masayoshi stated that Japan's relations with Africa represented a task that needed to be tackled. Not surprisingly, therefore, in 1974 Japan sent its Foreign Minister, Mr. Kimura Toshio, on a tour of sub-Saharan Africa. A similar tour took place in 1979, this time by Foreign Minister Sunao Sonoda.

The official Japanese explanation for the tours (which will be examined in detail in Chapter 6) was that they were aimed at deepening Japanese understanding of the problems and policies of the African states. Some observers of Japanese foreign policy, however, saw these new initiatives as nothing more than an attempt to reduce Japan's vulnerability to external pressures by diversifying its supply sources for raw materials, particularly fuels and minerals. Thus, to one observer, the 'oil crisis introduced a globalization of Japan's Asia-centric aid policy'[11] in pursuance of this 'resource diplomacy'.

I choose 1991 as the closing year for this study because, at the time of writing, it is the last year for which all the required data is available. Japan's economic power was by this time a global phenomenon. By the latter part of the 1980s, for example, Japan's net overseas assets of $240.7

bn. (1987 figures) were the world's largest. The latter part of the 1980s is also crucial in the sense that Tokyo emerged in that year as South Africa's leading trade partner. And in 1987 Japan made a generous donation of $500 m. non-project grant aid to eleven countries in sub-Saharan Africa. This donation, which was to be disbursed over a three-year period ending in 1990, was the first of a series of Japanese non-project grant aid to the region. Suffice to say that by 1990 the African states had become particularly aware of Japan's economic, if not political, importance in the international community.

CASE STUDIES

South Africa, Nigeria and Tanzania are the selected case studies for our analysis of Japan's foreign policy towards sub-Saharan Africa. Through these case studies the variegated nature of Japan's relations with the region will be demonstrated, by means of an examination of Japan's trade, investment and aid relations with the above countries. The countries are spread out across the region so as to cover all the major sub-regions (East, West and Southern Africa). These countries are, coincidentally, also prominent within the context of the region in the issue areas selected for our analysis. South Africa, of the three, was by far Japan's biggest trade partner in the period. Tanzania figured prominently in Japanese aid to the region: it was the largest recipient of grant aid and the second largest recipient of technical assistance from Japan. Nigeria held the largest declared Japanese manufacturing investments in the region. It may be appropriate to note, however, that the above issue areas are not in any way compartmentalized, since they naturally overlap and are mutually related. Suffice it to say that, analyzed together, they provide us with a broader but coherent picture of the nature of Japan's foreign policy towards sub-Saharan Africa.

The case studies, together with our analysis of Japan's voting behavior at the General Assembly, underline the apparent incoherence of Japan's foreign policy towards sub-Saharan Africa. It should be recalled, however, that the lack of coherence in the pursuance of goals which are, in principle, incompatible, does not necessarily translate into failure in the state's endeavour to achieve those foreign policy goals. In short, success cannot always be measured by the ostensible coherence that it displays.

I will now explain the organization of the book. It begins (in this chapter) by contending with the security problematic while also focusing on the *Sōgo anzen hoshō senryaku* Comprehensive National Security (CNS) policy and its various dimensions. In essence, the base of the theoretical argument is broadened to include theoretical questions relating to the main issue areas of the book. Following that, by identifying Africa's place in Japanese foreign policy, Chapter 2 brings out certain historical dimensions of the relations between Japan and Africa. Chapter 3 examines the economic realities behind Japan's relations with South Africa. South Africa is used here particularly to show the commercially driven set of imperatives that complicated Japan's relations with the OAU states. It is argued that, because South Africa had the most healthy economy in Africa and controlled some metal raw materials that qualified as 'strategic resources', Japan was locked into an embarrassing relationship with it. Chapter 3 details the extent of trade between the two countries, and demonstrates that Japan was dependent on South Africa for some of these 'strategic resources'. Japanese investments in and divestments from Nigeria are examined in Chapter 4, where the study demonstrates the role and extent of Japanese finance capital in sub-Saharan Africa. In this section an attempt is made to show that the popular belief that Japan was interested in Africa's raw materials was exaggerated. Chapter 5 is devoted to diplomacy within the framework of the UN. By examining Japan's voting behavior at the United Nations General Assembly (UNGA) on apartheid issues an attempt is made to identify some of the conflicting exigencies of Japanese diplomacy. Specifically, an adjusted gross number of plenary session roll-call votes in the period 1973–1986 are examined. Using these votes, an attempt is made to answer the question of whether, during the period under study, Japan voted more like the USA, or more like the African group in the UN. Chapter 6 is an examination of Japanese Official development assistance (ODA) to Tanzania, and its implications for Japan's overall attitude towards sub-Saharan Africa. In the Conclusion I return to the broader questions of Japanese foreign policy towards sub-Saharan Africa, and seek to examine whether Japan was successful in its foreign policy towards the region.

THEMES

The obfuscating flavor in Japan's behavior towards sub-Saharan Africa is as attributable to the political demography of the region and the dynamics of Japan's own modern history as it is to the heavy dose of Anglo-American influence within that modern history itself. The latter point refers essentially to the centrality of the East–West conflict in the international relations of the time and the impact of that on Japan's foreign relations. The argument here is simply that the dilemma facing Japan's policy makers, especially those in the Gaimushō (Ministry of Foreign Affairs – MOFA), can be attributed to the following six factors (some of which overlap):

- Japan's interest in the strategic resources under South African control, and its policy of getting a foot in all the dynamic and successful economies of the world. The last point may be seen as a corollary of the operations of capitalism itself as well as a conscious policy of the government and domestic public of Japan, in tune with the country's foreign 'resource diplomacy'.
- The US–Japan alliance and its influence on Japanese foreign policy. At the risk of overemphasizing the point, it may be appropriate to identify within the 'US–Japan security' framework the primacy of East–West tensions that plagued international relations for over four decades. The study, however, attends (in passing) to how the recent developments in international politics, and in South Africa, might have impinged on Japan's relations with sub-Saharan Africa.
- Developments in the global political economy, especially since the early 1970s, starting with the 1973–1974 oil crisis and its impact on the Japanese economy; and how that in turn affected Japan's perceptions of its national security.
- Tokyo's economic interests in the OAU states in the region, even though these interests remain limited.
- The pressure on Japan's policy makers to play a more active role in the global political economy, including that of Africa, commensurate with its economic power. This led to changes in its aid policy towards sub-Saharan Africa, especially from the early 1980s.
- Japan's own sensitivity towards international perception of its place in the global scheme of things and its obsession with the prestige factor in international politics.

In view of the above factors, a pattern can be discerned in Japan's diplomatic behavior towards sub-Saharan Africa at the UN fora. At the UNGA, Japan's voting behavior was consistent in so far as its representatives voted against all resolutions that called for comprehensive sanctions against South Africa. This voting pattern was not unlike that of the USA and the other major advanced economies. This was, however, in contradiction to the Afro-Asian position, even though Japan had become a member of the permanent secretariat of the Afro-Asian Solidarity Organization in 1957. Tokyo was also firm in its opposition to resolutions supporting armed struggle against the minority regimes in Southern Africa. Yet it was also consistent in its support for all resolutions condemning apartheid. Nor was it hesitant in voting in the affirmative for resolutions advocating humanitarian assistance for the disadvantaged Africans of South Africa. The point needs to be reiterated, however, that the contradictions inherent in Japan's relations with sub-Saharan Africa are intrinsically rooted in Tokyo's conception of its national security requirements and how best to satisfy them.

Essentially, the contradictions reflect how an ideologically and commercially driven set of imperatives conflicted with Japan's professed solidarity with the OAU in the latter's fight against apartheid. One of the concerns of this study, therefore, is to show how moral considerations, very often, do not supersede a nation's assessments of its national (security) interests. This is not, however, to imply that Japan's policy makers approved of apartheid or wanted the instruments of apartheid to remain intact. Japan's votes and limited sanctions against South Africa were adopted to express disapproval of apartheid, however insignificant they might have been. And, as pointed out earlier, apartheid became rather unpopular with Japanese firms and business executives, in so far as international condemnation of it made it impossible for them freely to do business with South Africa.

It may be appropriate, then, to contend that the explanatory variable for understanding Japan's obfuscating behavior and the attempts to strike a balance in its approach to the African situation is its wider national security preoccupation. Thus, this study perceives Japan's CNS policy as a crucial point of reference. In view of the variegated nature of Japan's relations with the region, however, it may also be appropriate to widen the conceptual focus of the study to include other theoretical themes which should provide further insights into the debate on Japan's relations with Africa. The essence of such an exercise is thus to show, overall, (1) that Japan's relations with the African states were largely dictated by its economic security interests; (2) that the primacy of economic security – understood as accessibility to the strategic resources – does not necessarily translate into becoming dependent on states with supplies of such resources (as demonstrated with our Nigeria case study); and finally (3) that states, by their very nature, have a tendency to attempt to 'fine-tune' other states in order to secure their interests, and that weaker states have the proclivity to respond positively, but not necessarily on the basis of what Neil Richardson (1978) refers to as 'reward-compliance' – the threat and delivery of rewards and punishment by the dominant state with the result that the weaker state invariably complies with the dictates of the dominant state.

JAPAN'S COMPREHENSIVE NATIONAL SECURITY (CNS) POLICY AND THE QUESTION OF ACCESS TO RAW MATERIALS

In a report by the US Department of Defense concerning security issues in East Asia and the Pacific region 'security' is described as a concept the importance of which is often only confirmed by the fact that it is not there:

'Security is like oxygen. You do not tend to notice it until you begin to lose it.'[12] Without claiming to unravel fully the mystical folklore surrounding the concept of 'security' I would like to fashion a working definition of the notion to help with our analysis. According to the research group put together by Prime Minister Ōhira to look into questions of Japan's national security, 'security, in the abstract sense, can be defined as the state's protection of the people's mode of living from all forms of threat [*samazama na kyoi kara*].[13] Needless to say, the concept has been variously defined and described by generations of researchers. For our purposes, I would adopt the definition provided by the National Defense College of Canada, because it seems to go a bit beyond the abstract to identify specific variables within the myriad of problems and issues that need to be addressed. They view security as:

> a preservation of life acceptable to the . . . people and compatible with the needs and legitimate aspirations of others. It includes freedom from military attack and coercion, freedom from internal subversion and freedom from the erosion of the political, economic and social values which are essentially the quality of life.[14]

Using the above definition as a sub-stratum, we shall now refer to Frederick Hartman who, having noted that 'security is the sum of the total of the vital national interests of the state', points out, quite correctly, that as a consequence concepts of 'national security will vary from state to state in proportion to the concept of vital national interests that any given state entertains at any given time'.[15] In essence, the precise definition of 'security' will vary from state to state and will change for a particular state as its circumstances, and sometimes as its leaders, change. It is time now to proceed with the specific case of Japan's national security.

Richard Samuels contends that at the heart of Japan's ambitions to ensure a long-term relationship with such credible suppliers as South Africa and, indeed, the Arab oil-exporting countries, were two concepts: comprehensive (national) security and equidistance diplomacy.[16] His interpretation of the concept of comprehensive (national) security (CNS) is very useful for our analysis. He refers to the concept as 'the ways in which economic and resource issues are elevated to accompany more traditional geo-political (military) calculations in the determination of foreign policy'.[17] And Peter Katzenstein and Nobuo Okawara point out that the 'comprehensiveness' of Japanese security policy is shaped by the organizational structures of the Japanese state, the internal dynamics of which strengthen the economic and political dimensions of security while suppressing military concerns and interests.[18] Peter Drysdale, among others, concurs. He perceives the concept as stressing 'Japan's interests in maintaining a low defence posture and non-aggressive diplomacy, and constructive cooperation in settling international disputes and a high level of foreign aid'.[19] Yet Watanabe Osamu, in his interpretation of CNS over the period describes the concept as a smokescreen behind which the state was strengthening its military position.[20] The concept, needless to say, has been variously defined by different observers because it has different connotations for different analysts.

Drysdale attributes the essential values of the CNS that came to influence Japanese thinking and policy primarily to Okita Saburō, the economist, bureaucrat and Foreign Minister under Ōhira Masayoshi. When Prime Minister Ōhira presented the idea to the press in 1978, he explicitly referred to it as a strategy (*senryaku*), which 'will be concretely realized, not by military power alone but through the linked support of economic power, information, political power and diplomacy'. He then made the point that: 'It will not do if one link in the chain is too strong or too weak ... My meaning is that they should be well balanced',[21] he emphasized. He further noted that 'the application of the concept of comprehensive security entails a policy which establishes a chain of tightly stretched instruments of national power such as the economy, diplomacy, and politics and to ensure the security of the nation with these'.[22] Suzuki Zenkō, who, as a result of Ōhira's untimely death in 1980, took over the prime ministership of the country, did not understand the concept differently. He made the point that 'security should not be seen from the defensive point alone. I consider efforts ought to be made from a wider perspective which will include the economy, diplomacy etc.'[23]

Most analysts, including Katzenstein and Okawara, do not see the burgeoning military-force oriented security that Watanabe conjures up in his analysis of the Japanese state. Noguchi Yuichiro, for example, makes the point that 'Comprehensive Security' is another term for 'Comprehensive Economic Security'. He attributes this to the fact that the relative importance of the 'economic element of the concept is overwhelmingly high'.[24] Alan Rix equally sees the concept as a driving force behind Japan's resource policies. As he put it: 'the principles of Comprehensive Security can underpin an attempt by Japan to maximise its mercantilist[25] aims (particularly in resource and food import areas) within a liberal international regime.'[26] In essence, the concept was primarily designed to provide 'effective assurances of stable and reliable raw material supplies'.[27] It was, on the whole, as noted earlier, a response to the economic difficulties that seemingly threatened Japan's security in the 1970s.

The CNS debates started in the mid-1970s as a classic case of interest-group agitation; a bitter struggle over the question of how to organize and schematize the conceptual outfit of the different elements of Japan's foreign policy. In one sense, the CNS was a necessary development over the hitherto compartmentalized roles of economics and politics (*seikei bunri*) in Japanese foreign policy, in the sense that it brought the two, at least loosely, if not firmly, together.[28] And the concept, as suggested earlier, identifies military power as a distant constituent element of Japan's security. Yet Katzenstein and Okawara maintain that in this Japanese conception of security two sets of issues remain separate as they have done since the end of World War II: the economic and the military components of foreign policy. According to the authors, 'this separation rests on the premise that the use or threat of military force to ensure Japan's economic security is simply not a viable option'.[29] Thus, as noted earlier, the concept emphasized the application of effective diplomatic measures, as in expanding Japan's global aid initiatives, to ensure stability in strategically important countries and regions. These included areas that possessed strategic resources, such as Southern Africa and the Middle East.

Observers note that the debate that shaped the definition of national security involved three documents compiled, separately, by (1) the Nomura Research Institute in 1977; (2) Sōgo anzen hoshō kenkyū gurūpu (the Comprehensive National Security Research Group), headed by Inoki Masamichi, a private advisory body to Prime Minister Ōhira;[30] and (3) Heiwa mondai kenkyūkai (the Peace Problem Research Council – PPRC), a private advisory body to Prime Minister Nakasone Yasuhiro. The report of this last was completed in 1984.

The Nomura report made a proposal for a comprehensive package of measures to ensure Japan's security, essentially suggesting an increase in the financial resources to cover the cost of economic security items: stockpiling of oil, raw materials and food; prospecting for petroleum and uranium; and research for sources of energy, among other things. It also recommended outlays for (ODA), cultural exchange and, last but not least, military defense. As far as the latter recommendation is concerned, the report stated that Japan should remain within the US–Japan security arrangement, since an autonomous defense program would antagonize the neighboring Asian states.

Continuing with the tradition of de-emphasizing the military aspect of security, the report of the Sōgo anzen hoshō kenkyū gurūpu, *Sōgo anzen hoshō senryaku* (A Strategy for Comprehensive Security), recommended that the National Defense Council, which was the highest organ in charge of the nation's defense, should be replaced by a Comprehensive National Security Council.[31] The suggestion was based on the assumption that the former had outlived its importance, given the developments in the international political economy, for example the breakdown of Bretton Woods and the resurgence of economic nationalism. The report makes mention, for example, of the concern that the military balance between the USA and the USSR was no longer in favor of the former, indicating a concern about the relative decline of the USA's hegemonic position.[32] In that respect, the report aimed to fashion out a means of working with the two pillars of 'contributing to the maintenance and strengthening of the international system', while at the same time maintaining and strengthening its own 'self-reliant efforts' (*jijo doryoku*).[33]

But the report also recommended, as did that of the PPRC,[34] that the nation's defense budget be increased beyond the 1 percent limit stipulated in the 1976 outline. The PPRC report set the whole question within the context of the dynamics of the international geo-political system, taking particular note of the USA's hegemonic decline and the threat this posed to Japan's security. It was on this basis that the report criticized the 1 percent ceiling as being grossly inadequate for Japan's defense. Suffice to say that the recommendations for an increase in the nation's defense budget and the fact that it was eventually ratified under the Nakasone administration, presumably prompted Watanabe to argue that the 1980s can be seen as a turning-point in the development of post-war Japan.[35] And it may well be the reason why he saw the CNS as a smokescreen behind which the state was reinforcing its war potential. Thus, he saw the 1980s as the period when the ideals of the military bureaucrats (*gunbu kanryō*) were incorporated into the ideals of the state. The point should be made, however, that the PPRC report, like its predecessors, emphasized the economic component of the nation's comprehensive security, that is, the need for security in energy, raw materials and food.[36] And it recommended, in relation to food security, for example, that the country's agricultural sector should be developed further.[37]

These debates involved the government ministries on various levels. The Ministry of Foreign Affairs, for example, put together an in-house Security Policy Committee in April 1979, headed by the Permanent Vice-Minister Mr. Takashima Masuo. This committee, however, concentrated primarily on the political and military aspects of the CNS.[38] When, in 1980, the government, in view of recommendations made by the Inoki group, started making institutional arrangements to incorporate the recommendations in its policy measures, it was apparent that the concept of CNS would revolve around the three pillars of 'military, economy, and diplomacy, all of which were to be applied in a comprehensive sense to protect the state and civil society from "external threats (*kokusaiteki yōin*)"'.[39] Most importantly, it postulated three interrelated elements of national security efforts which were (1) self-reliant measures to deal with the threats, (2) efforts to massage the whole international system into one favorable to Japan's security and (3) intermediate-range measures.[40]

It may be appropriate to elaborate on the above strategies. The first element concerned the principle of 'self-reliance', which was primarily to do with measures concerning energy security and having access to strategic resources. Specifically, this involved stockpiling the necessary energy reserves and was a testament to the 'national obsession with security of supply'.[41] It was also, essentially, concerned with being able to sustain the country's economic power through competitive production and exports. In a more narrow sense, it was about the preservation of the state.[42] The second element included efforts to support the system of international economic interdependence (*sōgo izon*), and involved working for the maintenance of the liberal trade system and finding solutions to North–South issues. This is where ODA was seen as a prominent feature of Japanese diplomacy, within the overall framework of CNS. This aspect of Japanese foreign policy is explored in more depth in Chapter 6, which concerns itself with Japanese aid to Tanzania.

Most important is the fact that, on the specific question of Japan's economic security, the report makes the recommendation that, in the interests of the national economy, the state should develop amicable relations (*yūkō teki*) with the relevant countries,[43] which, for the purposes of this study would include South Africa. It is important to note that on the above question, the PPRC report which can be seen as a follow-up to that of the CNS Policy Committee and a refinement of the latter in that it identifies the value of certain strategic resources (rare metals)[44] to the Japanese economy, and indeed for the whole of Japan's national security. It notes, for example, that these resources are indispensable to Japan's major industries, including the steel, machine, and electronics industries. The report categorically states that the lack or unavailability of these resources could have profound effects on the living standards of the people, since the production of consumer goods depends on these resources.

It acknowledges, therefore, that the indispensability of the strategic resources to the world of high technology, both in terms of quality and quantity, is bound to grow immensely, alluding to the extent of Japan's dependence on external sources for these resources. And it points out that Japan imports 100 percent of its cobalt and 99 percent of its chrome needs. Aware of the security risks in the extent of its dependence on imports for these resources the report then expresses concern about the fact that, even more than for oil, the high concentration of these strategic resources and their production in a few countries is phenomenal. It further concedes that most of these resources are unevenly concentrated in Southern Africa, the (former) communist bloc countries and politically unstable (Third World) countries.[45] The concern becomes more poignant when one considers that South Africa and the Soviet Union alone held 60 percent of the world's reserves of chrome and manganese, while Zaire was the producer of 50 percent of the world's cobalt.[46] Japan's policy makers were reiterating the point that, both in terms of quantity of supply and the value of these strategic resources, there is extreme uncertainty. For the sake of the security of the Japanese economy in these circumstances, therefore, the report put forward the advice that access to the strategic resources ought to be ensured by means of developing amicable relations with countries of economic importance to Japan, as mentioned above. It is in view of this that Japanese policy makers became trapped in the embarrassing situation of expanding their country's trade with South Africa; and by so doing becoming dependent on South Africa for some of the world's strategic resources, a case that is extensively examined in Chapter 3.

Suffice to say, it is undeniable that states' concern over adequate raw material supplies from abroad has long been the theme of international politics – 'first, as a means to enhance national power and prestige, but second, with the arrival of mass democracy in the Western industrialized world, as a vital ingredient for the welfare state'.[47] Needless to say, the importance of raw materials for national power has thus been a traditional aspect of economic security. Historians do not, for example, underestimate the fact that the US embargo against Japan in 1941 threatened oil supplies to the country and in turn greatly contributed to the Japanese invasion of Pearl Harbor. Robert Gilpin, for example, argues that Japanese imperialism in the 1930s was partially inspired by Japan's lack of secure access to vital raw materials, which the countries it perceived as competitors – the US, UK, and the USSR – had.[48] Given their country's historical experience with raw materials, therefore, Japanese policy makers are particularly aware of the need for assured and easy access to those resources that would sustain their country's economic growth, and therefore they keep on producing policy measures designed to realize such goals. Their policies towards sub-Saharan Africa were thus indicative of their deep interest in the 'strategic' resources in Southern Africa, and in South Africa in particular. Indeed, Japanese policy makers saw Southern Africa as being equal in importance to the Middle East as a source of certain important raw materials.[49]

It is worth noting at this juncture that the particular importance of a specific mineral for industrial production and the functioning of a modern industrial economy is not eternal. A particular mineral might lose its strategic value as a result of new developments in industrial technology; or its strategic importance could be drastically reduced because of the availability of a substitute. (It could also happen through changes in the dynamics of international politics, as in the case of the collapse of the Soviet Union, which effectively made certain scarce resources under its control accessible to those who previously did not have access to them.) Thus, the question of whether a mineral is of strategic value or not is time- and place-specific.

Noguchi's point about the primary factor behind the conception of the CNS should be brought into perspective here. He attributes it to perceived threats against Japan, originating from systemic outcomes. Thus, he marginalizes concerns about natural disasters/earthquakes as security issues in the overall conception of the CNS. The emphasis, as he notes, is on Japan's relations with the international community.[50] And these relations are, unequivocally, about trade and investments and accessibility to natural resources. They are, specifically, about how the state can function effectively in a hostile economic environment without losing its markets or access to the essential raw materials outside its borders; and they are about circumventing protectionism, through the promotion of foreign investments, for example. Needless to say, market-oriented investments are mostly induced by trade barriers, as in the form of tariffs on final products. Our discussion of Japanese Foreign Direct Investment (FDI) in Chapter 4 also shows that among the 'push factors' determining investments, especially in developing countries in the period, was the absence of domestic raw materials. That is to say, to a very large extent, Japanese FDI in developing countries is natural resource-oriented, and in the advent of the oil crisis has been diversified to pre-empt another jolt of such dimensions to the economy. Thus, Noguchi's point that CNS was essentially oriented towards crisis prevention (*kiki yobō*), as opposed to crisis management (*kiki taishō*),[51] is poignant. With the benefit of hindsight, Japan's policy makers concentrated their energy on preventing a recurrence of the crises that hit the country in the 1970s.

Thus CNS as a policy strategy involved, primarily, three aspects of national power – economic, diplomatic and military/defense-related – to be used, as a chain, to protect Japan from external threats. The economic component, however, remained the most crucial variable of the equation, and it was supported with diplomacy, which is usually understood to refer to aid to the developing countries, the custodians of most of the strategic resources upon which Japanese industries depend. Investment was thus crucial in this equation. It was in view of this that Rix made the point that the concept of CNS was primarily designed to provide 'effective assurances of stable and reliable raw material supplies', pointing out, in essence, that the conceptual base of the framework was the efficacy of the national economy.

Foreign aid and the power of states

In a seminal paper entitled 'Japan and the Third World: Coincidence or Divergence of Interests', Ronald Dore notes[52] that:

> The considerable space devoted to Tanzania in the 1977 White Paper on international trade and the attempts to step up aid to Tanzania were explained by a Foreign Ministry official as having to do with Tanzania's position, along with Japan, as an elected member of the Security Council, and Tanzania's role as a leading castigator of industrial countries with extensive dealings with South Africa and a suspected role in breaking Rhodesian sanctions. Tanzanian attacks on Japan in the Security Council during 1977 had, he thought, been somewhat tempered as a result.

The issue of Japan's economic assistance to Tanzania and the actual diplomatic objectives behind it will be examined in Chapter 6. Suffice to say, that, in looking at Japanese relations with Tanzania, especially concerning the issue of aid, it is imperative that the subject is approached by first making reference to the political dynamics of the international community, and the motivation and objectives of states as individual entities within that community. It is important in this respect to refer to a couple of debates which are relevant to the analysis of Japanese aid to Tanzania and to attempt to account for the behavior of these two actors (Japan and Tanzania) by first referring to the systemic (outside-in) and unit-level (inside-out) analysis of states' behavior. By so doing, it is hoped that the question of how the systemic impacts on the behavior of states will be brought into perspective. First, it may be worth noting that 'systemic analysis of the international political economy begins by locating actors along the dimension of relative power on the one hand and wealth on the other'.[53] And it invariably refers to the location of each actor relative to others.[54] This suggests that nation-states, at best, coexist in a global hierarchy, a fact that in itself is a truism. In attempting to provide a systematic explanation for the resultant relations stemming from the hierarchy within which states operate, Neil Richardson teases out the political ramifications of the economic (trade) interactions between strong states and weak states. He then makes the point that 'because the larger economy dominates the smaller one through their mutual trade, the latter will be constrained to exhibit "cooperative" behaviour born of economic dependence; it should behave deferentially'.[55] Based on the above assumption Richardson then makes the proposition that nations are differentially constrained according to their rank in the hierarchical international system. Such differential 'political' behavior as emanates from the relationship he refers to as 'compliance'. Thus, the usual explanation of the foreign policy of weak states, as developed around the theory of 'reward-compliance', therefore rests on (1) the concept of power and (2) the empirical fact that the formal code of (foreign policy) behavior of weak states tends to conform to the dictates of dominant states.[56] The theory identifies a causal relationship (the threat and delivery of rewards and punishment by the dominant state) that ultimately ensures compliant behavior by the weak state.

There is, however, a more carefully crafted argument by Bruce Moon, according to which he suggests a different explanation for the empirical findings central to the above theory.[57] The alternative explanation Moon offers is based on what he refers to as a theory of 'constrained consensus', which implies much less confidence in the ability of the dominant state to violate and 'fine-tune' the foreign policies of other nations without a prior and massive penetration of their economic and political systems.[58] Moon's explanation 'also rests on more realistic assessments of the goals and constraints of actors in both dominant and dependent states'.[59] Nevertheless, as he points out, considerable evidence suggests that at least some characteristics of foreign policy are central to the determination of aid-worthiness, and that 'there is strong evidence . . . that the perceived importance of a nation substantially influences the aid allocations it receives'.[60] That in itself suggests that weak states, in so far as they remain important in (a) certain respect(s), could also be in a position of influence, even over stronger states, and that they may indeed exercise this influence in the form of 'power'. This then suggests that 'power must be analysed as something which circulates in the form of a chain', as Michel Foucault[61] puts it. And it should be seen as circulating in a manner that makes it possible for a country like Tanzania also to wield some influence on an economically powerful country like Japan, as the latter attempts to influence the former for its own interests. In essence, power is 'never localised here or there'[62], and should therefore be 'analysed as something which circulates, or rather as something which only functions in the form of a chain'. Foucault's conception of power as 'a multiform production of relations of domination which are partially susceptible of integration into overall strategies',[63] is relevant to the analysis of Japanese aid to Tanzania, and makes possible our conception of power as a mode of political and economic management which exploits the difference(s) between the weak and the strong.

International organizations and bloc/national interests

Moon's critique about the compliance behavior of weak states in their relations with strong states is equally relevant to our analyses of Japan's voting behavior at the UNGA. He is critical of the fact that:

Various analysts have used cross-sectional research designs to demonstrate that the UN voting patterns of nations linked to the United States through trade or aid are likely to resemble the voting of the United States. From this evidence they conclude that weaker states abandon their preferences on foreign-policy matters and instead seek the approval of the United States, anticipating that future American policy will reward and punish states in proportion to their compliance. In turn, American trade or aid is calibrated to the level of compliance, thereby justifying and reinforcing the compliance logic. Thus this theory simultaneously explains the behaviors of both the dominant and the dependent state in an asymmetrical dyad.[64]

With reference to the above quotation, it should be noted that although Japan was highly dependent on its economic relations with the USA, and was covered by the American security umbrella through the US–Japan alliance, the evidence shows that in UNGA votes relating to apartheid issues Japan did not necessarily vote as the USA. Moon's arguments further suggest that the agreement in votes such as might have existed between Japan and the USA might have been the result of a sharing of interests and perceptions. Thus, the observed voting agreement as existed between them (on questions relating to comprehensive economic sanctions) 'may be primarily the result of *consensus*, not *compliance*'[65] between the policy makers of the two countries. It may be added that Japan's voting pattern on such resolutions could be more attributable to the obsessive desire to have access to the strategic raw materials in South Africa which would have been lost to it if the Security Council had instituted comprehensive sanctions against South Africa. Needless to say, if Japan had voted in support of such resolutions it would have found itself in a far more disturbing foreign policy dilemma, especially if it had continued to trade with South Africa after supporting the resolutions. On the other hand, if it had been true to its votes (having voted in favor of sanctions) and discontinued trade with South Africa, its economy and its growing standard of living might have suffered as a result.

In relation to the above point, it may be interesting to note, as Jack Vincent points out,[66] that in general the higher the average per capita gross national product (GNP) of the groups the more negative their attitude tended to be towards the major organs of the UN, especially the General Assembly. In that sense, Hayward Alker, Jr.'s[67] point that, despite the composite nature of bloc politics in the international organization, national interests rather than anything else are the primary determinant of states' behavior at the UN is apt. He further makes the point that:

The suggestion that political conflicts preoccupy members of the UN implies that the national interests of the UN members, shaped as they are by domestic, regional, political, economic, and ethnic considerations, are more causally determinative of UN policy positions than caucusing group pressures at the UN.[68]

And Ernst Haas interpreted UNGA politics in terms of a balancing process between Cold War demands and the political, economic and anti-colonial demands of Third World countries.[69]

Japan's dilemma as a member of the Afro-Asian bloc (which evolved out of the Bandung conference of 1955) was eloquently confirmed in its voting at the UNGA on issues relating to apartheid. This goes to underline the argument above, and in so doing gives credence to the reference to Japan's raw material interests as stated within the framework of the CNS policy. Vincent's point about per capita GNP and how this reflects on the voting behavior of states is clearly illustrated in the way Japan voted on apartheid issues even as a member of the AA bloc, compared to how the rest of the members of the bloc, on the whole, voted. Chapter 5 is devoted to this issue. Suffice to say that Japan's voting behavior is attributable to its rather high standard of living, which is a product of high economic growth which, in itself is infinitely dependent on raw material imports. In short, the ambition to sustain and improve upon its economic achievement was the primary factor behind Japan's deviation from the overall voting behavior of the rest of the AA member states. As explained in Chapter 2, despite its participation in the Bandung conference, in reality, Japan was outside the 'culture' and euphoria that brought the underdeveloped countries together for that historical event.

This is not, however, to say that the AA group was a monolithic entity. Indeed, the cohesion of the AA group was far from complete, obviously because of the polarized nature of world politics at the time. Yet when it came to voting on a straight racial issue, as in the case of apartheid, they were very likely to vote as a bloc.[70] This is where Japan often fell foul of the bloc's interests, although, as would be shown later, it did not necessarily vote with the USA, its most important political and economic ally and the leading opponent of anti-apartheid proposals at the UNGA. In essence, Japan's voting behavior cannot be seen as simply a complaint behavior in response to US demands.

Despite the factors that divided the members of the AA group, its UNGA voting record reveals, seemingly because of the level of its membership's economic achievement (or lack of it), that as a caucusing group the AA was very effective in going with the Assembly majority. And, most importantly, the AA as a caucusing group brought a new theoretical addition to the whole concept of the UN, and invariably to the political issues that the Assembly had to try and resolve. The theory of the UN Charter was in effect upset by the intrusion of certain fundamental interests clamoring for recognition in their own right rather than as adjuncts to the preservation of peace, as envisaged by its originators. Needless to say, the Charter as it was written by its originators 'essentialized' peace and security as the fundamental aim of the UN, with collective security as its basic purpose. The functional tasks, including in particular the advancement of economic development and the emancipation of colonial peoples, 'were considered in 1945 as means towards the end of security, not as basic aims in their own right'.[71]

The developments in world politics from the end of World War II thus lend themselves to the argument that indeed there were two Cold Wars: the conflict between the West and the USSR, on the one hand, and the struggle of the Afro-Asian countries to free themselves from colonial domination and to achieve racial equality within the framework of the new international order, on the other.[72] The latter factor brought into perspective what Ali Mazrui referred to as the 'philosophical clash' between the ideal of peace as the moral foundation of the UN in the view of the older members,[73] and the ideal of human dignity and justice deemed as the foundation of the UN by the newer members.[74] The Charter's embodiment of such a philosophical conflict inevitably ushered on to the UN platform the demands for a re-evaluation of the priorities of the UN. As far as the newly independent states were concerned, they were 'in', as it were, to create reality by re-inventing politics in a way that would ultimately upset the *status quo*. Japan, however, was clearly ambivalent on this issue, as will be shown in Chapters 2 and 5.

The re-orientation of the theory of the Charter and the displacement of the concept of power as the instrument of security, not to mention the intrusion of the functional aspirations of the new states into the political intercourse of the UN, highlight Haas's point that, in allowing for such flexibility beyond the Charter, we must 'put conduct in the UN and regional organizations into the overall context of foreign policy aims and clashes'.[75] It is undoubtedly within this context that this study intends to take stock of Japan's voting behavior on apartheid issues at the UNGA. It should be pointed out, however, that Japan's stance on this question appeared more delicate than that of most nations, primarily because of its position between blocs which held divergent philosophical views concerning the essential (moral) responsibility of the UN. On the one hand, it was considered part of the AA bloc, bestowing upon it a greater responsibility (even at the cost of its viable economic interests) in questions relating to apartheid than would be the case with, say, the USA or indeed the Scandinavian countries. On the other hand, Japan is, to all intents and purposes, an economic superpower and was bound, when necessary, to act to protect its national security interest in this key area. This draws the analysis into yet another phase of theoretical discussion, and one that impinges directly on the issue of access to raw materials.

Foreign direct investment (FDI): raw materials and Japan's national security

Despite the economic basis of Japan's conception of its national security, this study shows that its 'obsession' with raw materials does not necessarily force Japan into striking up economic deals with any country simply because that country happens to have a resource that is essential to Japan's economic interests and its overall CNS. The analysis of theoretical arguments concerning FDI should help us to appreciate the nature of Japanese investments (or lack of them) in Nigeria, one of the world's leading producers and exporters of crude oil. It should also help us to understand the manner in which Japan has approached the question of accessibility to raw materials (through FDI) in sub-Saharan Africa as a whole.

This exploratory analysis of Japanese FDI should start with a mention of the fact that theories of the multinational enterprise include many definitions of what a multinational enterprise is. A useful definition is that of Kojima Kiyoshi. He states that they are often enterprises that maintain networks of branches and subsidiaries in more than one country. 'Thus a company may be considered a Multinational Company if it possesses at least one FDI project'.[76] Most important for this analysis, however, is a proper operational definition of FDI which includes a consideration of the non-traditional forms of equity acquisition. This implies a distinction between what the literature identifies as the 'traditional FDI' and the 'new forms of investment (NFI)'.[77] The NFI include 'joint ventures in which foreign equity does not exceed 50 percent, licensing agencies, franchising, turnkey and "product-in-hand" contracts, and international sub-contracting (when the sub-contracting firm is at least 50 percent locally owned)'. Charles Oman observes that 'some NFI operations combine two or more of these arrangements'.[78] This is confirmed by Yanaihara Katsu, who makes the point that 'for Japanese direct-investment enterprises, in particular . . . manufacturers and trading companies join hands with banks participating sometimes directly and other times indirectly through the parent manufacturing companies that belong to specific banking groups'.[79] It may also be worth making the point that investment invariably implies an interest on the part of the participant to generate a surplus over time, and a means to appropriate or control at least part of that surplus.

Kojima specifically articulates a thesis of Japanese-style FDI which is more directly related to the Nigerian case study considered here. His thesis primarily revolves around the difference between Japanese and US investments:

- Japanese investments are more export-oriented, because this approach complements the Japanese comparative advantage position.
- US investments are more oriented towards domestic markets, because US FDI displaces its comparative advantage position, thus becoming anti-trade-oriented.[80]

The suggestion in the above dichotomy is based on Kojima's understanding of the behavior of American multinationals as being designed primarily to protect markets through direct investment, whereas Japanese firms invest abroad to serve international markets. His conclusion, based on the above observation, is that the latter, therefore, comes nearer the optimum of fostering trade and technology transfer based upon comparative advantage. Thus, a major portion of Japanese FDI is directed towards securing the natural resources Japan lacks. It is also directed towards labor-intensive industries such as textiles, and assembly of automobiles and parts of components for electrical appliances. Such activities, effectively, involve shifting labor-intensive processes out of the whole process of production to another country where wages are lower.

Kojima notes in his analysis of Japanese style FDI that the future of the world economy or the economic outlook of the Asian-Pacific region under Japanese-type direct foreign investment is easily predictable. First of all, textile and other labor-intensive manufacturing industries would be transplanted to developing countries, resulting in a reorganization of North–South trade. Next, the steel industry, other intermediate goods production, and then various machinery industries would establish networks of intra-industry specialization between advanced and developing countries.[81]

The indications are that the initial stage of Japan's investments in Nigeria seem to have followed the above pattern. The second stage of the process, however, was never realized. On the contrary, there is confirmation that the first stage of the process in fact 'retrogressed', given the number of cases of Japanese textile and other labor-intensive industries that have divested from Nigeria. Nor has Nigeria had the advantage of the market access and other benefits that Japanese FDI supposedly brings to the host country.[82] Peter Buckley, for example, argues that:

of key importance are the market access which the link with a Japanese distribution network brings, and the organizational skills of Japanese management when working with relatively unskilled or semi-skilled labor. The host country unit, when taken over or set up by Japanese FDI, becomes integrated with a marketing network guaranteeing market access. The Japanese imprint enhances the quality image of the product. Japanese ownership therefore confers immediate benefit.[83]

Generally, three main forms of motives for foreign investment, all of them trade-oriented, may be discerned. These are: (1) natural resource-oriented investment, (2) labor-oriented investment and (3) market-oriented investment. Kojima's argument presupposes that Japanese foreign investment in developing countries is determined by either one of the first two, or by both. From the Nigerian case study, however, it seems obvious that Japanese investments in Nigeria were primarily induced by the potential huge market in the country. It may be worth pointing out that market-oriented investments are mostly induced by trade barriers, as in the form of higher tariffs on final products. The point to stress here is that, whilst theoretical explanations of FDI emphasize either the endowment of resources or micro-policies, such as trade barriers and taxes as incentives for FDI, this case study shows that the macro-economic management and performance of the recipient country was a factor strong enough to influence the decision of potential investors. Indeed, the political climate prevailing in the host country also influenced the structure of foreign investment in Nigeria. This suggests that, despite the plethora of natural resources (listed in Chapter 4), including a very important strategic resource like oil in Nigeria, Japan hardly showed any interest in investing there for the purposes of prospecting for raw materials. This is an indication that, apart from South Africa, Japan was hardly interested in investing in sub-Saharan Africa. As will be demonstrated in Chapter 4, while certain Japanese companies were attracted to the potential market in the region, they did not, on the whole, find the resources in the region competitive enough to invest in.

In effect, as far as Japan was concerned, not even the oil in Nigeria was worth investing in. This attitude suggests at least two things: (1) that the Japanese economy was less desperate for natural resources than assumed and (2) that the argument that Japan's interest in Africa as a whole was primarily determined by the resources in the region was perversely exaggerated. The main thrust of the argument proposed in this study remains, therefore, that if Japanese firms had found it viable to invest in Nigeria for the purposes of prospecting for oil, for example, Japan's attitude towards the anti-apartheid debate at the UNGA might have been markedly different. It is tempting to suggest that it would have conceivably been more in tune with that of the AA group of states. In essence, if the OAU states had had the strategic resources to fit the strategic interests of Japan's CNS policy, Tokyo's voting pattern on comprehensive sanctions would have been more favorable to the cause of the OAU states.

One last caveat about the overall dimensions of Japanese foreign policy as epitomized in the CNS might be useful here. Without prejudicing the concept, it should be noted that the CNS was a conceptual framework for already existing themes in Japanese foreign policy. It was, therefore, simply a tale of plot-repetition – a new label for an old idea, as it were; thus giving credence to the thought that Japanese policy making was saturated with immobilism. The notion of 'immobilist diplomacy' was used to describe some of the recurrent, almost static and monotonous rhythms in Japanese foreign policy. An example of this is what is referred to in Chapter 2 as Japan's 'traditional diplomacy' – moving with the powerful, that is. It suggests an inability to do more than accommodate competing pressures and effect a 'lowest common denominator compromise between them.' The idea is borrowed from J.A.A. Stockwin.[84] His conception of 'dynamic and immobilist' politics is in relation to 'the effectiveness and responsiveness of political decision making in Japan'.[85] As he further argues:

A dynamic decision-making process, on the contrary, is where in retrospect it would be possible to say that the decision makers had not simply been constrained by a complex environment, but had succeeded in transcending the limitations provided by the nature of the political system, pressures of competing demands and so on, so as to arrive at policy based on the merits of issues and incorporating structural change where necessary.[86]

It is important to note that the terms 'dynamic' and 'immobilist' are not used here in contrast to each other. They are instead used to connote the idea that Japan's foreign policy, especially with regard to sub-Saharan Africa during the period under review, was essentially 'immobilist'. The phrase is further used to suggest that this 'immobilist' tendency had its own dynamism which helped it to sustain itself. Suffice to say, the dynamic aspects of this 'immobilist' foreign policy behavior were called into play when Japan was faced with complex or potentially contradictory policy goals, as in the case of its relations with the two main competing interests in sub-Saharan Africa. The term 'immobilism' is, therefore, not meant to signify a failure in policy making. On the contrary, 'immobilism', in essence, perpetuates hitherto successful policies.

CONCLUSION

An attempt has been made in this section to identify the imperatives behind Japan's post-war security policies. In doing so, the economic determinants of these policies have been highlighted by stressing the centrality of economic issues to the debate on Japan's national security. Power is considered as an inherent component of the security problematic, although an attempt has been made to show that power is not one-dimensional in terms of its applicants; that is, power is not localized, for it is an agent that exploits both the weak and strong. There is a vague suggestion here that power and security are not synonymous, for nation-states may seek both. In terms of priority, however, nation-states are more likely to seek security first. The foreign policies of post-war Japan in particular exemplify this essential fact.

Diplomacy was an essential ingredient in the overall equation of the CNS, as has been argued. Thus, within the context of the CNS the diplomatic net was made stronger and cast wider, as it were, with a view to smoothing out relations with the relevant others. Needless to say, giving economic assistance to the relevant countries was crucial to Japan's national security interests. Much of Japan's aid, therefore, went into developing friendly relations with countries of economic importance to it, especially those in possession of important raw materials. However, aid to Tanzania was primarily designed to contain any growing hostilities among the African states against Japan because of its expanding trade with South Africa. It must be noted, however, that the economic determinant was not lost here, either. On the contrary, it was the driving force behind such aid. We argue that, in this instance, Japanese foreign policy was 'proactive' rather than 'reactive', to adapt Kent Calder's point that Japanese foreign policy is essentially reactive:[87] reacting only to the pressures from the relevant others, notably the USA.

The above analysis has highlighted the importance of raw materials in the overall equation of Japan's CNS policy. Yet, in the inquiry into Japanese FDI in Nigeria it can be shown that despite the abundance of oil – a strategic raw material – in Nigeria Japan did not become dependent on Nigeria for oil. This suggests that dependence on an external source for (a) raw material(s) is a position arrived at judiciously. In other words, the decision to become dependent on another state for a strategic raw material on a long- or short-term basis is based on the economic viability of the action as defined within the context of Japan's national security interests, and not simply because a particular state also has the resource.

The indications, on the whole, are that the CNS was more than an adopted slogan, in the sense that its basic prescriptions became official policy, irrespective of which administration was in power.[88] According to Reinhard Drifte: 'Although the term "Comprehensive Security" is no longer in vogue, all Japanese governments since 1980 have based their responses on the analysis of the 1980 report, and followed its recommendations with more or less vigour and success.'[89] However, the internal dynamics of the concept are such that the itemization of areas of concern (as in threats to national security) were determined by developments within the international political economy, and therefore changed in relation to that. In short, the CNS was far from being a fossilized idea. Instead, it was a policy informed with a sense of time. It is in this respect that Akaha Tsuneo, and to a certain extent Katahara Eiichi, looked at the relevance of the concept in relation to the Gulf crisis, and indeed the dramatic changes that have occurred in world politics since 1989.[90] Akaha attempted to find out whether or not the CNS as it stood could be broadened in its themes and objectives, in order for it to be able to accommodate and respond to situations such as the ones presented by the Gulf crisis, for example. It is in a similar vein that this study attempts to measure the extent to which the CNS (and the analysis of the centrality of economic security in Japan's foreign relations) is relevant in an analysis of Japan's foreign policy towards sub-Saharan Africa during the period under review. The above discussion should help us to appreciate, in the next chapter, the history and essence of Japan's relations with South Africa.

NOTES

1 In this study, I use the definition of sub-Saharan Africa adopted by Gaimushō (the Japanese Ministry of Foreign Affairs – MOFA), which does not count Sudan as part of the region, but designates it as part of North Africa.

2 Kitagawa Katsuhiko, 'Japan's Economic Relations with Africa Between the Wars: A Study of Japanese Consular Reports', *African Studies Monographs*, vol. 11, 1990, p. 125.

3 Morikawa Jun, in *Afurika kenkyū*, No. 47, September, 1995, p. 65.

4 A number of journalistic articles published in Colin Legum (ed.), *Africa Contemporary Record* and certain popular magazines in the 1960s and 1970s were, however, useful in informing us about, mostly, trade relations between Japan and some of the African states. Some of these articles were written by David Morris and Godfrey Morrison. Several of such (English-language) articles were published in weekly and monthly magazines, including *West Africa*, and *Africa Report*. My own article, published in *West Africa* (28 November–4 December 1988, pp. 2220–2222), is a typical 'bus-tour' piece. Academic (English-language) articles written in such a fashion include Oda Hideo and Aoki Kazuyoshi, 'Japan and Africa: Beyond the Fragile Partnership', in Robert Ozaki and Walter Arnold (eds.), *Japan's Foreign Relations: A Global Search for Economic Security*, London, Westview Press, 1985.

5 Morikawa Jun, 'The Anatomy of Japan's South African Policies', *The Journal of Modern African Studies*, vol. 22, no. 1, 1984; Morikawa Jun, 'The Myth and Reality of Japan's Relations with Colonial Africa, 1885–1960', *Journal of African Studies*, vol. 12, no. 1, Spring, 1985; Morikawa Jun, *Minami afurika to nihon: kankei no rekishi, kōzō, kadai*, Tokyo, Dōbunkan, 1988; Kitagawa Katsuhiko, 'Senzenki nihon no ryōji hōkoku ni mirareru afurika keizai jijō chōsa no kenkyū – gaimushō tsūshōkyoku [tsūshō-kōhō] o chūshin toshite' *Afurika kenkyū*, vol. 35, 1989; Kweku Ampiah, 'British Commercial Policies Against Japanese Expansionism in East and West Africa, 1932–1935', *The International Journal of African Historical Studies*, vol. 23, no. 4, 1990. A handful of Nigerian academics have also written on this subject. These include Bukar Bukarambe, 'Nigeria's Economic Relations with Japan: The Direct and Indirect', in R.A. Akindele and Bassey E. Ate (eds.), *Nigeria's Economic Relations with the Major Developed Market-economy Countries, 1960–1985*, Lagos, The Nigerian Institute of International Affairs, 1988; S.O. Agbi, *Japanese Relations with Africa, 1868–1978*, Ibadan, Ibadan University Press, 1992; and Jide Owoeye, whose writings on various aspects of Japan's relations with Africa (as separate articles) were eventually published as *Japan's Policy in Africa*, New York, The Edwin Mellen Press, 1992.
6 Ozaki and Arnold, *Japan's Foreign Relations*. We should also note that James R. Soukup's article on the subject, 'Japanese-African Relations: Problems and Prospects', appeared in the *Asian Survey*, vol. 5, no. 7, July, 1965.
7 Kitazawa Yōko, 'Aparutoheito e no nihon no katan–nihon, minami afurika keizai kankei chōsa hōkoku', *Ajia taiheiyō shiryō sentā*, 1975; Kitazawa Yōko, 'Japan Imports Namibian Natural Resources Illegally', *Pacific Asia Resource Centre*, 1976.
8 S.O. Agbi, 'Africa – Japan's Continent-sized Blind Spot', *Japan Times*, 6 June, 1982.
9 Ronald Dore, 'Japan and the Third World: Coincidence or Divergence of Interests?', in Robert Cassen, *Rich Country Interest and Third World Development*, London, Croom Helm, 1982, p. 141.
10 Namely, the US suspension of the convertibility of the dollar into gold, the establishment of a 10 percent surcharge on imports and the announcement in July 1971 of Nixon's trip to China, which was unexpected by Japanese policy makers.
11 Dennis Yasutomo, 'Why Aid? Japan as an Aid Great Power', *Pacific Affairs*, vol. 62, no. 4, Winter, 1989/90.
12 Quoted in Chalmers Johnson and E.B. Keehn, 'The Pentagon's Ossified Strategy', *Foreign Affairs*, vol. 74, 1995, p. 104.
13 Naikaku kanbō naikaku shingishitsu, *Sōgo anzen hoshō senryaku* (Ōhira sōri no seisaku kenkyukai hōkokusho – 5), Tokyo, Ōkurashō insatsukyoku (3rd edition), 1985, p. 21
14 Cited in Barry Buzan, *People, States and Fear: An Agenda for International Securities Studies in the Post-Cold War Era*, London, Wheatsheaf, 1991, p. 17.
15 Frederick H. Hartman, *The Relations of Nations*, New York, 1967, p. 14.
16 Richard J. Samuels, 'Consuming for Production: Japanese National Security, Nuclear-free Procurement, and the Domestic Economy', *International Organization*, vol. 43, no. 4, Autumn, 1989, p. 640.
17 Ibid.
18 Peter Katzenstein and Nobuo Okawara, 'Japan's National Security: Structures, Norms and Policies', *International Security*, vol. 17, no. 4, 1993.

19 Peter Drysdale, 'Foreword', in Okita Saburo, *Japan's Challenging Years: Reflections on my Lifetime*, Canberra, George Allen & Unwin, 1985, pp. viiii-ix.
20 Watanabe Osamu, *Sengo seijishi no naka no tennōsei*, Tokyo, Aoki shoten, 1990, p. 334. Umemoto Tetsuya, 'Comprehensive Security and the Evolution of the Japanese Security Posture', in Robert A. Scalapino *et al.* (eds.), *Asian Security Issues: Regional and Global*, Berkeley, University of California Press, 1988, is among those who see the CNS as a vehicle for expanding Japan's defense capabilities. He argues that, 'somewhat paradoxically, a concept which in the abstract implies a reduction of the relative weight of military efforts on behalf of national security has in fact served as a vehicle for promoting such efforts'. In 1985 Prime Minister Nakasone scrapped the 1976 policy of limiting the nation's defense expenditure to less than 1 percent of its GNP. Japan has, without doubt, expanded its defense capabilities substantially since the 1970s. Since 1978 its defense expenditure has risen at the rate of 6.5 percent a year, and in dollar terms in 1996 it has the world's third-largest defense budget after the USA and Russia. While Japan's defense expenditure is said to be approximately 1 percent, if it were calculated using the common method employed by NATO countries who include in their calculation military pension and benefits, the actual level of Japan's defense spending would be closer to 1.7 percent of GNP.
21 Cited in J.W.M. Chapman, R. Drifte and I.T.M. Gowe, *Japan's Quest for Comprehensive Security: Defense-Diplomacy, Dependence*, London: Francis Pinter, 1983, p. xvi.
22 Ibid.
23 Ibid., p. xv.
24 Noguchi Yuichiro, 'Sōgo anzen hoshō kōzō e no gimon', *Sekai*, no. 420, 1982, p. 200.
25 A number of observers analyze Japan's economic policies within the context of the trade friction between Japan and the US, and conclude that the former's economic policies are informed by neo-mercantilism. For an analysis of Mercantilism see Barry Buzan, *People, States and Fear*. William Nester, *Japan's Growing Power over East Asia and the World Economy: Ends and Means*, London, Macmillan, 1990, refers to Japan as a neo-mercantilist state.
26 Alan Rix, 'Japan's Comprehensive Security and Australia', *Australian Outlook: The Australian Journal of International Relations*, vol. 41, no. 2, August, 1987, p. 79.
27 Ibid.
28 Donald C. Hellmann, 'Japanese Security and Post-war Japanese Foreign Policy', in Robert Scalapino, *The Foreign Policy of Modern Japan*, Berkeley, University of California Press, 1977, p. 326, notes that 'the separability of economics and politics (*seikei bunri*) in foreign policies has been an implicit (and often explicit) premise in the policies of all post-war Japanese governments'.
29 Katzenstein and Okawara, 'Japan's National Security', p. 92.
30 The report was submitted to acting Prime Minister Itō Masayoshi in July 1980 when Ōhira died, unexpectedly, shortly before the task force completed the report.
31 Naikaku kanbō, *Sōgo anzen hoshō senryaku*, p. 86.
32 Ibid., p. 50.
33 Ibid., p. 21.

34 Naikaku kanbō naikaku shingishitsu, *Kokusai kokka nihon no sōgo anzen hoshō seisaku* (Heiwa mondai kenkyūkai hōkokusho), Tokyo, Ōkurasho insatsukyoku, 1985.
35 Watanabe Osamu, *Kigyō shihai to kokka*, Tokyo, Aoki shoten, 1991, p. 203.
36 Ibid., pp. 8–62.
37 Ibid., pp. 62–64.
38 Noguchi , 'Sōgo anzen hoshō kōzō e no gimon,' p. 199.
39 Ibid.
40 Naikaku kanbō, *Sōgo anzen hoshō senryaku*, p. 23.
41 Samuels, 'Consuming for Production', pp. 640–41.
42 Naikaku kanbō, *Sōgo anzen hoshō senryaku*, p. 24.
43 Ibid.
44 Naikaku kanbō, *Kokusai kokka nihon no sōgo anzen hoshō seisaku*, p. 59.
45 Ibid.
46 Ibid.
47 Hanns Maull, *Raw Materials, Energy and Western Security*, London, Macmillan, 1984, p. 8.
48 Robert Gilpin, 'Economic Interdependence and National Security in Historical Perspective', in Klaus Knorr and Frank Trager (eds.), *Economic Issues and National Security*, Kansas, University Press of Kansas, 1982.
49 Naikaku kanbō, *Kokusai kokka nihon no sōgo anzen hoshō seisaku*, pp. 58–62.
50 Noguchi, 'Sōgo anzen hoshō kōzō e no gimon', p. 200.
51 Ibid., p. 201.
52 Dore, 'Japan and the Third World,' p. 131.
53 Robert Keohane, *After Hegemony: Cooperation and Discord in the World Political Economy*, Princeton, NJ., Princeton University Press, 1984, p. 25.
54 Kenneth Waltz, *Theory of World Politics*, Reading, Mass., Addison-Wesley, 1979, pp. 19–79, 67–73.
55 Neil Richardson, 'Political Compliance and US Trade Dominance', *The American Political Science Review*, vol. 70, no. 4, December, 1976, p. 1099.
56 Neil Richardson, *Foreign Policy and Economic Dependence*, Austin, University of Texas Press, 1978; Adrienne Armstrong, 'The Political Consequences of Economic Dependence', *Journal of Conflict Resolution*, vol. 25, no. 3, 1981.
57 Bruce E. Moon, 'Consensus or Compliance? Foreign-policy Change and External Dependence', *International Organization*, vol. 39, no. 2, Spring, 1985.
58 Ibid., pp. 297–298.
59 Ibid., p. 298.
60 Ibid., p. 301.
61 Michel Foucault, 'Two Lectures', in Colin Gordon (ed.) *Power and Knowledge: Selected Interviews and Other Writings, 1972–1977*, Brighton, Harvester Wheatsheaf, 1980, p. 98.
62 Ibid.
63 Ibid., p. 142.
64 Moon, 'Consensus or Compliance?', p. 248.
65 Ibid., emphasis in original.
66 Jack E. Vincent, 'Predicting Voting Patterns in the General Assembly', *The American Political Science Review*, vol. lxv, no. 2, June, 1971, p. 471.
67 Hayward R. Alker Jr. 'Dimensions of Conflict in the General Assembly', *The American Political Science Review*, vol. lviii, no. 3, September, 1964, p. 179.

68 Ibid.
69 Ernest B. Haas, 'Regionalism, Functionalism and Universal International Organization', *World Politics*, vol. 8, no. 2, January, 1956, p. 238–41.
70 Conor C. O'Brien, *To Katanga and Back*, London, Hutchinson, 1966, pp. 17–18.
71 Ernst Haas, 'Regionalism, Functionalism and Universal International Organization,' p. 239.
72 Ibid., p. 240.
73 Ali Mazrui, 'The United Nations and Some African Political Attitudes,' *International Organization*, vol. xviii, 1964, p. 501.
74 Ibid., p. 508.
75 Ernst Haas, 'Regionalism, Functionalism and Universal International Organization', p. 240.
76 Kojima Kiyoshi, 'Japanese-style Direct Foreign Investment', *Japanese Economic Studies*, vol. xiv, 1986, p. 61.
77 Charles Oman, *New Forms of Investment in Developing Country Industries: Mining, Petrochemicals, Automobiles, Textiles, Food*, Paris: OECD, 1989.
78 Ibid., p. 11.
79 Yanaihara Katsu, 'Japanese Overseas Enterprises in Developing Countries Under Indigenization Policy: The African Case', *Japanese Economic Studies*, vol. 4, no. 1, 1975, p. 33.
80 Kojima Kiyoshi, 'A Macroeconomic Approach to Foreign Direct Investment', *Hitotsubashi Journal of Economics*, 14, 1973.
81 Kojima Kiyoshi, 'Japanese-style Direct Foreign Investment', p. 72.
82 Kojima Kiyoshi and Ozawa T., *Japan's Trading Companies: Merchants of Economic Development*, Paris: OECD, 1984.
83 Peter J. Buckley, 'A Critical View of Theories of the Multinational Enterprise', in Peter J. Buckley and M. Casson, *The Economic Theory of Multinational Enterprise*, London, Macmillan, 1985, p. 17.
84 Stockwin, J.A.A. 'Dynamic and Immobilist Aspects of Japanese Politics', in Stockwin *et al.* (eds.), *Dynamic and Immobilist Politics in Japan*, Macmillan, London, 1988.
85 Ibid., p. 2
86 Ibid.
87 Kent E. Calder, 'Japanese Foreign Economic Policy Formation: Explaining the Reactive State', *World Politics*, vol. xl, no. 4, July, 1988.
88 See Noguchi, 'Sōgo anzen hoshō kōzō e no gimon'; Akaha Tsuneo, 'Japan's Comprehensive Security Policy', *Asian Survey*, vol. xxxi, no. 4, 1991; and Umemoto, 'Comprehensive Security and the Evolution of the Japanese Security Posture'.
89 Reinhard Drifte, *Japan's Foreign Policy*, London, Royal Institute of International Affairs, 1990, p. 30.
90 Akaha, 'Japan's Comprehensive Security Policy'; Katahara Eiichi, 'The Politics of Japanese Security Policy-making: A Case Study of Japan's Participation in UN Peace Keeping Operations', paper prepared for the Institute on Global Conflict and Cooperation Conference on Pacific Security Relations after the Cold War, June 15–18, 1992, Hong Kong.

2 The historical dimensions of Japan's relations with sub-Saharan Africa

Japan's relations with Africa seem to have followed the pattern of the changes that evolve with the shift in hegemonic powers in global politics. Its relations with the African countries, as colonial entities and as independent states, were largely dictated first, by its relations with the UK (until the early 1930s), and second, by the USA (since the end of World War II). Implicit in this phenomenon, however, was a rather complex behavior of immobilist diplomacy. The new bilateral alliance with the USA was, in effect, a new version of a 'traditional diplomacy'[1] following the principle, according to John Welfield, of *nagai mono ni makareyō* (move with the powerful).[2] It is instructive that both alliances were directed primarily against Russia, with the US–Japan security pact further cemented by another strong legacy from the pre-war era: anti-communism.[3] And it is largely within this anti-communist framework that Japan's relations with the African countries were shaped.

But it is also plausible to argue that, at least in the post-World War II period, Japan's policies towards the region were punctuated by elements of the race politics in Southern Africa. Thus, Japan's policy makers, while supporting the minority (white) regimes in the region, particularly in South Africa, through trade,[4] none the less, or as a corollary, developed constructive responses towards the demands of other African states that reflected, to some extent, the interests of these countries. Thus, Japan's relations with the region were based primarily on a dual structure policy (*nigen kōzō*), as Morikawa puts it.[5]

JAPAN, BRITAIN AND AFRICA: FROM THE INTER-WAR PERIOD TO 1945

While in the 1930s Japan's leaders introduced a dramatically new flavor into their country's foreign policy, particularly from 1931 when Japan invaded Manchuria and subsequently set up the puppet state of

Manchukuo, we can argue that the circumstances within which these changes in Japanese foreign policy occurred were abnormal. They were abnormal, first, because, as far as the debate on hegemonic stability goes, the international community lacked a true hegemon at the time. During that transition Japan's policy makers made decisive moves to join forces with the other 'restless' powers (Germany and Italy) who thought it strategically appropriate, as far as their interests were concerned, to undermine the *status quo*.

Second, Japan's civilian-controlled political system had become too weak to stop the military from completely usurping power in the country. Thus, although Japan's foreign policy signals towards Africa changed during the above period, those changes represented nothing more than a deviant phenomenon in Japan's foreign policy behavior since modern times. An example of such a change in Japanese foreign policy towards Africa, which also signified a change in attitude towards its former ally, Britain, was the Italian invasion of Abyssinia in 1935.

Divorced from the League of Nations and therefore from the latter's position on the matter, the Japanese government supported the invasion. In fact, it has been argued that the Italian invasion of Abyssinia was made possible as a result of Japan's invasion of Manchuria in 1931, and its flagrant disrespect for the dictates of the League of Nations. Effectively, Japan's behavior evoked the sense that a policy of aggression, which ignored international public opinion, was operational;[6] although Agbi has cogently argued that Japan's support for the Italian invasion of Abyssinia was not automatic, but protracted and delayed. As he points out, Japan was initially antagonistic to the invasion because it trampled on Japan's economic interests in Abyssinia and totally disregarded the affinity between the monarchies of Japan and Abyssinia.[7] Despite all these developments, however, one fact remained constant in the minds of Japan's conservative leaders even in the 1930s, and that was the fear of the communist threat.

Japan's relations with Britain in the early twentieth century, as defined within the Anglo-Japanese Alliance (1902–1922), made it possible for Japan to participate in the Convention of St Germain en Laye, in 1919. The terms of this convention effectively replaced the Congo Basin Treaties of 1885, and reiterated the importance of East Africa as a free trade zone. Taking advantage of the above liberal economic principle, Japan's policy makers and manufacturers expanded their exports into the region. By the latter part of the 1920s, however, British manufacturers and policy makers had begun to observe a rapid expansion of Japanese exports to the Empire's colonies in Africa. With pressure from Lancashire and in the face of losing its markets to Japanese manufacturers, Whitehall decided to initiate measures to protect the interests of Lancashire against what it saw as a trade offensive from the latter's competitors. By 1932 Whitehall had introduced measures giving the UK particular advantages in trade with its colonies, except those in the Congo Basin region, to the exclusion of foreign countries, especially Japan. An examination of the actual effects of the quota system reveals that in West Africa (Sierra Leone, the Gambia, Nigeria and the Gold Coast) Whitehall was able to control Japanese exports to the region and to a large extent was successful in damaging Japanese commercial activities in these four West African countries.[8] These events, among others, led to far more complicated issues which ultimately wrecked a previously healthy relationship between Britain and Japan and led to a war situation in the Far East, from 1939–1945. Needless to say, an important aspect of Anglo-Japanese relations in the inter-war period often overlooked by historians is how the expansion of Japanese trade in Africa might have affected Anglo-Japanese relations, especially in the 1930s.

As Japan confronted Britain in war, many Africans, as colonial subjects of His Majesty's Government, found themselves fighting against Japan. African soldiers, including the 81st and 82nd West Africa Divisions and the 11th East Africa Division, directly confronted the invading Japanese Imperial Army on the Burmese Front.[9] Yet African intellectuals and leaders, in a rather convoluted way, admired Japan for standing up against white supremacy; overlooking the fact that Japan was equally imperialistic in its external relations. They chose to see in Japanese foreign policy and achievements the 'beginnings of the end of White supremacy'; and along with that they naively imagined the impending freedom of Africa from European domination.[10] As Jeremy Murray-Brown tells us, the fall of Singapore to the Japanese set off waves of optimism in Jomo Kenyatta concerning the possibility of the end of colonial rule in Kenya.[11]

The political configuration of South Africa, and Japan's emergence as a power to be reckoned with, drew African patriots like Walter Sisulu, Oliver Tambo and Nelson Mandela towards politics, Mary Benson informs us.[12] And the threat that Japan's aggressive policy posed to Madagascar and South Africa was even seen as positive by the Africans. The Africans in the Cape were not at all alarmed by this prospect. Indeed, they viewed the Japanese victories with almost open jubilation. Their sympathies and hopes were with the Japanese, who had proved too smart for the British and Americans.[13]

Interestingly, the same war that destabilized Japan's ambition to become a world power and, by implication, the deluded hopes of the political elites of Africa that a victorious Japan would liberate Africa from colonialism, even though it was won by the leading colonial powers and their allies, seems to have facilitated the African countries' political transition to modern statehood. It is conceivable, however, that had the Axis powers, including Japan, won the war, this transition would not have taken place when it did.

JAPAN WITHIN THE AFRO-ASIAN FRAMEWORK

The end of the war ushered in a new concept of spheres of influence, as dictated by the ideological positions of Washington, on the one hand, and Moscow, on the other. Both superpowers – the USA and the USSR – incidentally saw the end to colonialism as crucial to their own economic, political and strategic interests. As a result, they both pushed for decolonization. Needless to say, their efforts to bring about the end of Western European domination of extensive regions of the world did put pressure on the European powers, especially Britain, France and Portugal, to make concessions to the African nationalists who were demanding independence from colonial rule. These efforts, it must be mentioned, were made within the context of the Cold War, which in itself was a great strain on the process of decolonization.[14]

As the Cold War developed, and the two superpowers made moves for spheres of influence: 'they both began to perceive the strategic value of Japan in their contest for power'.[15] In effect, the politics of the peace settlement between Japan and the Allied powers became entangled with the politics of the Cold War. Both the USA and the Soviet Union thus attempted to detach Japan from the other.

A combination of factors, notably Washington's decision to commit Japan, spiritually and politically, to the cause of the Western democratic states[16] and the policy of the Yoshida Shigeru (Prime Minister of Japan, 1946–1947, 1948–1954) administration to ensure the country's security with the presence of US forces in Japan against communism, ultimately found Japan on the side of the ideological divide orchestrated by the USA, the hegemonic power. In the words of J.A.A. Stockwin, 'rather than a conquered enemy to be set on the true road of democracy and peace, Japan was . . . seen as a potential ally in a worldwide struggle against International Communism'.[17] Thus, Japan became rehabilitated as an ally of the USA, within the framework of containing the expansion of communism in the Far East. This culminated in the signing of the US–Japan Security Treaty of 1951, immediately after the signing of the San Fransisco Peace Treaty.

And, despite all the debate in the late 1950s and early 1960s surrounding the question of a neutral foreign policy for Japan, with calls from certain sectors of the community to the effect that Japan's security could be safely entrusted to the UN, in 1959 the Foreign Ministry Blue

Book confirmed that 'under the prevailing world situation Japan cannot survive independently as a free and democratic nation by taking a neutral policy'.[18] The suggestion, even from some of Japan's policy makers, that a security treaty cast in the mould of the UN would be more acceptable to the Japanese people, was ignored. Yoshida saw a policy of replacement of US forces by UN troops,[19] as suggested by some members of the Japan Socialist Party (JSP) and the intellectual community, as bankrupt and unrealistic.

In 1964 Ōhira Masayoshi reiterated the Liberal Democratic Party (LDP) government's position that the only way in which Japan could ensure its security in the international community was by means of a 'collective security by alliance with bona fide friendly powers'.[20] Following the previous argument concerning Japan's relations with the hegemonic powers, the contention put forward here is that Japan's post-war foreign policy – including its foreign policy towards the sub-Saharan African states – was heavily influenced, if not dictated, by its relations with the USA. Consequently, Japan's foreign policy position was to a large extent influenced by the rivalry between Washington and Moscow.

In the event, Japan, under pressure from the USA, adopted a pro-Taiwan rather than a pro-China policy. On 18 April 1952 Japan signed a separate peace treaty with Taiwan, and effectively sanctioned Koumintang (KMT) control of territories under its control. Further to complicate Japan's position on the 'two-China' issue, Yoshida had earlier in the year signed a letter drafted by the American Secretary of State, John Foster-Dulles. The 'Yoshida Letter', as it came to be known, condemned the People's Republic of China (PRC) and reiterated Japan's support for the KMT.[21] However, the letter held open the possibility of future relations with the PRC if it 'changes its present ways'.

It is appropriate to mention here that the Yoshida administration remained unconvinced by the US government's view that communist China was a threat to the region. Yoshida argued that 'Sino-Japanese contacts could be built to mutual advantage'. With his eyes on the economic development of Japan, Yoshida further said: 'I don't care whether China is red or green. China is a national market and it has become necessary for Japan to think about markets.'[22] That Japan could not formulate and implement its own independent foreign policy proved a dilemma for the US–Japan alliance, at least in some respects. It proved more of a problem for Japan, especially on the question of its relations with the developing countries.

Japanese diplomacy at the Bandung conference

Previous to some of the developments in its diplomatic initiatives as noted above, representatives of Japan had been at the Bandung conference of 1955. It was the first major international conference that Japan attended since the war. It was also its first attempt to gain re-admission into the 'Asian family of nations' since the end of World War II, or even since Fukuzawa Yukichi's exhortations to Meiji Japan to desert Asia (*'Tōhō no akuyū o shazetsu suru'*).[23] Japan's presence at the conference (which eventually culminated in the Afro-Asian Solidarity Movement) was seen among certain sectors of the Japanese leadership as important to Japan's membership in the international community. It is worth noting that Japan's membership of the UN, for example, did not occur until 1956. Thus, Japanese attendance at the conference deserves our attention, if only because it provides an illustrative precedent to Japan's concern for its broader image in international relations. It also furnishes us (through an analysis of some of the correspondence between a number of top-ranking Japanese ambassadors and ministers, as well as Gaimushō documentation about the conference) with an insight into what is appropriately referred to as Japan's dual policy towards sub-Saharan Africa.

Some background information about the conference may be appropriate at this juncture. The conference was held in Bandung, in Indonesia, from 18 to 24 April 1955. It was initiated by, and convened upon invitations from, the Prime Ministers of the Colombo Powers – Burma, Ceylon, India, Indonesia and Pakistan. The conference was organized to promote the highest aspirations of the peoples of Asia and Africa; that is, positive life chances for the disadvantaged nations of the international community. These ambitions were to be further channelled into an articulate and coherent 'third force' in a world supposedly frozen into two camps by the Cold War. The conference, therefore, was concerned with themes and problems of common interest to the participants, namely, economic co-operation, cultural co-operation, human rights and self-determination, the problems of dependent people, and the promotion of world peace.

The one underlying theme that ran through the economic, cultural, and political objectives of the conference was a sense among the members, irrespective of their individual ideological orientation, that they would not be trapped with their experiences as 'dependents' or appendages of colonialism. This was clearly expressed in the conference's universal declaration that 'colonialism in all its manifestations is an evil which should speedily be brought to an end'. Essentially, the spirit of the conference hinged on the determination of the member states to preserve their newly won freedoms and to reach out for more through their persistent opposition to colonialism and imperialism, as well as through a systematic attempt to advance the economic well-being of the people they represented, thereby questioning the essence of the UN as pointed out in Chapter 1. The conference, in short, was overwhelmingly critical of all aspects of colonialism in its past and present manifestations; and Japan as the only former colonial power at the conference was condemned to listen to the vitriolic pronouncements against 'the evils arising from the subjection of peoples to alien subjugation, domination, and exploitation' alone.

In view of the determination on the part of these countries to try and solve their problems without help from the villains, it was no surprise that the USA and the Western European countries were not invited to the conference. Nor was it surprising that these countries were very apprehensive of the real essence of the conference, which they saw as communist-inspired and therefore a fertile ground for communist propaganda. The *Nippon Times*, for example, was concerned that 'as Asia deplores the colonialism that has strutted throughout the Far East in the past century communist blandishments will urge the nations to accept a "Red" version of the same system to fill the vacuum'.[24] The living embodiment of the 'Red' threat at the conference was Zhou Enlai, the 'announced attraction' who was 'expected to pilfer the allegiance of "neutralist" nations'.[25] With its response to the conference predicated on controlling this threat, the USA advised its friends, especially Japan and the Philippines, to attend, 'hoping to counteract any put-up deals promoted by communists or their fellow travellers'.[26] Thus, among the *Nippon Times*' editorial comments was a plea that the 'Japanese delegate to Bandung will exercise discretion in the face of some likely temptations' from the PRC, suggesting a suspicion among the paper's editorial board of Japan's pan-Asianist inclination.

Japan's preparation for the conference is worth examining. In a letter to Foreign Minister Shigemitsu Mamoru, Ambassador Okamoto Suemasa (The Hague) expressed the point that, 'this is a big step in Japan's foreign policy, in the sense that both China and Japan have been invited to the conference and the whole world would be watching Japan's movements'. He also noted that how Japan performed at the conference could form the basis of Japan's leadership role within the Afro-Asian community.[27] But Japan's participation in the conference was from a distance. In a letter to Ambassador Yamagata Kiyoshi (Pakistan), Shigemitsu expressed an explicit note of caution. He stated that while 'Japan is looking forward to developing good relations with the[se] countries . . . it needs however to be careful of the international ramification of the conference, and how that may affect Japan's standing in global affairs. It needs to be particularly careful about participating in a conference involving South East Asian countries.'[28] He expressed a similar concern in a letter[29] to Ambassador Iguchi Sadao (Washington).

Attitudes towards the conference, needless to say, reflected the ideological leanings of both participants and observers. Ambassador Okamoto expressed what was obviously a concern of the Japanese government. This was 'that China would use the occasion to attack the West, which might then lead to conflict between the two ideological camps'. Thus, the USA, as he noted further, 'was rather nervous about China's participation in the conference'.[30] In view of this, he suggested that 'Japan should take the initiative to prevent conflict'. Shigemitsu was surprisingly optimistic about what his country could do, hinting that 'Japan might be able to change the negative tone of the conference into a positive one'.[31] This necessitated a careful balancing of the situation, however, which would be best achieved by keeping a low profile at the conference.[32] On the whole, Tokyo was of the opinion that it was venturing on to hostile territory, and therefore had to tread lightly.

The assumption of a low profile by Japan's representatives at the Bandung conference was predicated on multiple factors. In the first place, it was only sensible that, in the midst of Asian countries, the majority of whom were suspicious of, if not hostile to, Japan for its behavior towards them as an imperialist force, Japan's leaders should restrain their enthusiasm, if they had any at the time. There was also the immediate political issue of China's participation at the conference, on the one hand, and the absence of the Soviet Union and Taiwan, both of which were countries with an affinity to Asia if only because of their geographical location, on the other. Taiwan was not invited because none of the five sponsor nations of the conference recognized it.

The membership of the conference provided Japan with added reason to pursue 'tiptoe' diplomacy. In addition to the five sponsoring countries (Burma, Ceylon, India, Indonesia and Pakistan), twenty-four other countries, amongst them Japan, took part in the conference. Needless to say, due to their ideological leanings, the sponsoring countries disagreed over inviting certain countries, notably Japan and the PRC. Burma, Indonesia and India were very keen to have the PRC participate in the conference, after Burma suggested it. Pakistan and Ceylon, on the other hand, opposed it initially. The proposal to invite Japan was made by Pakistan with the support of Ceylon, but also with a certain amount of contention from the others.[33]

It is conceivable that in their attempts to establish a peace treaty with the Soviet Union, Japan's leaders thought it appropriate not to be seen to be active at the conference, for fear of offending Moscow. And of immense importance to the Japanese leadership was the question of their country's membership at the UN, which largely depended on the response of the Soviet Union. Tokyo's attempts to join the organization had been frustrated twice by Moscow's veto at the Security Council. It was necessary, therefore, at least for Japan's leaders, not to worsen an already troubled relationship.[34]

The absence of Taiwan from the conference while the PRC participated also effectively meant, at least in tactical terms, that Japan had to be careful as to how it related to the PRC. We should mention that, at a private meeting with Takasaki Tatsunosuke, the head of the Japanese delegation, Zhou Enlai reiterated China's desire to achieve better relations with Japan,[35] without the benefit of any positive response from him. Takasaki responded cautiously; it was not appropriate for him to express an opinion on the matter,[36] he said.

The composition of the Japanese delegation was another key factor in explaining Japan's performance at the conference. While the conference organizers hoped that each country's chief delegate would be either the Prime Minister or the Foreign Minister,[37] Japan neither sent its Prime Minister, Hatoyama Ichirō, nor its Foreign Minister, Shigemitsu. Instead, Takasaki Tatsunosuke (Minister of State, Director-General of the Economic Counsel Board) was named as the chief delegate.[38] A critical observer, therefore, expressed concern that Japan could not send a resolute (*shikkari shita*) representative.[39] It is not surprising that Mr. Takasaki could not articulate an opinion in response to China's request for diplomatic relations with Japan, much less give a resolute answer to the proposal. Takasaki, nevertheless, had no difficulty agreeing with Zhou Enlai for an expansion of trade between their two countries.[40] They agreed to discuss the trade further. Takasaki's primary appeal as representative was presumably that he was a prominent businessman who had worked in Formosa, had been a war-time president of Manchurian Heavy Industries Company and, most importantly, as John Welfield seems to suggest, he was an Asianist[41] – someone who could relate to the Asian delegates at the conference and to the aspirations of their countries for economic development. The government's inability to send the Foreign Minister to the conference was, however, viewed as an indication of Japan's lack of respect for Asia by certain concerned observers.[42] And yet, the fact that Japan was not represented by either Hatoyama or Shigemitsu is not so surprising. After all, the Japanese suspected that Zhou Enlai would demand a meeting with their chief representative; and that it would be a diplomatic blunder to agree to a meeting between either Hatoyama or Shigemitsu and the Chinese Prime Minister, when the two countries had no diplomatic relations.

In any case, the political fact that the conference itself was effectively a gathering for the Third World countries – states with a history as peripheral economies and sharing a history as former colonies,[43] or semi-colonies in the case of China, made Japan's presence at it a special case, as viewed by the rest of the members.[44] In short, Japan was outside the euphoria that had brought the other countries together. This can be construed to mean that Japan was incapable of understanding the essence of the conference, which was effectively a demonstration against colonialism and imperialism and a vehicle of support for the liberation movements in Africa. Nor was Japan capable of appreciating the real aspirations of these nations. And, after all, Japan was confounded by the overzealous ideological groupings within the framework of the conference: the supporters of the USA, on the one hand, and the anti-imperialist group, on the other. In fact, the latter group was split up into the pro-socialist group and the collection of non-aligned countries. But Japan's position was also blurred by its desire to renew links with the Asian countries, especially the PRC, when faced with the constraints put on its diplomatic freedom by its alliance with the USA.

Most importantly, Takasaki's speech at the conference contained an element of apology to Japan's neighbours for the atrocities Japan committed against them: 'In World War II, Japan I regret to say, inflicted damages upon her neighbours.' And he tried, obviously as instructed, to use the occasion to assure them that Japan had no intentions of repeating its past vicious foreign policy: 'Japan has reestablished democracy, having learned her lesson at immense cost. Chastened and free, she is today a nation completely dedicated to peace.' The indications were that Japan was, even at a time when it had not been admitted as a member of the UN, already showing signs of what subsequently became its UN-centred foreign policy. As its chief delegate noted, 'our fundamental policy is to uphold the principles and purposes of the United Nations which we believe is the best system yet devised for the maintainance of international peace and security on a basis of mutual trust'.[45] The invocation of the UN was conceivably meant to reassure Japan's neighbors in particular that it was, sincerely, a 'born-again' pacifist nation. But it was also designed to let the international community know how desperately Japan wanted to become a member of the international body. Takasaki's main responsibility at the conference, however, was to emphasize Japan's interest in (1) international peace, (2) economic cooperation and (3) cultural exchange. The most important of these three themes to Japan was economic cooperation with its neighbours. 'Japan is anxious to contribute her share to the promotion of economic co-operation for the common prosperity of the region', Takasaki declared at the conference. It was in this respect that the head of the Japanese delegation, without any hesitation, agreed with Zhou Enlai to hold further negotiations between their two countries on the question of Sino-Japanese trade.[46] Japan was, in essence, placing itself at the disposal of its neighbours – offering aid as a technical expert, hoping thereby to stimulate trade and gain access to the raw materials it needed to sustain economic growth. Takasaki must have made an impression on the Chinese with his speech, in the sense that he emerged in the 1960s as the person responsible for negotiating Japan's informal trade agreements with the PRC.[47]

The Japanese delegation also availed itself of the opportunity to state that Japan, as an Asiatic nation, had a destiny 'identical with that of Asia' and therefore attached the greatest importance[48] to the conference. 'We, the peoples of the Asian African region . . .', Takasaki proclaimed in an awkward attempt to venerate and celebrate a united front. It is, however, the intention of this study to show, by analyzing its voting behavior at the UNGA in Chapter 5, that Japan on the whole had a different set of political values and ambitions to the rest of the members of the Afro-Asian community.

Japanese foreign policy and the decolonization process in Africa

In the words of Roger Louis, 'the anti-colonial attitude of the United States gave powerful impetus to the decolonization of the European colonial Empires'.[49] Yet while the attitude of the USA towards decolonization, especially during the period of Roosevelt's presidency, was significantly firm in its opposition, it nevertheless increasingly assumed a position of ambivalence on the matter 'as World War II ended, and the Cold War began to emerge'.[50] The point to make here is that Japan's policies towards decolonization can be seen as having been heavily influenced by the US policies on the matter.

According to Charles O'Lerche.

> The United States mildly encouraged the colonial states to continue imperial rule, but on a more enlightened and humanitarian basis while at the same time giving studiously non-specific indications that it retained its traditional adherence to the principle of self-determination.[51]

It is pertinent to note in this respect that, by 1952, American anti-colonialism had melted to mere rhetoric. Eisenhower had won the elections on the issues of Korea and the spread of communism. Thus, the administration's main preoccupation, throughout its life-span, remained the containment of communism at the expense of decolonization.

Japan's attitude towards the decolonization process in Africa has to be seen within the context of the above US framework, especially in the period from the end of the war to the end of the 1950s, since during almost half of this period the sovereignty of Japan was in question due to its occupation by the Allied forces. From 1952 (when the occupation ended) to the end of the decade Japan also remained heavily dependent on the USA for economic assistance and security, as stipulated by the terms of the Security Treaty of 1951. From 1960 on, when Japan obtained a mutual security treaty with the USA, we can say that Japan became less constrained in its foreign policy behavior and presumably on the question of the decolonization of Africa.

Japan's entry into the UN, in 1956, seemed to have given its policy makers a greater latitude within which to play a role in the Afro-Asian framework. Technically, this became even more feasible when Japan gained membership of the permanent secretariat of the organization in 1957, for it specifically gave Japan a chance to participate in the debates concerning the future of the colonial empires, and how the demands of the liberation movements for self-government and independence were to be resolved in the face of persistent colonialism. But Japan's attitude remained one of following America's position on the issue. By this time, in the heat of the Cold War, the US was less enthusiastic about decolonization *per se*, given that the rhetoric surrounding the whole decolonization process had assumed a leftist slant. In fact, there were indications that Japan was more concerned about the grievances of the colonial powers than it was about the concerns of the 'subjects'. In one of his correspondences with Shigemitsu in relation to the Bandung conference, Ambassador Okamoto (The Hague) wrote that, on the question of self-determination and national independence for the colonies, which would be one of the preoccupations of the conference, Japan should treat the colonial powers' anxieties with the utmost concern (*Jūbun kōryo no yō aru beki*). He noted that the colonial powers were particularly nervous about the conference. [52] This is hardly surprising, since, according to a former British diplomat, 'British "advice" when provided tactfully in the course of political consultations . . . on African issues . . . influenced Japanese thinking'. [53] In addition, the media reports in Japan about the liberation struggles tended to favor[54] the position of the colonial powers.

In fact, it seems as though Japan's policy makers were not even catching on to what was happening in Africa at the time. For example, while very high-ranking dignitaries, like Vice-President Nixon of the USA, represented their respective countries at the independence celebrations of Ghana in 1957 – the first sub-Saharan state to be liberated from colonial rule in the post-war period – Japan was merely represented by its Ambassador to the country, Mr Kajima, who apparently kept a very low profile at the celebration.[55]

Japan's conservative leaders spoke of supporting self-determination in principle. But they also made clear their abhorrence of the application of revolutionary means to achieve it. They constantly reminded the leaders of the liberation movements to work within the constitutional framework to achieve their objectives, a somewhat understandable suggestion from a people who had experienced the worst consequences of the last world war. And if Japan had renounced war as an instrument of national policy and had foresworn force as a means of settling international disputes, then it was right, at least in principle, that it did not support the application of violence as an instrument for decolonization. One cannot help but also make the point that political chaos in raw material producer countries would make them unable to maintain the flow of supplies.[56] Japan needed assured access to the Third World's raw materials. It is therefore no surprise that the report of the 'Heiwa mondai kenkyūkai' on Japan's comprehensive national security expressed concern about the political and racial problems in the Southern Africa region, which it notes as housing some of the world's strategic resources. The report equates the strategic importance of this region to that of the Middle East,[57] in view of its strategic value, on the one hand, and the extent of the political instability of the region, on the other. As one quasi-government report notes, it would, therefore, have been counter-productive on the part of Japan to support anything that would exacerbate the tensions in any of its sources for raw materials supply.

At the UNGA on 9 September 1957, for example, the Japanese Foreign Minister Fujiyama Aiichirō spelt out Japan's position concerning the liberation struggles in the world:

> As a member of the Asian community, the people of Japan feel a deep sense of sympathy with the hopes and aspirations of the peoples of Asia and Africa . . . It is the belief of my delegation that in the settlement of disputes involving the principle of self-determination, the aspirations of the people should be fully respected, and primary considerations given to ensuring them their basic human rights and freedom, and to promoting their welfare.

Mr. Fujiyama went on to say that any system that denied these peoples their aspirations was bound to fall eventually.

These reassuring words to the liberation movements were, however, always followed with a caveat, even if a necessary one:

> It is also incumbent upon the peoples who are in the process of attaining independence to desist from narrow-mindedness and arbitrary actions and work for their political, economic and social progress in a spirit of tolerance and trust.[58]

Not surprisingly, therefore, on 19 September the Foreign Minister expressed his country's disapproval of the Algerian war and called for a quick end to it.[59] He called for providence, patience, tolerance, a sense of reality and proportion. On the specific question of supporting either of the parties involved in the conflict, the Japanese government adroitly chose to remain neutral. It refused to give diplomatic support to the provisional government of Algeria proclaimed by the nationalists in September 1958, for fear of offending General de Gaulle. Japan nevertheless held to its official declaration at the UN in support of decolonization.

Japan's security policy, as defined within its constitution and the framework of the US–Japan Security Treaty, proved rather static when confronted with the most serious crisis to have evolved from the decolonization process in sub-Saharan Africa. The Congo crisis of 1960 brought Japan's (military) security policy in general, and its policy towards the political upheavals in sub-Saharan Africa in particular, into question. On the question of whether Japan should contribute forces to the UN mission designed for the crisis, Japan's policy makers argued that Article IX of its constitution forbade it to deploy its armed forces overseas.[60] There was, however, a confusion within Gaimushō and in Japanese politics as a whole, on the matter.[61] Ambassador Kōtō Matsudaira, Japan's chief UN representative, had publicly stated, obviously contradicting Foreign Minister Kosaka Zentarō, that Japan's refusal to send a force to support the UN's peacekeeping mission in the Congo contradicted its commitment to support the ideals of the UN. He advised the country's policy makers to reflect on Japan's position on the issue. The Ikeda Hayato administration's position was, however, that Matsudaira's opinion was entirely private and had nothing to do with the government's position on sending Japanese forces outside Japan – which, in the words of the Foreign Minister, was (*impossible*) *arienai*.[62]

The Congo crisis, no sooner than it began, was to be embroiled in the Cold War conflict.[63] And Japan's attitude towards the problem reflected its ideological orientation, and by implication its relations with the USA. Japan's attitude towards Patrice Lumumba, seemingly pushed into the hands of the Soviet Union as a result of American intransigence, was ambivalent. Foreign Minister Kosaka, however, suggested at the UN in 1961, 'the implementation of a machinery to ensure the implementation of the Assembly's decision against the provision' of military aid to the factions in Congo.[64] No doubt, the suggestion was a reflection of the fear of Soviet dominance in the Congo. The country was too vital, resource-wise, to be allowed to fall into the hands of the Soviet Union. In retrospect, it can be said that it is by no means accidental that one of Japan's major raw materials-oriented investments in sub-Saharan Africa was in Zaïre (previously Congo).

As many more countries became independent, the momentum for action against colonial rule in Africa gathered more force. The 1960s and 1970s ushered in an avalanche of anti-colonial public opinion on the continent against the minority regimes and settler colonies in Rhodesia, Portuguese-ruled Mozambique, Angola and Guinea Bissau, South Africa, and Namibia. The newly independent states of Africa championed the 1960 'Declaration on the Granting of Independence to Colonial Countries and Peoples'. As the liberation movement in the Afro-Asian political block became more impatient with colonial rule and supported radical measures to destabilize it, Japan's position remained the same: the application of peaceful measures. As argued more cogently in Chapter 4, when the UNGA suggested the imposition of economic sanctions against Portugal, Japan's conservative leaders, along with their Western partners, rejected the proposal. And Japan did not vote in favor of UN Resolution 2017 (XX) at the twentieth UNGA session in 1965, which called for an end to diplomatic relations with Portugal. Our examination of Japan's UN policy towards aspects of the liberation process in Africa in Chapter 4 will further reveal the nuances of Japan's lukewarm position on the matter.

By the early 1960s Japan's economic interests were evidently dictating the pace of its foreign policy objectives. The Prime Minister, Ikeda Hayato, had issued a long-term economic plan for 'income doubling' over a ten-year period, and hoped to achieve this by adopting a 'low posture' (*teishisei*) in his foreign and domestic policies. This was in fact nothing new. He was only endorsing what his mentor and predecessor Yoshida Shigeru recommended as the appropriate tool for building the country's economy. Thus, as the domestic scene became more peaceful and the economy grew, Japan substituted economics for politics as the determining factor of its foreign relations. In the process, it instituted what Shibusawa Masahide refers to as an 'economistic' foreign policy.[65] Aurelia George aptly put it this way:

> Although it began as an extension to the foreign relations sphere of Japan's high-growth domestic policies, the primacy of economism was reinforced by the belief that economic involvement was much less likely to involve Japan in political or military disputes than taking the political high ground, and in fact exerted a positive and constructive effect on foreign relations at the same time as it maximised trade opportunities and market access . . . Japan refined and specialised in all the economic instruments of diplomacy. Economic strength was seen as the source of international status.[66]

It was more than just that. In fact, it was an illustration of the political and security importance that Japan's policy makers attached to economic growth. But the more they harped on this economistic foreign policy, the more they found themselves having to justify it by evoking the paradoxical idea of the separation of politics and economics (*seikei bunri*). And the more the country's economy grew, the more, ironically, the political leaders found themselves embroiled in the dynamics and tensions of international politics, and the more, also, Japan became dependent on other countries economically, obviously because of the growing inter-dependence of the world economy. This, by implication, at least, demanded an ability to understand the political grievances and interests of as many of its trade partners as possible, irrespective of the country's political orientation and irrespective of which region of the world the country belonged to. It is appropriate, however, to note that *seikei bunri* did exist as an orthodoxy. Nevertheless, despite its orthodoxy, *seikei bunri* was an ambiguous concept capable of accommodating change and even inspiring criticism of the *status quo*, as events later proved.

But the LDP's 'economistic' foreign policy met with serious criticism in relation to Africa and decolonization. Japan's first trade agreement with a sub-Saharan African country was signed between the Ikeda Cabinet and the government of Southern Rhodesia in 1959.[67] While Japan admonished the freedom fighters to negotiate for an end to minority rule, the Ian Smith regime announced its Unilateral Declaration of Independence from British rule in 1965. The idea of peaceful negotiations in Rhodesia therefore became bankrupt within the Afro-Asian group in general and within the OAU in particular. Yet Japan adamantly persisted with it.

When in 1966, the UN Security Council voted on a draft resolution – sponsored by Mali, Nigeria and Uganda – calling for the use of all the necessary measures, including the use of force, to abolish the minority regime in Southern Rhodesia, Japan abstained from voting on the matter. Along with the USA, Japan declared that, as long as the slightest chance of a peaceful settlement existed, the Security Council should not take any precipitate action.[68] Japan again abstained from voting on Resolution 2138 (XXX) introduced by Tanzania on October 1966, which condemned the 'talks about talks' between the British government and the minority regime as jeopardizing the inalienable rights of the African people of Zimbabwe. Japan, like the USA and the UK, abstained because, as its representative explained, time had not been allowed for consultations with its government.[69]

The problem became more complicated, at least for the Japanese government, when it became apparent that Japanese companies were circumventing the economic sanctions imposed by the UN Security Council on Rhodesia. Tokyo was heavily criticized by the international community, especially the Afro-Asian group. Yet its policy makers weathered the storm, skilfully. In 1968 they closed down the consulate that they opened in Salisbury in 1961. The Ministry of International Trade and Industry (MITI) had announced, previous to that, that it would no longer underwrite export insurances for goods destined for Rhodesia, and would revise the import–export control order suspending all trade. These measures go to confirm our previous argument that Japan's 'economistic' policy was not fossilized. It was, as previously mentioned, dynamic and flexible, within limits.

By the late 1970s, Japan seemed to have assumed a more pro-African position, while still not committing itself too deeply into the complex landscape of the African political economy. It voted in favor of General Assembly Resolution 33/38 B, among others, which condemned those governments, particularly the Pretoria regime, which continued to collaborate with the Smith regime and violated the mandatory sanctions adopted by the Security Council. It also condemned the failure of certain governments to enforce the sanctions, and deplored the decision of the US government to allow Ian Smith and some members of the illegal regime to enter the US, in flagrant violation of the UN decision.[70] This new diplomatic stance has to be seen within the context of developments in the global political economy, and Japan's attempts to contend with them.

JAPANESE FOREIGN POLICY AND THE SOUTH AFRICAN CONUNDRUM

Japan's relations with South Africa have parallels with its relations with Rhodesia, even though the former are of a more complex nature. Presumably because of this complexity, there seemingly developed a well-coordinated policy involving government, bureaucrats, and *zaikai* (the business community) to deal with it. Morikawa argues that in order to offset international criticism of Japan's economic relations with Pretoria, for example, policy makers in Japan found it convenient to make *zaikai* responsible for certain important aspects of Japan's relations with South Africa, and Africa as a whole.[71]

By 1952, Japan had set up a consulate in Pretoria to give meaning to its growing economic relations with South Africa. Trade expanded dramatically from 1960, leading to the establishment of a Japan External Trade Organization (JETRO) office in Johannesburg in 1961.[72] By 1967, Japan had already become South Africa's second most important market for its agricultural and mineral exports. South Africa, on the other hand, had become Japan's most important market in Africa for the latter's manufactured products in Africa.[73] In essence, South Africa assumed a very important position in Japan's relations with Africa, because it was one of the largest producers of natural resources within the liberal international economic regime, as demonstrated in Chapter 3.

Morikawa's thesis, as previously mentioned, is that Japan's relations with sub-Saharan Africa were based primarily on *nigen kōzō*: supporting Pretoria, on the one hand, and appeasing the other African states, on the other. Thus, he contends that Japan had, as a policy, different policies for 'black' and 'white' Africa. His opinion is that by supporting the regime, Japan gained access to the much-needed resources for the expansion of the nation's economy. By appeasing the 'black' African states, on the other hand, Japanese governments, substantially curbed African criticisms against Japan for its expanding relations with South Africa. Japan increased its popularity among the Africans, and its prestige internationally, by giving them symbolic support both politically and economically.

What is also worth noting here is that in their relations with the African states, particularly on matters relating to the racial policies of the minority regimes in Southern Africa, Japan's post-World War II governments constantly evoked the 1919 Makino proposal at the Versailles conference for the League to adopt a 'racial equality clause'. This reference was, without doubt, designed as a signal of solidarity (from an Asian country) with the Africans in their struggle against racial discrimination. However, Morikawa contends that the reference to the 1919 Makino statement by Japan's policy makers in their relations with Africa was nothing more than a camouflage, behind which Japan continued expanding its economic relations with Pretoria.[74] As he rightly points out, the Makino proposal, which was rejected by the European powers, was to all intents and purposes a plea on behalf of the Japanese people; and in fact was against extending equality to those of 'backward cultures'.[75]

Japan's relations with South Africa reveal that the two countries' diplomatic relations, re-established in 1961, had ambassadorial status, despite Tokyo's claim to the contrary.[76] Following Morikawa's thesis about Japan's dual structure policy for sub-Saharan Africa, we could argue that it was just simply politically expedient for Japan to keep its proper diplomatic relations with Pretoria out of sight from its critics.

Within Japan's diplomacy towards sub-Saharan Africa was a systematized criticism of South Africa by Gaimushō. Critics point out that these criticisms were directed not so much at the South African government but at apartheid.[77] This view is supported by a Gaimushō statement which said that 'We cannot support . . . the view that questions the legitimacy of the Government of South Africa . . .'.[78] But this position was also in line with the governments' position that the problems in the region should be resolved through negotiation, as opposed to confrontation. Alternatively, Japan's approach to the problem could be seen as an attempt by the LDP governments, with the assistance of *zaikai*, not to offend the sources of their valuable resources, such as South Africa.

Evidently, the dynamics of Japan's relations with South Africa is a matter that complicated Japan's foreign policy towards the other African states and muddled Japan's standing in the Afro-Asian group. This is due to the fact that, as many of Japan's critics were eager to point out, in 1961 Japanese citizens were granted what is popularly known as 'honorary-white'[79] status by the minority regime, upon request by the Japanese government. As argued in Chapter 4, this status conferred on the Japanese was merely a 'status of convenience', designed by the South African government to make it possible for the two countries to trade freely. Whatever the reasons for this flamboyant designation, it did not make Japanese diplomacy towards sub-Saharan Africa any better in the eyes of the Africans. Nor did it make Japan any more popular among the Afro-Asian group. On the contrary, it called into question Japan's projected solidarity with the Africans on the issue of racial discrimination. In fact, it exposed the myth surrounding the 1919 Makino proposal for an all-embracing universal racial equality clause.

Trade between Japan and South Africa, the main factor that sustained the growing relationship between the two countries grew astronomically, as is shown in Chapter 3. Trade with the other sub-Saharan African states increased too, but only slightly. Japan's largest trade partner, after South Africa, was Nigeria. In 1975, for example, the value of Japanese exports to Nigeria more than doubled to $585.3 mn. from the previous year, due primarily to the huge increase in Nigeria's oil revenue by this time. Imports, on the other hand, fell by about 38 percent in value (from $448.8 mn. to $278.5 mn. respectively). Comparable figures for South Africa show that in 1975 Japan exported $871.8 mn. worth of merchandise to Pretoria (about a 9 percent fall from 1974). Its imports, on the other hand, increased by 13.7 percent from $763.3 mn. in 1974 to $868.2 mn. in 1975.[80] The figures for 1980 show that exports to Nigeria were $1,493.6 bn., compared to $120.1 mn. for imports. For South Africa they were $1,800.2 bn. and $1,740.8 bn., respectively.[81] By 1987, when Japan's emergence as South Africa's leading trade partner became a 'serious' international issue, trade with Nigeria had become a mere shadow of what it had been in the 1970s. In that year, Japan exported $345.9 mn. (49 percent drop from 1986) worth of goods to Nigeria and imported a mere $5.2 mn. (1 percent increase over 1987) worth of goods from Lagos.[82]

Already, by 1972, trade between Japan and South Africa had assumed political significance. On a visit to Japan in 1972, the OAU mission headed by President Mokhtar Ould Daddah of Mauritania raised the issue with Foreign Minister Fukuda Takeo, and urged the Japanese government to control its trade with Pretoria. Fukuda's response was that Japan was a free nation and not a socialist state, and as a result its government was not in a position to control trade by private firms.[83] This is a fairly reasonable argument if one overlooks the fact that in Japan there is in most cases a 'managed' agreement between the bureaucracy, the business community and the government on the question of state interests. But Fukuda's statement underlines the point that the Japanese government used *zaikai* to ward off criticisms against it, especially on questions pertaining to Japan's relations with South Africa.

THE 1970S AND JAPANESE OVERTURES TOWARDS SUB-SAHARAN AFRICA

The Arab–Israeli war of 1973 brought into perspective changes in the global political economy that forced a number of states, seemingly, to do things that they would not otherwise have done. Specifically, the oil crises of 1973–1974 and 1979 were responsible for this. Japan's leaders also had to respond to the times if they wanted to keep their assembly lines, and the whole economy, running. Suffice to say, the oil crisis made Japan's policy makers aware of the political ramifications of international trade, for the Arab states had demanded that Japan support them against Israel, and ultimately the USA, since they provided it with over 80 percent of its oil requirement. This demonstrated to the Japanese the dangers involved in working within the framework of the world political economy, on the one hand, while, on the other, claiming, as Japan's leaders did, that it was possible, within that very framework, to separate economics and politics. It also proved that the Japanese economy was potentially vulnerable to raw material shortages.

The implications of Foreign Minister Kimura's trip to Africa

By way of managing the above crisis, attempts to diversify Japan's sources for raw materials, as far and as much as possible, gathered momentum within the MITI and the *zaikai*. It is no surprise, therefore, that in the Autumn of 1974 Kimura, the Foreign Minister, went on a carefully planned tour of Africa, as already mentioned in Chapter 1. It is instructive to note that this was the first highest official visit from Japan to the region. The official Japanese explanation for the tour was that it was aimed at deepening Japanese understanding of the problems and policies of the African states. It has, however, been argued that Kimura's trip was designed to safeguard Japan's resource interests in the region. Aoki Kazuyoshi, for example, argues that it is only when resource-related problems become evident that Africa emerges in Japan's diplomacy.[84] This is partly because another Japanese Foreign Minister, Mr. Sonoda, was dispatched to the region in the wake of the second oil crisis of 1979.

It seemed that certain policy makers in Africa were aware of this, for at a press conference in Tokyo in May 1973 to commemorate the tenth anniversary of the OAU, Japan was heavily criticized by the African ambassadors in Tokyo on the question of Japan's relations with South Africa, and in the same breath the Ethiopian Ambassador representing his colleagues attempted to use the 'resource card', which the Arab states did more effectively later in the year. He proclaimed that:

> we are ambassadors and we have to be polite but our message is very clear today. Japan is interested in Africa's natural resources and we welcome you to invest and develop Africa. But economic ties are not enough. We expect Japan as an Asian nation to give its political support to the struggle against the [minority] regimes. All other Asian nations – India, Pakistan, Indonesia – have supported us and I warn you that Japan will be isolated from the Afro-Asian group unless it joins us now.

In conclusion, the ambassadors once again made reference to the issue of Japan's resource needs, effectively threatening Japan this time: 'Africa has a tremendous potential to provide Japan with natural resources, but we will only support those countries who support us'.[85] The performance of the ambassadors, orchestrated without doubt by their governments, signified the frustration of the African states in their dealings with the Japanese governments on matters concerning Japan's economic and diplomatic relations with the minority regimes in Southern Africa. In this respect, it could also be argued that Kimura's tour was primarily prompted by the political significance of the ambassadors' statement and not necessarily by the issue of resource procurement, as suggested above. In any event, the latter interest cannot be completely ruled out, given that access to all possible resource sources is one of Japan's main diplomatic objectives. The implications of Kimura's trip is more critically analyzed in Chapter 6.

In response to the above statement, and following Kimura's tour of the region, the Tanaka administration warned the *zaikai* against making any capital investments in South Africa, apparently in direct response to requests from the South African Iron and Steel Industrial Corporation (ISCOR)[86] team visiting Japan from South Africa in June 1973. The government was concerned that such transactions could greatly offend even Japan's friends in the Afro-Asian bloc.[87] The indications were that, even with respect to Africa, the Japanese government was quickly responding to issues that they saw as having the potential to disturb Japan's standing in the global scheme of things.

The dynamism of Japan's diplomacy showed itself once again in 1974. While the European states and the USA were dragging their feet on the issue of recognizing, diplomatically, the newly established socialist state of Guineau Bissau, the government of Japan under the leadership of Miki Takeo did so. This reflected, once again, a shift in Japanese diplomacy in the mid-1970s to a value-free diplomacy (*issai no kachi handan o shinai gaikō*). The policy itself was widely criticized as being self-centred, but in a way it showed a perceptive awareness on the part of the leadership in Japan of the need for positive responses towards the OAU member states (and other problem areas) if their resource policies were to work.

At this point it may be appropriate to note the fact that Japan's diplomatic approach towards the African states has not been necessarily 'economistic', in the literal sense of the word. Its diplomacy towards Tanzania has been supportive, despite the latter's lack of any worthwhile resources. Japan's relations with Tanzania, indeed, have been motivated by political pragmatism and a desire to assist it on humanitarian grounds, following the example of countries like Norway and Sweden, whose development assistance to Tanzania and other developing countries have been widely noted. Japan's aid to Tanzania has been high within the context of its economic assistance to the countries in the region.

It has, however, been widely said that Japan's supportive diplomacy to Tanzania is attributable to the charisma of Julius Nyerere, the country's first president and a former leading statesman in Third World politics.[88] As argued in Chapter 6, the conservative leaders of Japan saw it as politically expedient to be supportive of Tanzania, on the matter of aid, because Nyerere was a useful asset to have for the purposes of either assuaging rising feelings among the OAU membership should Japan blunder in its relations with any of the minority regimes in Southern Africa, or for gathering support among Third World states, especially at UN fora, when necessary.

It is appropriate to reiterate the point that it was in response to the events in the 1970s which heightened Japanese awareness of their economy's extreme sensitivity to external pressures, that the Ōhira administration initiated the guiding principles, known in the official lexicon as *sōgo anzen hoshō senryaku* (comprehensive national security – CNS – policy). The main tenets of this policy have been outlined in the Introduction, pointing out that the policy aimed to provide a chain of orderly balanced national power, including factors such as economy, diplomacy and military to counter both potential and actual threats. These threats were mostly defined as systemic-related threats. The policy, needless to say, and not unlike policies of past administrations, emphasized the economy as the primary determinant of national security. As Alan Rix put it, security was seen to comprise two major elements: a narrow military security concept and a wider area of economic security.[89] Thus, economic power was seen almost as an end in itself.

As has been noted, central to the above policy was the question of the role of ODA as a policy instrument. Suffice to say, aspects of Japan's aid policies in the 1980s were influenced by reasons of political expediency. In response to requests from the USA in particular, Japan strengthened its aid to countries bordering areas of conflict and areas important to the maintenance of peace and stability in the world. In essence, starting from the 1980s, Japan's policy makers introduced strategic considerations into the country's aid policy, even though the provision of economic aid remained a major pillar of Japan's foreign policy as a whole, as articulated in its CNS policy. Japan's aid policy towards sub-Saharan Africa largely reflects this.

Most of Tokyo's prominent aid recipients in the region were countries with the necessary natural resources or markets, or both. Thus, Kenya, Zaire and Nigeria, among others, were regular recipients of Japan's economic aid, starting in the 1960s. On the other hand, Japan's aid to Somalia, for example, 'went up sharply' in 1982, and remained high until the end of the decade. This was because of close Soviet involvement in Ethiopia from around 1980. Zimbabwe (since 1980) and Zambia, not to mention Tanzania, were regular recipients of Japanese aid, because of their importance to stability in the Southern Africa region. Zimbabwe's importance in this respect is also attributed to the fact that it is a crucial source for a strategic raw material, chromium. Aid to Tanzania, as is shown in Chapter 6, was determined primarily by the latter's political importance in regional and international politics.

JAPANESE RESPONSES TO SPECIFIC AFRICAN ISSUES IN THE 1980s AND BEYOND

As Japan's economy expanded globally, Tokyo's importance in the economic, if not in the political, sphere increased among the African states. At the 39th UN Conference in 1984, Japan was nominated by some of the African states to head a UN team that was put together to look into Africa's economic crises. African business delegations and governments made several requests (during this decade) to Japanese governments and business enterprises to invest more in the region, but to no avail.

During the 1980s, pressure was also kept on Japan to minimize its dealings with South Africa. In response, the Nakasone administration enacted a law prohibiting the sale of computers to the South African defence and police forces. It also imposed a limit on the imports of kruggerands into the country. Further, there was also a government-proposed rule that requested Japanese companies operating in South Africa to give equal employment opportunities to all the races in the country. In addition, the administration made proposals (which they called *hito tsukuri kyōryoku* – human resource development cooperation) designed to help Africans develop technical skills.

There were more symbolic gestures of solidarity with the liberation forces and with the OAU states as a whole in the mid-1980s, reflecting the dynamism of Japanese politics. In September of 1986, the Nakasone administration initiated measures discouraging imports of pig-iron from South Africa; prohibiting the establishment of air links between Japan and South Africa; and controlling tourism between the two countries. Government officials were also prohibited from travelling by the South African Airlines.

At the end of 1987, this time under the Takeshita Noboru administration, Japan announced $500 million non-project grant aid to be disbursed over a three-year period to mid-1990, to eleven countries in sub-Saharan Africa. This was partly in response to international pressures, particularly from the USA, for Tokyo to recycle some of its trade surplus to the Third World. In another dramatic diplomatic move, the LDP invited Oliver Tambo, the President of the African National Congress (ANC), to Tokyo in connection with the ANC's request for a liaison office in Tokyo. The indications were that Tokyo was attempting to build bridges using pragmatic political tools, towards the leading liberation movement in Southern Africa. It was no surprise, therefore, when at the end of 1988 an ANC liaison office opened[90] in Tokyo.

These, however, were not the only 'positive signals' sent towards the region from the Japanese government. Pretoria was being given its share of these 'positive' gestures, presumably in an attempt to balance the ledger of Japanese diplomacy in the region. In 1984, for example, members of the LDP and Minshatō (Japan Democratic Socialist Party) set up the Japan–South Africa Friendship Association. It was primarily designed to lobby for policies that would be favorable to South Africa. Six of its members went to South Africa on an official visit in August, two months after the society was set up.[91] Subsequently, in September of 1986, Japan played host to Pik Botha, the South African Foreign Minister. He was followed in October by South Africa's Minister of Finance and the Head of the Bank of South Africa.

Even though there were signals that Japan was reducing its trade with Pretoria, by 1987 Tokyo had evolved as South Africa's leading trade partner;[92] to the chagrin of policy makers in Africa, the international community, especially the US Congress and business community and, understandably, Gaimushō. It may be appropriate to mention that confusion within the Japanese bureaucracy, epitomized in this instance by the contemptuous rivalry between Gaimushō and MITI contributed to some Japanese companies increasing their exports to South Africa despite warnings from the government. The rivalry apparently manifested itself in conflicting signals from the two ministries to the *zaikai*; with the Gaimushō, on the one hand, advising restraint, and MITI, on the other, ignoring the former's cautious approach.

In the 1990s Japan's aid contributions to sub-Saharan Africa and its relations with post-apartheid South Africa continue to excite interest. On the question of aid it is important to note that Japan has given positive signals about assisting in the development of Africa. In this regard, Mr. Hirabayashi Hiroshi (Director-General of the Economic Cooperation Bureau of Gaimushō) has given assurances to the effect that, although many OECD countries are tired of giving economic assistance to Africa, Japan does not perceive the process as a hopeless exercise,[93] suggesting in effect that Japan's policy makers believe in the efficacy of providing economic assistance to developing countries; and they have examples in South-east Asia to prove this. Whether Japan will become as committed to the development of Africa as it has been in the case of East and South-east Asia is, however, a question worth asking. Japan's aid to the region for the 1993 period was $966.10 mn.; which was only 11.8 percent of its overall ODA commitments for that year. Of the above amount 21.1 percent were loans (given to only seven countries), 59.6 percent grant aid and 19.3 percent was earmarked for technical aid. Although the 1993 figure is an improvement over those of the three previous years, and higher than the 9.9 percent of Japan's global aid allocation that the region received in 1985 when Japan was enjoying booming economic growth, it falls slightly short of the figure for 1989, which was $1.039.64 mn. and 15 percent of Japan's global ODA commitments. But in 1993 Tokyo hosted and partly organized the Conference on African Development, the first of its kind in Japan.

The latest development in Japanese economic assistance towards the region concerns its aid program to South Africa. In June 1994 Japan decided to extend a two-year aid package to the tune of $1.36 bn. in economic assistance to Pretoria. Of this more than $300 mn. was to be allocated as grant aid for basic human needs: water supply, electricity, schools, housing, telecommunications, etc. among the black population. And $500 mn. of the total amount was designed as a loan from the Export–Import Bank of Japan, which would be for the improvement of the economic and social infrastructure of South Africa. The remaining $500 mn. was to be used for the purposes of a credit line for trade and overseas investment insurance. The latter case suggests that the MITI and indeed the Ministry of Finance are both relatively well-disposed to the idea of loan aid to South Africa, further suggesting that, unusually given the Japanese bureaucratic attitude towards the African economy, South Africa has a good credit rating.[94] This development in Japanese–South African relations notwithstanding, there were concerns among the South African media[95] that Pretoria had not shown any enthusiasm for the promised economic assistance from Japan. The case concerned the fact that by January 1995 bureaucrats in Japan had still not received from officials in South Africa a list of priority projects to be financed through the $1.3 bn. package pledged by Japan (as part of its annual budget, starting from April 1995). It was, for example, reported that the Japanese Ambassador, Mr. Sezaki Katsumi, said he had not been able to meet Minister without Portfolio, Mr. Jay Naidoo, for three months and was frustrated that he had not received any response regarding the priority list mentioned above.[96]

The good credit rating for South Africa underlined the potential viability of South Africa as a country to invest in; and indeed the popular perception before Japan lifted the economic sanctions (in October 1992) it imposed on South Africa, mostly in the latter part of the 1980s, was that Japanese firms would flood post-apartheid South Africa with investments.[97] This prediction has as yet not happened. On the whole, Japanese firms with investment interests in South Africa have adopted a wait-and-see strategy. There are a number of factors behind this cautious behavior of the Japanese firms. Aside from the question of political stability, there is the more important question of the economic viability of such investments, especially in the manufacuring sector.[98] The indications are that Japanese manufacturing firms see South Africa as a relatively small market. For example, the annual consumption of colour television sets in South Africa is approximately 400,000, and it is roughly the same for automobiles. However, a Japanese (television) tube manufacturer would expect sales of about 1,000,000 television sets in order to want to invest in the market. The other crucial concern of potential investors in the manufacturing industry is what they perceive as the high cost of skilled labor in South Africa. Thus, while the potential market for their products could be relatively widened by exporting to other neighbouring African countries, the high labor cost, it is argued, would not make the products competitive and therefore the investment may not be worthwhile. There is nevertheless a lot of interest in the potential of Southern Africa as a viable market.

Where Japan wants to see its firms invest is in the mining industry. This is where, in tune with its CNS policy, the country gets a sizable share of the strategic minerals for its economic security. In view of this, the Metal Mining Agency of Japan, which is supervised by MITI and executes the metal mining policies of the Japanese government in addition to implementing the programs and projects commissioned by MITI, set up an office in South Africa in 1993. The objective of this initiative is to give quasi-governmental help by way of subsidies, concessional loans or debt payment guarantees to private firms with mining interests in South Africa. The agency's functions also include the collection of data about mining in South Africa and its neighbors. It is not surprising, therefore, that just under a year after the agency set up shop in South Africa, Sumitomo Corporation bought a stake in Anglo-vaal's base metals and ferro-alloys producer Associated Manganese Mines of South Africa (Assoman).[99] The 1-percent stake ($2,82 mn.) was instituted, Sumitomo claimed, in an effort to stabilize supplies of manganese, chrome, iron ores, ferro-chrome and ferro-manganese. The point to stress here is that the main problem with the sector is not so much lack of interest in investing on the part of Japanese firms, but rather that the sector is monopolized[100] by five or six South African conglomerates whose aim has been to keep foreign investors out, and who therefore make it difficult for Japanese firms to invest in the mining industry.

Thus, contrary to the optimistic predictions concerning an influx of Japanese investments in South Africa by early 1995, only a handful of Japanese firms had established some form of investment in the country. These include the joint venture between Nippon Denko and South Africa's Samancor (the ferro-alloy branch of the General Mining Corporation) to produce ferrochrome, all of which would be exported to Japan. Marubeni (the sole agent of NEC) also set up a small joint venture with Plessy (a South African telecommunications equipment supplier), and Mitsubishi Corporation and Matsushita Industry set up a joint venture with Bophutatswana National Stone Company to produce granite plate.

CONCLUSION

The above scenario reflects Japan's resilience, even in the face of the most complex of issues. Indeed, it says much about how dynamic conservative politics in Japan can be. The analysis above shows that, especially before the 1970s, the USA constrained the fundamental choices in Japan's external relations; and indeed influenced its attitude to the politico-economic problems of sub-Saharan Africa. In the event, Japan's diplomatic formulae for the decolonization of Africa were fairly patterned after US models. In essence, until the 1970s, Japanese policy makers were operating basically within a realm of necessity rather than of choice; even though, ultimately, most of the necessary policy 'choices' imposed on Japan and orchestrated from Washington were used wisely to serve Japan's basic interests. Based on its resource policy, Japan's relations with sub-Saharan Africa seemingly took on a new turn. The two trips by Japan's

Foreign Ministers (in 1974 and 1979) showed signs of interest in the region. When it became necessary to make moves towards accommodating organizations like the ANC in the 1980s, Tokyo did so.

Yet Japan's policy makers did not give up their interests in South Africa, even though attempts were officially made to curb trade with it. Nor did they ignore the interests of Pretoria. All of these go to buttress Morikawa's argument about Japan's 'dual policy' towards sub-Saharan Africa. This dual structure policy may be seen as a facet of the dynamic components within that immobilist pattern of behavior. Suffice to say, what paddled and sustained the momentum of Japan's immobilist foreign policy towards sub-Saharan Africa was its policy makers' ability to apply the system's inherent, if low-key, dynamism in such an ingenious fashion. Since Japan's diplomatic formulae towards sub-Saharan Africa were based on a dual structure policy, Tokyo had to try to appease both the regime in South Africa, on the one hand, and the OAU states, on the other. The essence of this foreign policy behavior was not to offend any of the parties. The objective, understandably, was to sustain and expand Japan's economic and diplomatic interests in the region. Through an act of 'satisficing',[101] therefore, it gave only something of what the region wanted, while making sure that its interests were well secured.

NOTES

1 J.W. Dower, *Empire and Aftermath: Yoshida Shigeru and the Japanese Experience, 1878–1954*, London, Harvard University Press, 1979, p. 307.

2 John Welfield, *An Empire in Eclipse: Japan in the Post-war American Alliance System*, London, Athlone Press, 1988, Chapter 1.

3 It is interesting to note that anti-communism was a central theme in Japanese foreign policy, even when Japan supposedly deviated from its traditional diplomacy and joined Germany and Italy in the Axis pact.

4 It was widely noted, for example, that a Japanese computer manufacturer (Hitachi) sold computers to the South African police and armed forces. See, for example, *Asahi shimbun*, 29 January 1989.

5 Morikawa Jun, *Minami afurika to nihon: kankei no rekishi, kōzō, kadai*, Tokyo, Dōbunkan, 1988, p. 106.

6 Kibata Yōichi, 'Sekai no kiro to ichigonen sensō', in Rekishigaku kenkyūkai (ed.), *Nihonshi kenkyūkai, nihon rekishi kōza*, Tokyo, Tokyo University Press, vol. 12, kindai 4, 1985, pp. 6–7; Maruyama Masao, *Thought and Behavior in Modern Japanese Politics*, London, Oxford University Press, 1963, p. 10.

7 S.O. Agbi, *Japanese Relations with Africa, 1868–1978*, Ibadan, Ibadan University Press, 1992, pp. 49–65.

8 Kweku Ampiah, 'British Commercial Policies Against Japanese Expansionism in East and West Africa, 1932–1935', *The International Journal of African Historical Studies*, vol. 23, no. 4, 1990.

9 Central Office of Information, *The Campaign in Burma*, London, HMSO, 1946; Michael Crowder, *West Africa under Colonial Rule*, Evanston, Northwestern University Press, 1968, pp. 490 ff.

10 Ali Mazrui, 'The United Nations and Some African Political Attitudes', *International Organization*, vol. xviii, no. 4, 1977, pp. 122–124; 'Beiseifu ga osoreta kokujin no nihonbīki', *Asahi shimbun*, 15 July 1993.

11 Jeremy Murray-Brown, *Kenyatta*, New York, George Allen & Unwin, 1973, pp. 250–251.

12 Mary Benson, *The African Patriot*, London, Faber & Faber, 1963, p. 99.

13 Edward Roux, *Time Longer than Rope: A History of the Black Man's Struggle for Freedom in South Africa*, London, 1948, p. 314. See also L. C. F. Turner, 'The Crisis of Japanese Strategy, January–June 1942', *R.M.C Historical Journal*, vol. 1, March, 1972; Joseph Ephraim Casely-Hayford, 'Yellow Peril' in Casely-Hayford', *Ethiopia Unbound: Studies in Race Emancipation*, London, Francas, 1969, pp. 107–115.

14 Elie Kedourie, 'A New International Disorder', in Hedley Bull and Adam Watson (eds.), *The Expansion of International Society*, Oxford, Clarendon Press, (1975), p. 350.

15 Hosoya Chihiro, 'Japan's Response to US Policy on the Japanese Peace Treaty: The Dulles–Yoshida Talks of January–February 1951', *Hitotsubashi Journal of Law and Politics*, vol. 10, December, 1981, p. 1.

16 Ibid., p. 21.

17 J.A.A. Stockwin, *Japan: Divided Politics in a Growth Economy*, London, Weidenfeld & Nicolson, 1982, p. 63.

18 Ministry of Foreign Affairs, *Foreign Ministry Blue Book*, Tokyo, 1959.

19 Michael Yoshitsu, *Japan and the San Francisco Peace Settlement*, New York, Columbia University Press, 1983, p. 43.

20 Ōhira Masayoshi, 'Diplomacy for Peace: The Aims of Japanese Foreign Policy', *International Affairs*, vol. 40, no. 3, July, 1964, p. 392.

21 Dower, *Empire and Aftermath*, pp. 407–410.

22 Yoshida Shigeru, 'Japan and the Crisis in Asia', *Foreign Affairs*, vol. 29, no. 2, 1951, p. 171.

23 Keiō Gijuku (ed.), 'Datsu a ron', *Fukuzawa Yukichi zenshū*, vol. 10, Tokyo, Iwanami shoten, 1960, pp. 238–240.

24 *Nippon Times*, 10 April 1955.

25 Ibid.

26 Ibid.

27 Letter (in Japanese) from Ambassador Okamoto Suemasa (The Hague) to Foreign Minister Shigemitsu, 18 January 1955, Gaikō shiryōkan [Ministry of Foreign Affairs Archives], *Ajia–afurika kaigi e no nihon no sanka mondai*, B6.1.0.24–1. B0049.

28 Letter (in Japanese) from Foreign Minister Shigemitsu Mamoru to Ambassador Yamagata Kiyoshi, 17 December 1954, Gaikō shiryōkan, *Ajia–afurika kaigi e no nihon no sanka mondai*, B6.1.0.24–1. B0049.

29 Letter (in Japanese) from Foreign Minister Shigemitsu to Ambassador Iguchi Sadao, 4 January 1955, Gaikō shiryōkan, *Ajia–afurika kaigi e no nihon no sanka mondai*, B6.1.0.24–1. B0049.

30 Letter from Ambassador Okamoto to Foreign Minister Shigemitsu, 18 January 1955.

31 Letter (in Japanese) from Foreign Minister Shigemitsu to Ambassador Iguchi,

27 January 1955, Gaikō shiryōkan, *Ajia–afurika kaigi e no nihon no sanka mondai*, B6.1.0.24–1. B0049.

32 Ibid.

33 'The Afro-Asian Conference', *Nippon Times*, 10 April 1955; Letter (in Japanese) from Consulate General Wajima Eiji (Jakarta) to Ambassador Shigemitsu, 5 January 1955, Gaikō shiryōkan, *Ajia–afurika kaigi e no nihon no sanka mondai*, B6.1.0.24–1. B0049. In a previous letter to Shigemitsu (31 December 1954), Wajima expressed concern about speculations in an Indonesian newspaper that Indonesia might oppose Japan's participation in the conference, even though he did not think the Indonesia government would do so. It is worth noting that the two Koreas were omitted because these were both considered 'too hot'. The Mongolian People's Republic was also omitted from the Asian countries; and Taiwan was not invited either. In the Middle East and Africa, Israel and the Union of South Africa were not invited.

34 Donald C. Hellmann, *Japanese Foreign Policy and Domestic Politics: The Peace Agreement with the Soviet Union*, Berkeley, University of California Press, 1969, p. 35.

35 Shū On Rai, 'Ware ware no unmei wa ware ware no te de', *Sekai*, no. 114, June, 1955, p. 62.

36 This meeting was initiated by Zhou En-Lai and took place on 22 April 1955, at the latter's hotel. *Asahi shimbun*, 23 April 1955; *Asahi shimbun* (evening edition), 24 April 1955.

37 *Bogor Conference Final Joint Communique* (text in English), December 29 1954, Gaikō shiryōkan, *Ajia–afurika kaigi e no nihon no sanka mondai*, B6.1.0.24–1. B0049. This was the final communique from the conference of the Prime Ministers of Burma, Ceylon, India, Indonesia and Pakistan, held on the 28 and 29 December 1954. It was at this conference that it was agreed that an Asian–African conference be convened.

38 Apparently, there were some last-minute changes in the cast. The Japanese delegation was initially to be led by Shigemitsu. Veteran Tani Masayuki was suggested when Diet sessions precluded the choice of Shigemitsu. Tani was eventually relegated to the second position. The other delegates were Kase Toshikazu (Ambassador Extraordinary and Plenipotentiary), Ōta Saburō (Ambassador Extraordinary and Plenipotentiary to the Union of Burma), Asakai Kōichirō (Envoy Extraordinary and Minister Plenipotentiary) and Wajima Eiji (Envoy Extraordinary and Minister Plenipotentiary to India). There were seven advisers to the delegates, five of whom were members of the House of Representatives. They were Uehara Etsujirō, Nadao Hirokichi, Sata Tadataka, Sone Eki, and Kajiwara Shigeyoshi. The delegation also included Fujiyama Aichirō, President of Ajia kyōkai (The Society for Economic Cooperation in Asia) and Takata Gisaburō. In all, Japan had thirty-one representatives at the conference including Ōkita Suburō.

39 *Asahi shimbun* (evening edition), 26 April 1955, p. 1.

40 Ibid.

41 Welfield, *An Empire in Eclipse*, pp. 175, 211.

42 *Asahi shimbun*, 18 April 1955, p. 2.

43 Leslie Wolfe-Phillips, 'Why Third World?', *Third World Quarterly*, vol. 1, no. 1, January, 1979, pp. 105–146; Peter Worsley, 'How Many Worlds?', *Third World Quarterly*, vol. 1, 1979; Joseph Love 'Third World : A Response to Professor Worsley', *Third World Quarterly*, vol. 2, no. 2, April, 1980.

44 *Asahi shimbun*, (evening edition) 26 April 1955, p. 1; Robert A. Mortimer, *The Third World Coalition in International Politics*, London: Westview Press,1984, pp. 8–9.

45 Address (in English) of Mr. Takasaki Tatsunoske, principal Japanese delegate, before the Asian–African Conference, 19 April 1955, Gaikō shiryōkan, *Ajia-afurika kaigi e no nihon no sanka mondai*, B6.1.0.24–1. B0049.

46 Letter (in Japanese) from Shigemitsu to Takasaki Tatsunoske, 15 April 1955, Gaikō shiryōkan, *Ajia–afurika kaigi e no nihon no sanka mondai*, B6.1.0.24– 1. B0049; *Asahi shimbun*, 17 April 1955. See also address of Mr. Takasaki Tatsunoske; Japanese delegation, *Proposal for Economic Cooperation*, 18 April 1955; Gaikō shiryōkan, *Ajia–afurika kaigi e no nihon no sanka mondai*, B6.1.0.24–1. B0049 (text in English).

47 Ogata Sadako, 'The Business Community and Japanese Foreign Policy: Normalization of Relations with The People's Republic of China', in Robert Scalapino (ed.), *The Foreign Policy of Japan*, Berkeley, University of California, 1977, p. 182; Chalmers Johnson, 'MITI and Japanese International Economic Policy', in Robert Scalapino (ed.), *The Foreign Policy of Japan*, Berkeley, University of California Press, 1977, p. 259.

48 Address of Mr. Takasaki Tatsunoske, 19 April 1955.

49 Roger Louis, *Imperialism at Bay, 1941–1945: The United States and the Decolonization of the British Empire*, Oxford, Oxford University Press, 1977, p. 3.

50 A. S. Cleary, 'The Myth of Mau Mau in its International Context', *African Affairs*, vol. 89, no. 355, April, 1990, p. 231.

51 Ibid.

52 Letter (in Japanese) from Ambassador Okamoto to Foreign Minister Shigemitsu, 18 January 1955, Gaikō shiryōkan, *Ajia–afurika kaigi e no nihon no sanka mondai*, B6.1.0.24–1.B0049.

53 Sir Hugh Cortazzi, *British Influence in Japan Since the End of the Occupation (1952–1984)*, Nissan Occasional Paper Series, no. 13, 1990, pp. 7–8.

54 Kawabata Masahisa, 'Afurika no dokuritsu wa donoyōni nihon de tsutaerar-etaka', *Ajia-afurika kenkyū*, no. 318, 1987, p. 8.

55 Hoshino Yasuo, 'Gana dokuritsu e no ayami to sono shōrai', *Sekai*, no. 137, May, 1957, p. 199.

56 Bruce Russet, 'Security and the Resources Scramble: Will 1984 Be Like 1914?', *International Affairs*, Winter, 1981/82, p. 45.

57 Naikaku kanbō naikaku shingishitsu, *Kokusai kokka nihon no sōgo anzen hoshō seisaku*, (Heiwa mondai kenkyūkai hōkokusho), Tokyo, Ōkurasho insatsukyoku, 1985, p. 60.

58 Ministry of Foreign Affairs (UN Bureau), *Statements Delivered by Delegates of Japan During the XIIth Regular Session of the General Assembly*, Tokyo, 1958, p. 4.

59 Ibid.

60 In June 1992, the Miyazawa administration pushed through the Upper House of the Diet a law enabling the Self-Defense Forces (SDF) to participate in UN peacekeeping operations. Aurelia George 'Japan's Participation in U.N. Peacekeeping Operations', *Asian Survey*, vol. xxxiii, no. 6, June, 1993, p. 562, argues that, in fact, 'there is no specific prohibition – constitutional, legal or otherwise – in cases where the dispatch is not for the purpose of using force. Hence, the deployment for other purposes such as peacekeeping becomes permissible under the constitution'.

61 *Asahi shimbun*, 22 February 1961, p. 1; *Asahi shimbun* (evening edition), 22 February 1961; *Asahi shimbun* (evening edition), 23 February 1961; Shūgiin kaigi roku, *Kampō*, no. 9, 23 February 1961.
62 *Asahi shimbun*, 28 January 1961, p. 1.
63 'Afurika dokuritsu no nagare no naka de', *Sekai*, no. 177, September, 1960, p. 142; *Asahi shimbun*, 6 March 1961, p. 1; *Asahi shimbun*, 9 March 1961, p. 1; Evan Luard, *A History of the United Nations: The Age of Decolonization, 1955–1965. Vol. 2.* London, Macmillan, 1989, pp. 217–316.
64 United Nations, *Yearbook of the United Nations*, 1960, p. 94.
65 Shibusawa Masahide, *Japan and the Asian Pacific Region*, London, Croom Helm, 1984, pp. 23–25.
66 Aurelia George, 'Japan and the United States: Dependent Ally or Equal Partner', in J.A.A. Stockwin *et al.* (eds.), *Dynamic and Immobilist Politics in Japan*, Macmillan, London, 1988, p. 256.
67 Morikawa, *Minami afurika to nihon*, p. 155.
68 United Nations, *Yearbook of the United Nations*, 1966, pp. 99–100.
69 Ibid., pp. 63–64.
70 United Nations, *Yearbook of the United Nations*, vol. 32, 1978, p. 932–3.
71 Morikawa, *Minami afurika to nihon*, pp. 109–110.
72 Ibid. p. 115.
73 Ibid.
74 Ibid., pp. 41–43.
75 Ibid., pp. 38–43; see also Shimazu Naoko, 'The Japanese Attempt to Secure Racial Equality in 1919', *Japan Forum*, no. 1, April, 1989 and Murakami Hyōe, *Japan: The Year of Trial, 1919–1952*, Tokyo, Kodansha International Ltd.,1983. It is instructive to note that the Japanese government, in concluding a new treaty with The Netherlands in 1896, had demanded equal treatment for Japanese citizens whether in The Netherlands or in the Dutch East Indies (Indonesia). In 1899 the Japanese in Indonesia were therefore equated with the Europeans. This privilege granted to the Japanese apparently offended the indigenous Indonesians and the Indonesian Chinese. See C. Fasseur, 'Rulers and Ruled: Some Remarks on Dutch Colonial Ideology', *Journal of the Japan-Netherlands Institute*, vol. II, 1990. It should be mentioned that, not surprisingly, colonial rule in the Dutch East Indies was partly based on legal racial classification. It is equally interesting to note that at the Bandung conference an Indian representative, M. Panekal, mentioned Japan as the leader in the struggle for racial equality for Asians with reference to the 1919 Makino statement. See 'Dokuritsu no shōchō', *Sekai*, 1955, June, p. 73. This is a common misconception among ill-informed Afro-Asians of Japan's position on the question of racial equality before World War II.
76 Morikawa, *Minami afurika to nihon*, pp. 23–24. The Japanese government maintains that the two countries had nothing more than a Consular relationship. See also Morikawa Jun, 'The Anatomy of Japan's South African Policies', *The Journal of Modern African Studies*, vol. 22, no. 1, 1984.
77 S.O. Agbi, 'Africa: Japan's Continent-sized Blind Spot', *Japan Times*, 6 June 1982, p. 12.
78 *Policies of Apartheid of the Government of South Africa (item 28), Explanation of vote by Mr. Sezaki*, 16 December 1980.
79 The term was coined by the press in reaction to South African Minister of the Interior Mr. Jan de Klerk's statement in Parliament in April 1961 to the effect

that Japanese nationals would be regarded as whites in view of their honorary status. There was no official South African or Japanese terminology for this status.

80 Japan External Trade Organization, *White Paper on International Trade*, 1976.

81 Japan External Trade Organization, *White Paper on International Trade*, 1981.

82 Japan External Trade Organization, *White Paper on International Trade*, 1988.

83 Singe Landgren, *Embargo Disimplemented: South Africa's Military Industry*, Oxford, Oxford University Press, 1989, p. 217.

84 Aoki Kazuyoshi, 'Nihon to afurika: hyo na kankei kara mitsunaru kankei no kōchiku', in Oda Hideo (ed.), *Afurika no seiji to kokusai kankei*, Tokyo, Keisō shobō, 1991, p. 318–19.

85 Godfrey Morrison, 'Japan's Year in Africa, 1973–74', in Colin Legum *et al.* (eds.), *Africa Contemporary Record, Annual Survey and Documents*, London: Rex Collings, 1974, p. A104.

86 While the Japanese steel companies were not equity participants in any of ISCOR's projects, they nevertheless offered long-term procurement contracts (as discussed in Chapter 3) to the corporation. The latter, presumably, used these contracts to raise additional capital.

87 Morrison, 'Japan's Year in Africa', p. A106.

88 Tsūshō Sangyosho, *Tsūshō hakusho*, Tokyo, 1977, pp. 166–71; Morikawa, *Minami afurika to nihon*, p. 108.

89 Alan Rix, 'Dynamism, Foreign Policy and Trade Policy', in Stockwin *et al.*, (eds.), *Dynamic and Immobilist Politics in Japan*, p. 304.

90 Interview with Mr. Jerry Matsila (Head of the ANC liaison office in Tokyo), October, 1991; 'Japan: ANC Office Opened', *Sechaba* (Official Organ of the ANC, South Africa), August 1988, pp. 18–19.

91 Interview with Mr. Matsila, Tokyo.

92 *Nihon keizai shimbun*, 9 December 1988, p. 2; *Asahi shimbun*, 1 February 1989; *Asahi shimbun*, 28 February 1989, p. 1.

93 The *Star*, 23 January 1995.

94 The *Star*, 27 October 1994.

95 *Business Daily*, 23 January 1995; *Pretoria News*, 23 January 1995.

96 The *Star*, 23 January 1995.

97 Masatoshi Ohta, 'For a Smaller Indian Ocean: Japan–South Africa Relations, their Past, Present and Future', *The Round Table*, No. 336, 1995. p. 423.

98 Interview with Mr. Yoshino Kyoji (Second Secretary, Economic Attaché) Japanese Embassy, Pretoria, South Africa, January 1995.

99 *Nikkei keizai shimbun*, 24 May 1994.

100 Interview with Mr. Yoshino Kyoji, Pretoria.

101 The term 'satisficing' is used by J. A. A. Stockwin to describe a variant of Japan's immobilist diplomacy. It involves 'giving everybody something of what they want but nobody everything of what they want'. See J.A.A. Stockwin, 'Dynamic and Immobilist Aspects of Japanese Politics', in Stockwin *et al.*, (eds.), *Dynamic and Immobilist Politics in Japan*, p. 2.

3 South Africa

Strategic raw materials and Japan's economic security

To say that since the end of Pacific War international trade has been Japan's lifeline is to state the obvious. But international trade has also presented Japan with some unpleasant experiences; and sometimes with some of its close friends. Since the 1960s, its trade relations with the USA, for example, have been locked up in what seems to be a permanent state of tension, or what is known as *boeki masatsu* (trade friction). Japan's trade relations with South Africa were also of that ilk, plagued with difficulties, although of a different flavor. The usefulness of that relationship to Japan was also clear. And, no doubt, the extent of trade between Tokyo and Pretoria strengthened the intimacy between the two countries. With a two-way trade of $762.9 mn. in 1972, trade reached $2.3 bn. in 1979. By 1980 it had grown to $3.5 bn. And Japan was South Africa's fourth-largest trading partner in that year, after the USA, Britain, and West Germany, in that order. A year later, at a two-way trade of $3.4 bn. in 1981, Tokyo became South Africa's second-largest trade partner, after the USA. When it eventually emerged in 1987 (as shown in Table 3.9, p. 82) as Pretoria's leading trading partner in the face of the rising temperature of the sanctions debate, Tokyo found itself shouldering the full impact of the political implications of trading with South Africa.

The trends in the volume and value of imports and exports, and changes in the content of these in response to the changes in, and development of, the respective economies of the two countries is interesting to observe, especially from 1974 to the latter part of the 1980s. It is particularly interesting when analyzed in relation to the question of South Africa's strategic importance to Japan; that is, Japan's dependence on Pretoria for strategic resources during this period. What is also relevant to this analysis is an examination of the end uses of some of these resources, to show how these strategic resources contributed to the sustainable growth of the Japanese economy. Thus, although Japanese exports to South Africa are mentioned in this discussion, they are not explored in any great detail. In essence, the chapter attempts to demonstrate the importance of South Africa to Japan's economic security, specifically in relation to the question of Japan's raw materials imports.

There is an implied flirtation here with the notion that Japan's resource diplomacy in sub-Saharan Africa can be seen as a political response to problems of economic insecurity, at least since the 1960s and especially in the 1970s and 1980s. While the concentration of the discussion is on the 1970s and 1980s, it may be appropriate to attempt to explore the origin and history behind the ever-expanding trade relations between Tokyo and Pretoria. It may be worth exploring the general pattern of trade between the two countries, first, while making periodic references to their respective comparative advantage. The second part of the study will concentrate on the question of South Africa's strategic raw materials, and will examine the extent of Japanese dependence on Pretoria for some of these resources.

As stated earlier, Japanese policy makers viewed the Southern African region as strategically important in the economic sense, and they singled out South Africa as a country with strategic resources. This chapter should therefore serve as an empirical explication for the argument concerning Japan's CNS plan and the centrality of raw materials in this economic-oriented strategy for security. As will be demonstrated in Chapter 5, nowhere was the insatiable interest in South Africa's raw materials demonstrated more clearly than at the UNGA, where Japan, year after year, consistently voted in opposition to the rest of the AA group of states on apartheid-related resolutions. And, as has been stated several times earlier, Japan's votes at the General Assembly on comprehensive sanctions in particular should be seen within the context of the 1973 oil crisis and indeed the CNS strategy that was to be implemented in its aftermath.

THE GENERAL CONTEXT OF THE JAPANESE–SOUTH AFRICA TRADE RELATIONSHIP

Since Japan had to import increasing amounts of raw materials to sustain and augment its growing economy, a steady expansion of exports was considered vital for economic independence. 'Export or die' was the proverbial mercantilist attitude Japanese policy makers adopted in their confrontation with this most vital security problem of post-war Japan. Trading with a pariah state like South Africa was therefore part of Japan's active and frantic search for appropriate strategies – excluding military aggression, of course – for meeting the challenge of national security.

In essence, for a country with an expanding economy and few local raw materials, every relevant primary resource producer was a viable trade partner. It is in this respect, rather than for its immoral principles, that Japan's policy makers and business executives disapproved of apartheid; for apartheid, in practice, created the circumstances that made it impossible for Japan to trade and invest freely in South Africa.[1] According to a General Manager of Mitsui (& Co.) in South Africa, 'We need the raw materials South Africa can provide and we would like to invest here.'[2] The frustration was confirmed by the General Manager of the Johannesburg branch of the Mitsubishi Corporation, who confessed that: 'We are certainly facing difficulties on the political side. Japan is concerned about it because South Africa is so important to us with its mineral wealth.' Another Japanese business executive, the head of the Mitsubishi Corporation (Johannesburg), said that his government's ban against direct investment in South Africa was disadvantageous to the interests of Japanese firms doing business in the country. As he put it:

> The investment ban puts us at a distinct disadvantage vis-a-vis our foreign competitors . . . If you have a factory employing thousands of workers . . . you have far more say with government. We don't have that push and consequently lose business to other firms.[3]

Bearing in mind this fact and the importance of investments to advanced capitalist economies, Japan's inability to compete freely where its competitors could, and did, must have been extremely disturbing for Japanese companies operating in South Africa, especially because of their distinct interest in the latter's primary resources.

Japan profited a great deal from the successful conclusion of the Kennedy Round (KR) of talks (1964–67) which, among other things, reduced tariffs on manufactured goods by its major trading partners. As trade in the Western hemisphere expanded through the trade liberalization principles of the KR, Japanese exports accelerated, with great international reverberations. In fact, by 1960, economic relations between Japan and South Africa had started to show signs of tremendous growth. Between 1955 and 1961 Japan had almost doubled her exports to the South African market, while at the same time importing large quantities of industrial raw materials from South Africa, which was overtaking both Germany and France and rapidly catching up with the USA in its relative importance as a market.[4] For South Africa, this was an indication of a significant change in the geographical direction of its trade since World War II. It must be noted that in 1961 South Africa had become a republic by leaving the Commonwealth. As a result, it welcomed anything that made it less economically dependent on that institution and its traditional trade partner, Britain.

These developments meant that South Africa had to tinker with its racial policies in order to smooth the path for trade with an Asian nation. Accordingly, in April 1961, the Verwoerd government passed a decree to the effect that Japanese were to be regarded as whites for the purposes of the Group Areas Act. In fact, albeit a new development, this was a reaffirmation of a policy by the Nationalist–Labor Pact government[5] in 1930, which removed the restrictions (imposed by the South African Party) that Japanese merchants could only enter South Africa subject to government sanction. The restrictions, as stipulated in the Union Immigration Act of 1913, meant that Asians, including Japanese, could not do business in South Africa.[6]

These racially nuanced historical events, culminating in the 1961 decree, are significant in one particular respect: they gave the Japanese 'an economic free hand in South Africa' although, as we have pointed out above, it was an economic free hand that was not conducive to free economic activity, due to the constraining political connotations of doing business with South Africa. Nevertheless, the 1961 decree amounted, essentially, to the freedom to participate in economic activities in South Africa without the political, administrative and social impediments faced by other Asians.[7] It is important to note that, for purposes of the Population Registration Act, Japanese were categorized as 'Other Asiatics'. All these attempts to accommodate the Japanese were, indeed, an indication of the importance of foreign trade to South Africa, just as such trade was important to Japan. And it was also a sure indication of the importance of South Africa to Japanese economic security. Thus, the two economies complemented each other in terms of their individual comparative advantage within the international trade system. South Africa's exports to Japan (during the period under observation) were still heavily dependent upon primary products – agricultural and mineral exports – despite the expansion and diversification of its export products, at least since 1961. Japan's exports to South Africa from the 1960s onwards advanced from light consumer goods like textiles to machinery, transport equipment, computers and other high-technology products; a testimony to the industrial progress in both countries.

THE 'WAR EFFECT' ON JAPANESE TRADE WITH SOUTH AFRICA

World War I gave meaning to the fledgling but negligible trade between Japan and South Africa. On this subject Kitagawa Katsuhiko's seminal paper on Japanese consular reports on the economic situation in Africa suggests that trade between Japan and South Africa started before 1898, when a branch of Mikado Shōkai was set up in Cape Town.[8] However, while trade continued steadily, mostly in the export of Japanese products to South Africa, it was not until World War I that trade relations between the two countries began to take proper shape. Japan's imports from South Africa accounted for a mere £45 in 1910.[9]

The war brought striking changes in the volume and direction of South African trade. For example, whereas in the first half of 1913 US exports to South Africa totalled £1.7 mn. or 8.8 percent of total imports for the same period, in 1916 South Africa's American imports came to the value of £2.8 mn. or 14 percent of total imports. The *Weekly Cape Times* reported that 'A large portion of this increased US business is due of course to the diversion of trade formerly enjoyed by Germany'. It further noted, in defense of the poor performance of British trade with South Africa, that 'the US has probably secured more than would otherwise have been her share if the factories of the UK had not been absorbed in the production of munitions'. Another war effect was the 'striking case of rapid trade' between Japan and South Africa.[10] It may be worth noting, however, that as part of the war effort, Germany was cut off completely from South African trade, as well as from contact with the whole of the British Empire. Thereafter the Board of Trade exhorted[11] British manufacturers to recapture the gap left by the Germans.

While the Board of Trade was 'strategising'[12] to capture the German markets for the British merchants, the Japanese government was also actively researching how best to compete for at least a sustainable share of that market. Kitagawa's paper effectively identifies Japan's interests in South Africa at the time. He points out that a report sent to the Gaimushō (Bureau of Commerce) by its contact person in Cape Town said, among other things, that the German products on the South African market could be easily replaced by Japanese products, primarily because Japan, like Germany, had a comparative advantage against the USA in providing cheap consumer goods for the 'African' market. Presumably in response to this valuable information another report emerged, during the war, from the Gaimushō – written by a Shimizu Yaoichi[13] – detailing how best Japanese merchants could enter the South African market.

As has already been pointed out, by 1916 Japan was seen on the South African scene as a viable competitor, simply by doing what it did best: selling to the cheap end of the market. 'The Japanese can turn out two or three wooden boats for a few pence' wrote the The *Weekly Cape Times*.[14] Japanese exports to South Africa during this period included cotton goods such as underwear, shorts, shirts, blankets, socks, silk, bracelets for the natives (*dojin yō udewa*), ceramics, brushes, hats and other essential commodities. Kitagawa notes that these products sold quickly, leading to the increase in the direct imports of such products from Japan, and visits of merchants from Cape Town, Durban, and Johannesburg to Japan in search for the relevant goods and their manufacturers.[15] Previous to that many such Japanese products were originally intended for London.[16] Thus, until 1916 there were hardly any Japanese imports from South Africa.

Shimizu also identified in his report certain products in South Africa – mostly raw materials – that were relevant to Japan's manufacturing economy. These raw materials included wattle, bark, stone cotton, hides, and skins and wool. From an early stage, therefore, trade between the two countries was defined according to the comparative advantage that each of the parties held, meaning that South Africa would supply raw materials to and import manufactured goods from Japan. This continues to be the general pattern of trade between the two countries.

Wool, rather than gold, which held the dominant position in South Africa's exports, was identified after 1915 as possibly the most attractive commodity to Japan's manufacturing economy. The *Weekly Cape Times* reported that

> The dangers to shipping caused by submarine warfare in the mediterranean have deflected Japan's European liners Southward by the Cape Route . . . Prospects in this direction are regarded as especially auspicious at the present time, when Japanese mills are suffering for want of wool, a plentiful supply of tops being expected from South Africa. Owing to high freights and scarcity of shipping facilities, Japan has been finding it increasingly inconvenient to depend for her wool supplies from Australia; and as she's now busy filling enormous orders in army cloth for Russia, the delay means great loss. The wool exporters of South Africa are said to welcome the opportunity for opening a market in Japan, and have already begun to supply samples through Japanese Consular agents . . . The first order to South Africa is for 200,000 lb of merino tops; and though the wool is said to be somewhat inferior to that usually imported to Japan from Australia the cost is about 20 percent less, and the quality quite sufficient for Japan's need.[17]

Obviously the 'war effect' opened up avenues for South Africa as well, at least as far as its trade relations with Japan were concerned. The wool exports were subject to violent fluctuation due to the tendency to overproduction. The intervention of Japan, thus, was something of an act of redemption for the South African economy. The value of wool exports increased from £3.8 mn. in 1910 to £17.9 mn. in 1919. As shown in Table 3.1, the value of Japanese imports from South Africa in 1919 was £3.7 mn., compared to its exports at £1.7 mn. South Africa now enjoyed a favorable balance of payments with Japan after more than a decade of

Table 3.1 Japan–South Africa trade, 1906–1943

1906–1924			1925–1943		
Year	Exports	Imports (£)	Year	Exports	Imports (¥1000)
1906	70,329	–	1925	9,539	1,325
1907	53,835	–	1926	10,741	917
1908	54,128	–	1927	11,640	1,082
1909	51,787	–	1928	11,695	1,341
1910	78,706	–	1929	13,179	1,448
1911	94,702	–	1930	14,169	1,618
1912	104,604	–	1931	19,283	1,333
1913	109,812	–	1932	16,418	2,636
1914	110,259	135	1933	26,741	4,313
1915	221,593	765	1934	29,540	8,234
1916	540,884	14,452	1935	32,769	4,763
1917	730,998	2,842,037	1936	41,534	22,561
1918	2,663,421	2,816,249	1937	53,749	88,852
1919	1,754,268	3,752,313	1938	35,291	1,810
1920	1,463,282	5,981,646	1939	16,802	9,486
1921	747,666	467,139	1940	61,366	25,197
1922	628,608	155,743	1941	24,545	13,915
1923	525,880	66,679	1942	–	0
1924	699,627	87,875	1943	–	44

Note: Figures for 1906–1909 are based on total calculated for The Cape Colony, Natal, The Orange Free State and Transvaal
Sources: Kitagawa, 'Senzenki nihon no ryōji hōkoku', 1989, p. 57; Bureau of Statistics (Office of the of the Prime Minister), Japan Statistical Yearbook (Nihon tōkei nenkan), October 1956

buying from and not selling much to Japan. In 1920 (Table 3.2), Japan took £5.9 mn. of South African products, and had become the second-largest market for South Africa, although far behind Britain. The latter's share had declined from 91 percent in 1910 to 65.2 percent a decade later.[18] However, Japanese imports from South Africa decreased drastically in 1921, and continued along that path for a while.

Japanese exports to South Africa were at their peak in 1918 at £2.6 mn., compared to £730,998 the previous year, as shown in Table 3.1. As already noted, however, from 1919 onwards Japanese exports began to decrease, partly through loss of popularity, as German goods crept back into the market.[19] As post-war European goods came back onto the South African scene, even the cheap Japanese cotton and silk goods faced stiff competition, leading to a rather fatalistic comment from a Japanese official in the Cape Town Consulate. He noted that Japan was competing in a rather hostile environment: Japanese goods were 'surrounded by rivals on all sides [shimen soka]'.[20] The general perception in South

Table 3.2 Principal export markets of South Africa and their proportion of total merchandise exports, 1910, 1920 and 1933

	1910		1920		1933	
Country	(£1,000)	%	(£1,000)	%	(£1,000)	%
UK	49,819	91.0	59,458	65.2	55,042	78.4
Germany	1,814	3.3	515	0.6	1,942	2.8
Belgium	668	0.2	1,778	2.1	2,308	3.3
USA	402	0.7	3,917	4.7	–	–
Japan	–	–	5,982	7.2	–	–
S. Rhodesia	–	–	1,212	1.5	–	–
France	–	–	–	–	2,805	4.0
Italy	–	–	–	–	1,129	1.6

Source: Jones and Müller, *The South African Economy*, 1992, p. 117

Africa, however, was that although the Japanese were competing well, their cheap goods were of inferior quality because they were products of the 'very cheapest labor'. According to the General Manager of a large trading company in Cape Town, 'most of the stuff which comes from Japan is characteristic of the country . . . but when [they] have been educated up to our needs they will be able to send us anything we want'.[21]

The latter part of the 1920s saw the volume as well as value of Japanese exports to South Africa rising again with some consistency. As illustrated in Table 3.1, in 1926, for example, Japan shipped ¥10.7 mn. worth of goods to the Union. Its imports, on the other hand, were a mere ¥ 917,000. As this scenario continued into the early 1930s – when in 1933 (Table 3.3), for example, Japan emerged as South Africa's fourth largest supplier, after the United Kingdom, Germany and the USA – and the South African market became inundated with cheap Japanese products, it evoked anti-Japanese sentiments among South African manufacturers. The agitation concerned primarily the threat to South African-made shoes and shirts. The Union's manufacturers demanded higher customs tariffs for the above products when, already in 1930, for example, a very high duty of '1s. 9d [was] imposed on every silk shirt imported from Japan'.[22] And they rationalized their demand for higher customs tariffs with the slogan (popular at the time) that Japan employed 'sweated labor', although South Africa was the last country in the world entitled to criticize the exploitation of 'sweated labor' by another country. It must be noted, however, that the Union government had, in 1925, imposed tariffs on certain imports specifically to foster industrialization.

In spite of all the agitation, trade between the two countries continued

Table 3.3 Principal suppliers of imports to South Africa and their proportion of total merchandise imports, 1910, 1920 and 1933

	1910		1920		1933	
Country	£1,000	%	£1,000	%	£1,000	%
UK	20,048	59.0	50,244	47.4	23,711	49.9
Germany	3,513	10.3	–	–	3,067	6.5
USA	2,663	7.8	17,044	16.1	5,976	12.6
Australia	1,608	4.7	3,948	3.7	–	–
India	–	–	2,606	2.5	–	–
Canada	–	–	2,702	2.6	1,229	2.6
Sweden	–	–	2,037	1.9	–	–
Japan	–	–	–	–	2,065	4.3

Source: Jones and Müller, *The South African Economy*, 1992, p. 119

and exports to South Africa grew. Imports from South Africa, however, took a deep dive from 1938 onwards, with only periodic signs of resuscitation until 1941 when the war started, after which trade between the two countries faded into oblivion until the latter part of the 1940s. And although the value of Japanese exports to and imports from South Africa was a high ¥53.7 mn. and ¥88.8 mn., respectively, in 1937, by 1938 exports had reduced to ¥35.2 mn. Even then Japan was fifth among South Africa's major export countries, as shown in Table 3.4. It was, however, providing a mere 3.2 percent of South Africa's imports compared to 42 percent, 19.2 percent and 5.3 percent for the UK, the USA and Germany, respectively. And Japan's imports from South Africa in 1938 (Table 3.1) were rather negligible at a mere ¥1.8 mn., which did not allow it a place among South Africa's top six markets in 1938 (Table 3.5). The above discussion of the trade relations between the two countries in the pre-World War II period introduces us to the roots of the Japanese–South Africa relationship, its basis in comparative advantage, and some of the benefits both countries derived from the relationship, at a time when there were serious constraints on international trade and the international economy as a whole.

TRADE IN THE POST-WORLD WAR II ERA: EXPORTS TO JAPAN

As shown in Table 3.4, between 1955 when it joined the General Agreement on Tariffs and Trade (GATT) and 1961, Japan's exports to South Africa increased by over 70 percent in value. It had just started to import, in 1955, what became in the 1960s large quantities of industrial

Table 3.4 Principal sources of South Africa's imports and their proportion of total merchandise imports, 1938, 1947, 1955 and 1961

Country	1938	1947	1955	1961
UK	37,249	82,311	166,606	146,164
	(42.0)	(27.7)	(34.6)	(29.1)
USA	16,537	101,470	100,429	88,678
	(19.2)	–	–	(17.7)
Germany	5,024	–	–	54,624
	(5.3)	–	–	(10.9)
Canada	3,011	17,290	17,290	13,470
	(3.5)	(5.8)	(5.8)	(2.7)
Japan	2,785	–	10,220	17,880
	(3.2)	–	(2.1)	(3.6)
Belgium	1,825	6,631*	9,763	10,153
	(2.1)	(2.2)	(2.0)	(2.0)
Sweden	–	5,111	–	9,677
	–	(1.7)	–	(1.9)

Note: *Mostly from the Belgian Congo
Source: Compiled from Jones and Müller, *The South African Economy*, 1992, p. 220

Table 3.5 Principal export markets of South Africa and their proportion of merchandise exports in 1938 and 1961

Country	1938		1961	
	£	%	£	%
UK	58,791	74.4	111,854	26.2
Germany	4,992	6.3	20,578	4.8
France	2,129	2.7	17,741	4.0
Belgium	1,566	2.0	16,741	3.9
S.Rhodesia	1,352	1.7	–	–
Italy	1,021	1.3	–	–
Rhodesia and Nyasaland	–	–	48,481	11.4
USA	–	–	34,347	8.1
Japan	–	–	25,628	6.0

Source: Jones and Müller, *The South African Economy*, 1992, p. 216

raw materials from South Africa. Not surprisingly, in 1961 the Japanese government revised its tariff schedule extensively. These revisions included setting low tariff rates on the following items: (1) primary commodities, such as agricultural products and minerals; (2) goods that could not be produced locally or that could be produced only in limited quantities with no possibility of expanded domestic production in future; and finally (3) the products or raw materials of well-established export industries. The above prescriptions were designed, obviously, in favor of Japan's raw material-dependent industries, and suggests, as pointed out in Chapter 1, that raw materials were viewed as being eternally crucial to Japan's economic security, a fact that became essentialized in the CNS strategy. What is also important to note here is the fact that the above tariff prescriptions were eminently favorable to countries such as South Africa, whose exports were heavily dependent on primary products.

During the 1960s, three important changes occurred in Japan's international trade: (1) its share of world trade rose substantially; (2) the composition of its exports changed remarkably; and (3) the share of products heavily dependent on unskilled labor such as textiles, miscellaneous light industry products and domestic products declined, while the share of products of heavy engineering industries, such as steel and various kinds of machinery and automobiles, rose sharply. Corresponding with the above, was the fact that fuel (crude oil and coal) imports increased while the share of raw materials for textiles declined. Machinery imports for its steel and other newly expanding industries also increased slightly. These developments were a reflection of the advancement and expansion of the Japanese economy.

As the Japanese economy moved into the production of light industrial products and various kinds of machinery, the content of South Africa's import trade moved generally into manufactured capital and consumer goods, industrial raw materials and some foodstuffs, even though textiles still formed the largest group of imports. Prominent among these were machinery and metal wares (including vehicles and vehicle parts). According to Stuart Jones and Andre Müller, the process of industrialization in South Africa necessitated the importation of producer goods for manufacturing industry.[23] Thus, 'finished capital goods and processed intermediate goods accounted for 68.7 percent of imports in 1958', and 'machinery and transport equipment accounted for 36.2 percent of all imports in 1961'.[24] These changes to the South African import trade were responsible for the huge increase in the value of Japanese exports to South Africa in 1955 and 1961 (Table 3.4), at £10.2 mn. and £17.8 mn., respectively.

South Africa broadened its exports throughout the 1950s, 1960s and into the 1970s, as it diversified its export markets abroad. Throughout most of the 1960s and early 1970s, Japan was fourth among Pretoria's principal sources of exports, as indicated in Table 3.6. Nevertheless, gold as a single commodity remained crucial to the country's export economy during this period, even though manufactured exports to the African markets north of the Limpopo also featured prominently in the country's foreign trade.[25] Most important in the country's overall trade was the boom in the export of

Table 3.6 The principal export markets of South Africa, 1961–1976 (R mn. and %)

Year	UK	USA	Japan	Germany	France
1961	252.2	68.8	51.3	41.1	34.0
	(29.9%)	(8.1%)	(6.0%)	(4.8%)	(4.0%)
1964	321.2	82.4	84.4	57.8	36.4
	(33.7%)	(8.6%)	(8.8%)	(6.1%)	(3.8%)
1967	444.8	107.4	175.2	85.7	35.2
	(32.7%)	(7.9%)	(12.9%)	(6.3%)	(2.6%)
1970	446.6	128.9	181.2	106.6	37.8
	(29.1%)	(8.4%)	(11.8%)	(7.0%)	(2.5%)
1973	696.5	163.7	246.4	157.7	68.9
	(29.5%)	(6.9%)	(10.4%)	(6.7%)	(2.9%)
1976	987.7	407.3	526.8	356.5	158.6
	(23.5%)	(9.7%)	(12.5%)	(8.5%)	(3.8%)

Source: Jones and Müller, The South African Economy, 1992, p. 346

the following raw materials: coal, platinum, chrome, copper, iron ore, manganese and diamonds. It has to be noted at this point that, from the 1960s onwards, the sanctions debate at the UN began to develop into a pressing political issue for South Africa and its trading partners, such as Japan. Even so, it was not until later, in the 1970s and 1980s, that sanctions seriously affected South Africa's international trade. It was also during this period that Japan's votes at the UNGA on apartheid-related matters became less supportive of the Afro-Asian position on the matter, as will be shown in Chapter 5.

As Pretoria's importance as a source for primary commodities grew, so its trade relations with, and its strategic value to, the Western industrialized countries, including Japan, became reinforced; and Hanns Maull poignantly points out that: 'Dependence on raw material imports . . . [gave] rise to diplomatic and political efforts at fostering close relations with supplier countries'.[26] Thus, it is no exaggeration to note, as Maull does, that 'Japan's resource diplomacy is an outstanding example of this'. Inevitably, this complicated Tokyo's diplomatic relations, especially with the OAU and at the UNGA, as Pretoria remained Japan's biggest trading partner on the continent. In 1969 South Africa took almost 25 percent of Japan's exports to the African continent as a whole, and shipped about 30 percent of Africa's total exports to Japan. And, in 1973, it took 38.2 percent of Tokyo's total exports to Africa. Japan's exports to the Republic grew a remarkable 63.6 percent, as Pretoria relaxed its import restrictions that year. As for Japan's imports from the region, South Africa was responsible for 29.9 percent of the total, compared to the previous year's 34 percent.[27]

In 1977, South Africa's principal export markets were the UK, the USA,

Japan, Germany, France, Switzerland, Belgium and Italy, in that order. In 1976, South Africa ran a US $-based trade surplus of $44.5 mn., after a 1975 deficit of $3.7 mn. and a 1974 deficit of $196 mn. Exports to Japan in 1977 outran imports by $138.7 mn. According to Japanese government figures, Tokyo's imports from South Africa rose 19.1 percent, while exports to South Africa increased by only 7 percent. Despite its third position among South Africa's principal export markets, Japan depended on it for a mere 1.3 percent of all its imports, down from 1.5 percent in 1975. Pretoria ranked nineteenth among countries exporting to Japan; and it did not rank in the top twenty of Japan's export markets. In 1979, Japan's bilateral trade with South Africa amounted to just 1.1 percent of Japan's total foreign trade, at the value of $2,291,783 mn.[28] Nevertheless, from 1976 to 1980 South Africa's exports to Japan increased by 84.5 percent in value, while imports went up by 33 percent. It must be noted, though, that a fair share of the increase in the value of exports was due to inflation.[29]

In the 1950s and 1960s, then, Japan steadily expanded its share of South Africa's exports. Albeit a small share of Japan's external trade, the qualitative significance of imports from South Africa were enhanced with the gradual shift from commodities like cotton and wool to other raw materials with greater strategic value. Suffice to say, in the post-World War II period, trade between South Africa and Japan remained rooted in comparative advantage but changed in composition with the evolving industrialization and modernization of the two economies.

THE NEW COMPLEXITY OF TRADE RELATIONS IN THE 1970s AND 1980s

As noted above, trade between Japan and South Africa continued to expand after the oil crisis. Indeed, in 1973, South Africa's Economic Affairs Minister, Lourens Müller, stated that his country considered Japan one of the best markets for South Africa's resources.[30] As far as sub-Saharan Africa as a market for Japanese products was concerned, Japan's policy makers were also aware of Pretoria's value, and therefore maintained its importance as a supplier of the relevant technology and merchandise to South Africa.

South Africa as an export market for Japan

In an international environment becoming increasingly hostile to Japanese exports, it is no surprise, despite its political implications, that South Africa's importance as a fast-growing market attracted Japanese producers. For example, in 1977, machinery and mechanical equipment accounted for 65.3 percent of Japan's total exports to South Africa compared to 62 percent in 1976.[31] Exports of general machinery rose by 14.6 percent, while exports of metal products for construction increased by 30.1 percent, despite the recession and the fact that the construction sector of the South African economy in particular was suffering during this period. On the other hand, the export of motor vehicles, the major export commodity, declined by 3.8 percent. In 1987, machinery exports, on the whole, went up 43.6 percent from the previous year and made up 79.9 percent of total exports.

As for light industry goods, exports of textiles fell 23.3 percent in 1976, as a result of fallen demand in synthetic fibre yarns and synthetic fabrics. But South Africa had, by this time, also become self-sufficient (except in acrylic fibre) in the production of these textile goods.[32] In 1987 textile goods were only a mere 2.9 percent of Japan's exports to South Africa.[33] These changes, as noted earlier, were a reflection of the structural changes constantly taking place in the South African and Japanese economies in general, and in their respective industrial policies in particular. As South Africa advanced in the process of industrialization, therefore, its imports of heavy industrial machinery became prominent in Japanese exports to South Africa while its imports of light manufactured goods declined. And the pattern of exports of many types of machinery equipment fluctuated in the 1980s, as illustrated in Table 3.7; except for automobile parts whose exports shot up dramatically from 1985–1987. Export of engines also increased significantly from 1986 to 1987.

From 1980 to 1984, Japanese exports to South Africa were greater than imports, except in 1982, as illustrated in Table 3.8. From 1985 to 1987, imports were far more than exports however. And South Africa remained by a large margin Japan's leading trade partner in Africa,[34] taking 32 percent of Tokyo's exports to and 56.5 percent of its imports from the continent in 1987. Crucial to this discussion is the fact that Japan emerged in both 1986 and 1987 as South Africa's leading trade partner. As noted earlier, this exposed Japan to severe criticisms at the UNGA and other

Table 3.7 Principal Japanese exports to South Africa – items, 1980–1987 ($ mn.)

Merchandise	1980	1981	1982	1983	1984	1985	1986	1987
Automobiles	363.7	504.9	346.9	372.2	400.8	188.3	278.8	373.8
Automobile parts	166.2	210.2	204.5	193.5	218.5	122.1	252.4	498.9
Electrical machinery	229.1	325.5	252.1	314.1	335.8	171.9	214.9	232.5
Metal (manfactured)	184.6	176.7	149.4	149.9	148.9	101.4	937.5	116.4
Engines	33.4	48.5	31.3	32.1	40.0	22.6	32.6	48.1

Source: JETRO, *White Paper on International Trade*, 1981–1988

international fora, especially in 1987. And, incidentally, 1987 was the year that the US House of Representatives recommended measures against non-American corporations actively trading with Pretoria. The USA had, by this time, become frustrated with Tokyo for not stopping its firms from moving into South Africa to fill the gap left by American firms that had supposedly divested. And in 1988 the US Senate recommended harsher sanctions against countries like Japan who were taking advantage of the US divestments from South Africa.

As the sanctions pressures increased in the latter part of the 1980s, for example, individual Japanese vehicle producers advised by Gaimushō to exercise restraint[35] imposed voluntary restrictions on their exports to South Africa. In 1988, the balance sheet of Tokyo's trade with South Africa showed a 'convenient' drop in the value of trade between the two countries; making Japan South Africa's second-largest trade partner after West Germany, as demonstrated in Table 3.9. Not surprisingly, the Japanese government was pleased with this 'change in position'.[36] It is interesting to note, however, that West Germany was spared the treatment that Japan received as South Africa's leading trade partner. At this juncture, it may also be appropriate to recall that within the multilateral trade system, and invariably in its economic relations with South Africa, Tokyo's trade policy evolved under the balance of power between MITI and Gaimushō.

Table 3.8 Japan–South Africa trade, 1980–1988

	1981	1982	1983	1984	1985	1986	1987	1988
Exports								
$1,800	2,222	1,655	1,738	1,840	1,020	1,355	1,863 (109.8)	2,047 (109.8)
¥4,050	4,878	4,085	4,133	4,344	2,448	2,284	2,692 (117.9)	2,622 (97.4)
Imports								
$1,741	1,728	1,840	1,587	1,611	1,844	2,229	2,259 (101.4)	1,931 (85.0)
¥3,960	3,813	4,558	3,770	3,816	4,419	3,787	3,284 (86.7)	2,476 (75.3)
Total								
$3,541	3,950	3,495	3,325	3,451	2,864	3,584	4,122 (115.0)	3,978 (96.5)
¥8,010	8,691	8,643	7,903	8,160	6,865	6,071	5,976 (98.4)	5,096 (85.3)

Note: Figures in parentheses indicate percentage change in value of trade from 1987 to 1988
Source: JETRO, *White Paper on International Trade*, 1980–1988

Table 3.9 Trend in trade between South Africa and its major trading partners, 1984–1988 (US $ mn.)

Country	1984	1985	1986	1987	1988
West Germany	3,391 (3)	2,775 (3)	3,267 (3)	3,797 (2)	5,058 (1)
Japan	3,451 (2)	2,864 (2)	3,584 (1)	4,122 (1)	3,980 (2)
UK	2,579 (4)	2,591 (4)	2,469 (4)	2,657 (3)	3,352 (3)
USA	4,732 (1)	3,262 (1)	3,493 (2)	2,598 (4)	3,275 (4)

Note: Figures in parentheses indicate country's ranking in trade with South Africa
Source: JETRO, *White Paper on International Trade*, 1985–1989

Japanese imports of South Africa's agricultural commodities and foodstuffs

Japan imported a variety of agricultural commodities from South Africa, some in great amounts. Corn and sugar were typical of such Japanese imports. By 1974, there were signs that the Japanese were in the market for South African maize (mainly for animal feed and corn starch), sugar, canned and dried foods, grapefruit and other produce.[37] In 1973, sugar exports alone to Japan earned South Africa $76.6 mn.[38] In 1974, the two countries signed a contract for the annual shipment of 350,000 tons of sugar to Japan from 1976–1978. While sugar exports increased 2.7 times in value in 1975, however, they went down 28 percent in quantity in the same year.[39] Nevertheless, this commodity remained the biggest single export to Japan for most of the 1970s and maintained a high prominence among Japan's imports even into the 1980s. In 1981, South Africa was Japan's second-largest source for sugar after Australia. It was third in 1985 and 1989 despite a cut in imports from a 25.5 percent share in 1987 to 16.5 percent of Japan's total sugar imports in 1988.

South Africa was also a source for a fair amount of Japan's maize requirements. In 1975 alone, maize (excluding maize for animal feed) imports rose 2.7 times both in value and quantity.[40] In 1980, Japan imported 908,402 tons of corn at the value of $151.1 mn. This was an increase of 8.4 percent and 30.5 percent, in quantity and value respectively, from the previous year.[41] In 1981, South Africa was Japan's second-largest source for corn, even though it was far behind the USA in terms of size of imports.[42] The following year, the volume of imports increased almost twofold from the previous year to 2,398,484 tons, and subsequently started to decline. In 1987 for example, South Africa sold only 1,682,737 tons of corn to Japan at the value of $150,987. It may be worth reiterating the point that a fair proportion of Japanese imports of maize was intended for animal feed and use as corn starch. Japanese maize imports, therefore, found a critic in Japan. Yoshida Masao[43] argued that so much maize should not be imported for the above uses, since maize (the staple food of the African population of South Africa) was often in short supply there as a result of drought and exports. The pressures for sanctions against South Africa in the latter part of the 1980s, however, led to a huge decrease in Japanese corn imports from Pretoria. From 12 percent in 1987, South Africa's share of Japan's total maize imports dropped to 1.4 percent.

Japanese contracts for coal, iron ore and uranium

Among the other commodities South Africa exported to Japan were manganese, iron ore, ferro-alloys, asbestos, chrome, platinum, copper and nickel. Suffice to say that by the early 1970s negotiations had started between the two countries for long-term export contracts for coking coal, iron ore and uranium, among others, to Japan. A team from one of Japan's major iron and steel industries went to South Africa in May 1970 to do feasibility studies on ISCOR's proposed iron ore transport facilities at Saldanha Bay.[44] This was part of the negotiations to participate, through a long-term purchase contract, in the construction of a deep water iron ore harbor at the bay with a 860 kilometer rail link to ISCOR's Shisen iron ore mine. The project entailed transforming Saldanha into a port substantial enough to accommodate the giant Japanese iron ore carriers. According to the terms of the contract, ISCOR would supply Japan with 7 million tons of ore annually, while two private companies – Consolidated African Mines (CAM) and Associated Manganese – would supply 5 million tons, over a fifteen-year period starting from 1976.

A similar contract was signed with CAM, the details of which were that Japan would be supplied 70 million tons of iron ore over a sixteen-year period, if the ore loading terminal at St. Croix island in Algoa Bay were completed. At the same time, CAM set up a contract leading to the supply of 3.8 mn. tons of manganiferous ore, over a period of eleven years starting from 1977, to the Japanese steel industry. Japan's first contract with ISCOR, however, involved the purchase of large volumes of semi-processed steel which, according to some observers, was the main justification for the siting of the steel works at Saldanha. South African observers noted that: 'It is an open secret . . . that the Japanese are the mysterious unidentified partner in the semis plant at Saldanha'.[45] Japanese participation in this and the Richard's Bay project,[46] which also involved an expansion of the harbor and a new railway link from Witbank coal mine to the harbor, was obviously contingent on their acquisition of iron ore. It is interesting to note, as shown in Table 3.10, that despite the above contractual arrangements, in 1974 only 2 percent of Japan's iron ore

Table 3.10 Percentage supplied by South Africa of total imports of particular mineral commodity to five main trading partners, 1974

Commodity	United Kingdom	West Germany	France	USA	Japan
Platinum group metals	37	–	22	19	38
Antimony	95	50	14	43	15
Copper	4	10	1	6	21
Iron ore	–	–	–	–	2
Nickel	–	11	14	–	21
Vanadium	60	50	31	57	62
Chrome ore	30	29	17	30	37
Ferro-chrome	15	43	20	35	87
Manganese	43	52	40	8	43
Ferro-manganese	27	14	–	36	–
Asbestos	–	–	–	3	35
Fluorspar	–	–	–	–	23
Vermiculite	100	14	19	100	100

Source: Van Rensburg and Pretorius, *South Africa's Strategic Minerals*, 1977

imports were from South Africa. This had increased to 5 percent by 1985/86 as shown in Table 3.11.

Japan's import dependence on coal became very high, since domestic coal mines were (in the 1970s and early 1980s) unlikely to produce more than a few million tons of coking coal per year; and its extensive diversification policy to ensure secure supplies brought in a fair amount of coal from South Africa. The importance of this resource to Japan was demonstrated in its exemption from the number of resources that Japan was forced to slam the door of sanctions on. The signing of a contract between seven Japanese steel mills and coke-works and the Transvaal Coal Owners' Association (TCOA) allowed for the importation of 27 million tons of coal, worth $350 mn., over an eleven-year period from 1976. The exemption of coal as a sanctioned commodity obviously pleased the TCOA, since a Japanese ban on coal imports would have cost them 7 mn. tons of coal a year. [47]

Japan's frantic search for alternative energy sources in the 1970s, therefore, led to spectacular increases in its uranium imports, and a further awareness of the importance of South Africa in this respect. In December 1970 the Kansai Electric Power Company (the second-largest in Japan), through its agent the Mitsubishi Corporation, signed a contract with the Rossing Mining Group of Namibia to which the South African and Japanese governments were parties. The agreement allowed for the sale of 8,200 short tons of uranium from the above mine. By 1973 Japan had contracted for the purchase of 38,000 tons (43 percent of total needs) from

Table 3.11 Percentage supplied by South Africa and other major mineral exporters to Japan, 1985–1986

	South Africa	USA	Australia	Switzerland	EC	Canada	USSR
Chromite	56	—	—	—	—	—	11
Ferrochrome	63	—	—	—	—	—	—
Ferro-manganese	27	—	—	—	—	—	—
Fluorspar	14	—	—	—	22	—	—
Gold	7	29	6	26	—	2	—
Industrial diamonds	42	—	42	—	—	—	—
Iron ore	5	—	5	—	—	—	—
Manganese ore	55	9	—	—	—	—	—
Platinum	36	—	—	—	13	—	36
Titanium	12	—	—	—	—	—	—
Vanadium	84	—	—	—	—	—	—
Zirconium	12	—	85	—	—	—	—
Uranium	N/A	—	—	—	—	—	—

Source: Compiled from Phillip Crowson, *Minerals Handbook, 1987–88*

South Africa and Namibia (which was then under South African rule, illegally) over the period from 1976 to 1985. Suffice to say that the Japanese government supported the contract, despite the United Nations Council for Namibia's ruling (Decree No. 1), in 1974, that the raw materials in Namibia could only be obtained with the permission of the Council. Kitazawa Yōko notes that when confronted on the issue the Japanese government's response was that the decree was not legally binding,[48] because it was not enacted by the Security Council, a point that was consistent with Japan's position against resolutions advocating comprehensive sanctions, as will be pointed out in Chapter 5. The strategic importance of uranium will be examined in detail in the second part of the chapter.

In view of the nature of some of the above agreements, which involved long-term import guarantees, it was reported that:

> principal and visible characteristic[s] of Japanese involvement in South Africa appear to be long-term guarantees for the import of commodities, like ore and coal, which helped South Africa get some of its massive infrastructure projects off the ground.[49]

Indeed, a Japanese consortium was actually involved in the construction of a huge steel plant for ISCOR in the latter part of the 1960s. It should also be noted that the Export–Import Bank (of Japan) financed a number of these projects, despite the Japanese government's announcement in May 1974 of a ban on the provision of finance by the Exim Bank for projects in South Africa. It must also be noted that the Japanese government had officially banned Japanese companies from investing in South Africa in 1968. With reference to that policy, the *Financial Mail* wrote that 'it appears . . . that the announcement was merely a political smokescreen',[50] although that policy did indeed make it difficult for Japanese firms to invest in South Africa.

JAPANESE DEPENDENCE ON SOUTH AFRICA'S 'STRATEGIC MINERALS'

To attempt to ascertain exactly which of the so-called 'strategic minerals' South Africa has may be appropriate at this juncture. In so doing it may be helpful, first, to define exactly what the term 'strategic minerals' means. Maull points out that the term:

> has been used repeatedly in economic security analysis with a sometimes obscure meaning. Criticality and vulnerability to supply disruptions have been implicit or explicit criteria for defining what

makes a mineral 'strategic'; importance for defence industries taken into consideration as yardsticks . . . Strictly speaking, strategic relates to requirements needed to win a war . . . For economic security analysis therefore, the term . . . tends to cloud, and overdramatize, rather than to clarify.

Within the context of this discussion the term is used in relation to economic security, and therefore to imply a minerals scarcity and a nation's vulnerability to supply disruptions of those minerals. The proposition put forward here, then, is that Japan was potentially vulnerable to supply disruptions of many of the minerals found in South Africa, not least because Japan is not itself endowed with such resources. From the point of view of Japan's post-World War II policy makers, therefore, accessibility to 'rare metals' would clarify the issue of the economic security of Japan rather than fudge it. This is primarily because Japan's leaders, as noted in Chapter 1, had placed emphasis on the economy as an instrument of national security.

By 1980, South Africa was seemingly basking in its perception of its own importance to the Western industrial countries and Japan, because these countries were 'becoming increasingly, irrevocably dependent on South Africa for most of its vital minerals'.[51] The growth of industry and, inevitably, the oil crisis, which accentuated the pressure of raw material scarcity and therefore the scramble among the industrialized states over scarce natural resources, in part made this possible. For example, the Director of the Institute for Energy Studies (Rand Afrikaans University), W.C.J. van Rensburg, proclaimed in 1977 that

South Africa is the world's biggest producer of precious metals and minerals, including gold, platinum metals and gem diamonds. It has vast resources of other important industrial minerals such as fluorspar, asbestos, limestone, phosphates and vermiculite. It has the world's largest reserves of important ferrous metals such as manganese, chrome and vanadium, and vast reserves of high-grade iron ore and almost unlimited resources of medium- and low-grade iron ore, and has smaller but significant resources of other ferrous metals such as niobium, tantalum, tungsten and molybdenum.[52]

This fact was not lost on the Western industrial states who 'are all very largely, if not vitally, dependent on South Africa for . . . a large proportion of the[se] minerals necessary to sustain'[53] their industries. Table 3.10 illustrates this point well. It was on the basis of this that Hanns Maull pointed out in 1986 that:

in view of this the growing tensions in South Africa . . . and the accumulating pressure of the industrialized democracies for the application of sanctions against apartheid could therefore pose a new risk to the economic security of the Western countries.[54]

This point was of great concern to Japan's policy makers, since their country's economic and national security, as shown in Table 3.11, depended largely on the accessibility of resources like those in South Africa.[55] Not surprisingly, several observers had noted, with good reason, that the importance of these resources to modern industrial production explains why it was unlikely that Western nations would ever agree to comprehensive Rhodesian-style sanctions against South Africa. As shown in Chapter 5, for example, Japan consistently voted against such measures, conceivably because voting in favor of comprehensive sanctions against South Africa would have amounted to destabilizing its own economic security.

This would have been especially so during the period of near Cold War build-up, with Western governments urgently trying to secure their future supplies of raw materials.[56] The implied strategic importance of South Africa within the context of the Cold War was accentuated by the contrived conception that the USSR would invade and take control of South Africa,[57] a scenario considered as implausible by Hanns Maull[58]. Nevertheless, South Africa's prominent clients and lobbyists kept up what some critics identified as the propaganda that exaggerated South Africa's importance in the resource market.[59] They highlighted supposed threats by Pretoria to close its resources to the industrialized countries if the latter imposed sanctions against it. The following are some of the strategic minerals for which Japan depends on South Africa and an attempt to explain their importance to Japan's industrial production and economic security. These should offer some insight into why Japan could not afford to vote in favor of comprehensive sanctions against South Africa.

Chromium

Chromium is crucial to the production of steel, and therefore very important to the steel industry. According to Maull, 'its importance in armour plates, gun barrels, projectiles, heat-resistant machine parts, crankshafts, axles and gears has given chromium a special strategic importance'. [60] While it has various other uses, including in the chemical industry, chromium's primary importance lies in its role as an alloy in the production of special steels. It is particularly useful for enhancing the resistance of steel to corrosion and oxidation and increases such properties as hardenability, creep and impact strengths, as well as longevity. The steel industry alone takes about 70 percent of total demand of chromium as alloy in the 'Western world', while the chemical industry[61] takes 12 percent.

There are different chromite (chromium ore) qualities. Ferro-chrome is produced from chromite by various reduction processes. South Africa has a very large ferro-chrome industry and provided Japan with 87 percent of its ferro-chrome imports in 1974. The figure for 1985–1986 was much smaller, at 63 percent, as shown in Table 3.11. The USA, UK and the EC countries (10 states) imported 60 percent, 40 percent, and 51 percent, respectively, of their ferro-chrome requirements from South Africa in the same period.

As in the case of ferro-chrome, sources of chromite supplies to the industrialized world are fairly concentrated, as noted by Japan's policy makers[62], with South Africa and Zimbabwe enjoying a competitive advantage in high-quality chromite. Japan imported 56 percent of its chromite needs from South Africa in 1985–1986. To underline Southern Africa's importance in the production of chromium it may be worth mentioning that, for the 1985–1986 period, the world reserve base for chromium totalled 6,800 million tons, of which 95 percent was held in South Africa and Zimbabwe. As illustrated in Table 3.12, South Africa's share of this figure was 78 percent. For the same period South Africa produced 36 percent of the world's chromium ore.

Manganese

Manganese is the most important alloying metal needed to produce any type of steel. The indications, however, are that manganese ore and ferro-manganese are found in concentrated sources which may continue for a long time. Ferro-manganese's principal functions are to 'counteract the detrimental effects of sulphur contamination, to de-oxidize the steel and to increase its strength and hardenability'. [63] The most important sources of supply are South Africa, Gabon, Brazil, Australia, India, Mexico and a few insignificant others.

Table 3.12 indicates that South Africa alone had 40 percent of the world's manganese ore reserves for the 1985–1986 period, compared to 35.5 percent for the USSR. Australia held only 7 percent of the ore in that period. As for world production of the ore, South Africa was responsible for 17 percent. The USSR and Australia produced 32.5 percent and 10.15 percent, respectively. For the same period Japan imported 55 percent worth of its ore needs from South Africa, as illustrated in Table 3.11. Maull contends that 'South African manganese ore enjoys a particular advantage

Table 3.12 South African shares of world reserves and production (percentages)

Mineral	Reserves	Primary production 1985–6 Averages
Antimony	6	13
Asbestos	6	3 (but 100% of amosite and crocidolite)
Beryllium	4	–
Cadmium	6	(a)
Chromium	78	36
Cobalt	1	–
Copper	1	2
Fluorspar	18	7
Gold	59	41
Industrial diamonds	7	13
Iron Ore	4	3
Lead	4	3
Manganese	40	17
Magnesite	n/a	–
Nickel	5	4
Phosphate	19	2
Platinum group	80	46
Silicon	n/a	3 (metal and ferro)
Silver	–	2
Sulphur	n/a	1
Tin	1	1
Titanium:		
Ilmenite	19	–
Rutile	5	11
Uranium	15(b)	13 (b)
Vanadium	20	47
Vermiculite	n/a	37
Zinc	7	1
Zirconium	15	20

Notes: No details available on mine output by country (Western world only)
Source: Phillip Crowson, *Minerals Handbook, 1988–89*, p. 15

because of its low phosphorous content', and identified South Africa to be in a 'particularly strong position as a producer'. He is, however, cautious about South Africa's prominence in this area: 'The principal risk appears to be the strong market position of South Africa; supplies from this country could be affected by internal instability, or by attempts to exploit consumer dependence for political ends',[64] as the Arab oil exporting countries did in the early 1970s. This is a concern eloquently expressed by the PPRC (Peace Problems Research Council – Heiwa mondai kenkyūkai) in their report on national security. A similar concern was expressed about the other resources in whose production South Africa enjoyed a comparative advantage.[65]

Vanadium

Over 70 percent of the world's reserve base (some 16.6 mn. tons) of vanadium was in South Africa and the USSR alone.[66] The bulk of the mineral is used in the steel industry, for the production of special steel. The production of steel pipes for the energy industries alone was said to account for some 25 percent of world demand of vanadium. The mineral is also used as super-alloys in the production of jet engines and airframes. Needless to say, Japan imports all its vanadium requirements. For the period 1985–1986, South Africa alone provided Japan with 84 percent of its imports;[67] and observers note that there are a number of substitutes for this mineral, although at higher cost or with lower performance.

Platinum group of metals (platinum, palladium, iridium, osmium, rhodium, ruthenium)

These non-fuel minerals are said to be among the rarest and most precious metals used by man. In industry they are mostly used for their resistance to corrosion, their chemical inertness over a wide range of temperatures, their high melting point and their outstanding catalytic capabilities. They are also extensively used in electric and electronic equipment. The automobile industry, for example, is highly dependent on certain particular properties of the metals, since they are vital ingredients for exhaust systems designed to meet stringent clean air requirements. The other industries that use them are the chemical, electrical and electronic industries, and ultimately the energy industries. Their main uses in the latter area are in fuel cells, for the direct conversion of solar energy to electricity.[68] Maull notes that the metals are also needed for the production of glass fibre and special glass production. But the strategic use[69] of platinum is in fertilizers and oil production.

Maull says, however, that in Japan (presumably in the 1970s), some 70 percent of total consumption of platinum was for jewellery.[70] Japan was therefore unique in its use of a large bulk of its platinum imports for jewellery. Yet, the Japanese automobile companies also used the metal for converters to satisfy the emission controls in their major exporting markets. The Japanese automobile industry consumed 14 percent of the country's platinum metals imports, compared to 25 percent each for the jewellery and electrical industries, as indicated in Table 3.13. Obviously, the end uses of platinum in Japan have become more diversified.

In order to highlight the extent of the Japanese economy's dependence on the platinum metals, it may be worth noting that in the 1970s Japan's consumption of platinum and palladium grew at an average rate of 10.1

Table 3.13 End use patterns of platinum group of metals by the USA and Japan, 1986 (%)

End use	USA	Japan
Automotive	38	14
Chemical	7	16
Dental	19	12
Electrical	22	25
Jewellery	1	25
Petroleum refining	4	5
Others	9	–

Source: Compiled from Phillip Crowson, *Minerals Handbook, 1987–88*, p. 210

percent per annum. This was subsequently reduced to 5.8 percent between 1980 and 1986. For the period 1983–1984, for example, Japan alone consumed 71,695 kg. of the Western world's total of 176,985 kg. of platinum and palladium. This compares with 63,765 kg. for the USA.[71] It is useful here to try and identify where the world's platinum originates.

All three industrialized regions (Western Europe, North America and Japan) are completely dependent on platinum imports. Of great importance to this discussion is the fact that more than 80 percent of the world's 3 million troy oz. of reserves of platinum-based metals were in South Africa alone, and produced by Rustenburg Platinum Mines[72], Impala Platinum Mines, and Western Platinum. South Africa produced, for the 1985–1986 period, 46 percent of world production of the metals, as shown in Table 3.12. The other major producer of this rare metal was the Soviet Union. Nevertheless, as Maull points out, only in South Africa was platinum mining undertaken for the platinum group metals themselves. In the USSR, as in other minor producing areas like Canada and Columbia, the metals came as a by-product of nickel copper ores. Thus, South Africa's prominence in this area gave it a measure of control over the producer price at least of platinum, by which it could influence world spot price by curtailing production and purchasing excess metal. Suffice to say that for the 1979–1980 and 1985–1986 periods, Tokyo obtained 33 percent and 36 percent, respectively, of its platinum metals from Pretoria, compared to 44 percent and 36 percent, respectively, from the USSR.

A degree of caution is necessary when considering the figures for South Africa, since most ores and concentrates imported into the UK for refining[73] and then re-exported to other places, possibly including Japan, were from South Africa.[74] In 1987, Japanese imports of Pretoria's platinum increased dramatically to 52 percent over the previous year's, in quantity. In terms of value, they increased by 78.8 percent. In 1988,

Table 3.14 Platinum imports from six major sources, 1988: differences in percentage from 1987 (tons)

Source	1987	1988
South Africa (producer)	16.63	−38.7
UK (non-producer)	16.14	116.5
West Germany (non-producer)	8.69	718.5
France (non-producer)	1.92	2700.0
USA (non-producer)	6.95	90.1
USSR (producer)	13.70	18.7
TOTAL	67.55	24.4

Source: JETRO, *White Paper on International Trade*, 1989

however, as critics raised their voices at this lucrative trade relationship between Japan and South Africa, and as MITI asked the relevant Japanese industries to act prudently in trading with South Africa, Japanese imports of platinum from the latter declined drastically. They fell by 38.7 percent (in weight). In value they reduced from $479 mn. in 1987 to $279 mn. in 1988, as shown in Table 3.14. Imports from other non-producer countries, on the other hand, increased astronomically. For example, Britain's exports of the metal (as indicated in Table 3.14) increased by 116.5 percent, while West Germany's increased by a huge 718.5 percent (both in weight). It is very important to emphasize here the fact that neither of these countries produce platinum. In short, they were 'third countries' who served as conduits for certain South African products. Suffice to say that 'platinum is a precious metal which figures prominently in many economic security risks analyses'[75] and the 'very heavy concentration of sources of supply and of reserves', which gave 'South Africa and the Soviet Union a near monopoly as suppliers', somewhat made it inevitable that Japanese companies would import platinum through third countries.

Uranium

The brief overview of Japan's contracts for uranium with South Africa, given earlier, demands further clarification in the form of an explanation of the importance of this resource to Japan's industrial production. This should help to advance our understanding of the extent of Pretoria's significance to Japan. Japan is 100 percent import-dependent on uranium. The need to develop alternative sources of energy supply, obviously as a result of the 1973 oil crisis, further enhanced the strategic importance of the mineral. For decades, Japan's electricity authorities promoted the use of nuclear energy as the only viable alternative to oil. The only uses for natural uranium are for military purposes, as in the production of nuclear weapons, and for civil nuclear power – the production of electricity. It must be noted, however, that the production processes for the two uses are closely related. Even though production and export statistics of this product were clouded in secrecy, to the extent that there was legislation in South Africa, for example, prohibiting the disclosure of its production, the figures given earlier should provide us with an idea of the extent of Japan's dependence on South Africa for uranium. Maull has also noted that during the 1980s Japan was expected to acquire 43 percent of its uranium from South Africa,[76] a great deal of which came from mines in Namibia, then under South African control.

The point that 'because of their sensitive nature, uranium exports are heavily controlled by host governments in all respects',[77] needs reiterating here. In addition, supplying countries imposed various restrictions on trade in, and the uses of, their exports. The Carter administration, for example, initiated a nuclear energy policy providing for, among other things, new international restrictions on enriched uranium and plutonium separation, thus aggravating an already strained relationship between the USA and its industrialized allies on the question of nuclear power as a source of energy. Some Japanese observers, for example, feared that the USA could place further restrictions on exports of uranium to their country.[78] In view of this, Maull suggests that, considering South Africa's 'generous interpretation'[79] of the non-proliferation guarantees, it became attractive as a source of import for Western Europe and Japan. In any case, policy analysts in Japan realized that it was strategically important for Japan to establish good relations with uranium-producing countries if it was to make good its comprehensive energy policy.[80] And given the fact that of the main producers – Canada, the USA, Australia and South Africa,[81] the first three had some kind of non-proliferation disputes with Japan, it was easier for Tokyo to target South Africa as the country to do business with, especially since Pretoria was generous with its non-proliferation rules. In fact, Japan and South Africa were jointly producing atomic energy as early as the early 1960s.[82]

Other minerals

While not claiming that the following are 'strategic minerals', it is still important in the analysis of the two country's economic relations that a mention is made of how much fluorspar, industrial diamonds, zirconium and gold Japan imported from South Africa, and how essential these minerals were to Japanese industries. The indications are that 37 percent of Japan's fluorspar consumption, for the 1985–1986 period, went into steel production, while 36 percent of it went into glass, enamel and other uses. Of the remainder, 11 percent went primarily into aluminium production and 16 percent into the chemical industry. Most importantly, South Africa provided Japan with 14 percent of its fluorspar imports, as illustrated in Table 3.11 (p. 85). Japan's dependence on South Africa for industrial diamonds was even greater. Pretoria supplied 42 percent of Japan's industrial diamond requirements for the period 1985–1986, even though the production of this mineral was not concentrated on a few producers. Throughout the 1980s, Japan's consumption of industrial diamonds grew by over 12 percent per annum. The figure was higher in the 1970s. The mineral had its most important uses for machinery and transport equipment, and was therefore crucial for sustainable growth of its automobile industry, for example. Also, for the period 1985–1986, 85 percent of Japan's zirconium requirement came from Australia. Of the remainder, South Africa provided 12 percent. Fifty percent of Japan's uses of the mineral in 1986 went into the production of refractories, while 23 percent of it was used for foundry sands. The mineral is also used in the chemical industry and for nuclear applications.[83]

Gold was another South African product that appealed very much to the Japanese, especially from the mid–1980s onwards. South Africa is the world's leading producer of gold. Its share of reserves and production of the mineral for the 1985–1986 period was 59 percent and 41 percent respectively, as shown in Table 3.12 (p. 90). Japanese imports of South African gold jumped from nothing in 1980 to 12.5 percent in 1985, at the value of $231,307. In 1986, Japan's share of South African gold exports was 16.4 percent, at a value of $366,387 as indicated in Table 3.15. The end uses of gold in Japan were as follows: jewellery took 30 percent, while 39 percent went into the production of coins and small items as investment mediums in the 1980s. An abnormally high percentage of it went into the production of coins to commemorate the sixtieth anniversary of the accession of Emperor Hirohito to the imperial throne. Yet, more than 20 percent[84] of Japan's gold imports managed to go into the electronics industry, while 5 percent went into dentistry. As in the case of platinum, however, Japan's imports of gold from South Africa declined sharply in

Table 3.15 Gold, platinum and ferro-alloy imports by Japan from South Africa, 1980–1989 (US$:1000)

Year	Gold	Platinum	Ferro-alloy
1980	–	293,308	128,814
1981	34,770	259,098	85,181
1982	61,723	209,400	90,786
1983	28,565	247,064	97,781
1984	52,320	199,932	160,451
1985	231,307	204,968	137,069
1986	366,387	267,947	155,809
1987	230,517	479,212	147,069
1988	64,676	278,707	219,813
1989	118,024	140,239	299,077

Source: JETRO, *White Paper on International Trade*, 1981–1990

1988 from the previous year; in an attempt to redirect its critics' attention Japan's import levels fell by 71.1 percent. Imports from Britain (a non-producer), on the other hand, went up by 80.9 percent. At the same time, gold imports from Switzerland (a non-producer) also went up (see Table 3.16).

On the whole, if gold imports were excluded, Japan took 14.9 percent of its mineral imports from South Africa in 1966, ranking it third after the UK (29.7 percent), and the rest of Europe (19.0 percent), excluding West Germany, which took 7.2 percent of South Africa's mineral exports. By 1971, Japan's imports had increased to 17.3 percent, raising it to the second position after the UK (26.5 percent). By 1975, the UK's imports of South Africa's minerals (excluding gold) had reduced to 16.6 percent, while Japan's stood at 19.6 percent, ahead of West Germany (18.2 percent) and very close to the 'rest of Europe'. Obviously, by 1975 Japan was the leading (single) importer of South African minerals, excluding gold, among the advanced liberal economies, as indicated in Figure 3.1. This shows that while the shifts in the international political economy in the early 1970s, culminating with the oil crises in 1973 and 1979, might have accentuated South Africa's strategic importance, there is every indication that Japan's dependence on Pretoria for some of these resources dates further back.

From the above account it could be deduced that, if the first oil crisis signalled the need for politically assured supplies of certain raw materials, then South Africa was bound to get all the attention that it wanted from a country such as Japan, which was dependent on imports for most of its required raw materials. It is not surprising, therefore, that Japan cultivated a relationship with even a pariah state in order to get the raw materials

Table 3.16 Gold imports from four major sources, 1988 (tons)

Source	1988	Difference (%) from 1987
South Africa (producer)	4.49	−71.1
UK (non-producer)	30.19	80.9
Switzerland (non-producer)	118.43	19.8
USSR (producer)	23.95	−17.9
TOTAL	293. 8	25.9

Source: JETRO, *White Paper on International Trade*, 1987–1989

needed for its industrial growth. In effect, Japan was simply taking advantage of the liberal economic climate of which it was an active and indeed a leading member.

CONCLUSION

The above discussion has attempted to explore Japan's trade relations with South Africa before and after the institution of apartheid, and has also attempted to show that the fulcrum of the two countries' economic relations was determined more by the industrial structures and the pattern of economic development of the two countries, than by any other factors. Surely it cannot be denied that government policies influenced the relationship: the two countries shared much in common in terms of their governments' interventionist role in their respective economies. And as has been pointed out, Japan's imports of raw materials from South Africa, especially after 1973, were essentially dictated by the government's desire to gain secure access to the world's strategic raw materials. This is part of what eventually became formulated as the CNS strategy.

Inevitably, trade relations between the two countries evolved and revolved around their relative comparative advantage in trade. Thus, South Africa exported mostly raw materials, and semi-manufactured products to Japan. For its part, Japan exported manufactured goods and heavy and chemical industry products to South Africa. The pattern of trade in specific items, following the relative dynamism of the two economies, was constantly changing in accordance with the economic demands of the two states. In concentrating on the strategic resources outlined above, an attempt has been made to show that Japan was dependent on South Africa

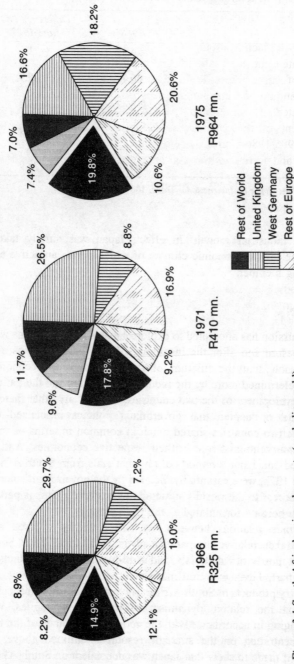

Figure 3.1 South Africa's mineral exports (excluding gold), 1996, 1971 and 1975

Source: Van Rensburg and Pretorius, *South Africa's Strategic Minerals: Pieces on a Continental Chess Board.* 1977, p.109

All efforts have been made to trace the copyright owner. The publisher and author would welcome any additional information.

for certain specific resources crucial for sustainable industrial growth. I have also sought to demonstrate how uranium is very important for the development of nuclear energy, which may be seen as a viable alternative to other energy-producing resources like oil.

As was pointed out, the platinum group of metals was central to the development of certain specific industries. Other resources, too, like vanadium, chromium and manganese, were of crucial importance to the production of steel. These resources were therefore critical ingredients to the development of the Japanese automobile industry, for example. According to 1985/1986 figures, Japan obtained 56 percent and 63 percent of its chrome and ferro-chrome requirements, respectively, from South Africa. Eighty-four percent and 55 percent of Japanese imports of vanadium and manganese ore, respectively, emanated from this same source. Japan, finally, took a fair share of its uranium requirements from Pretoria, against the ruling of the UNCN (United Nations Council for Namibia). One of the arguments put forward in the discussion was that, given South Africa's dominance in the production of some of these resources, Japanese dependence on the Republic for such 'rare metals' was inevitable. Needless to say, certain aspects of trade with South Africa, especially imports of the above strategic metals from the country, was very important to the Japanese economy. Indeed, it is in light of this that we can establish a meeting point between Japan's dependence on South Africa for certain resources, and its economic security: Tokyo's inability to vote in support of the UNGA resolutions that called for comprehensive sanctions against Pretoria, despite Japan's proclaimed opposition to apartheid.

Another argument put forward in the above discussion was that the apartheid policies of the Nationalist Party and the international pressures against South Africa's economic partners made it impossible for Japan to take full advantage of its economic interests in South Africa, despite Tokyo's anxieties over questions of raw materials scarcity. It was in this sense, as was suggested earlier, that Japan's policy makers abhorred apartheid. In short, the inability of Japanese companies to invest freely in South Africa because of their government's ban on investments to the country was a barrier to the real extent to which Japanese companies had wanted to expand their operations in South Africa.

Nevertheless, these restrictions did not stop Japan from acquiring the resources enumerated above from South Africa. Where necessary, Japanese companies indulged in some form of quasi-investment activities, as in the case of the Saldanha Bay and Richard's Bay projects, for the purposes of procuring iron ore and coal from South Africa. Furthermore, where Japan was forced by international pressures to roll back its imports from Pretoria, it found its way back in the South African export market, even if through a third party, as in the case of platinum and gold imports in the latter part of the 1980s. Suffice to say that all these factors go to show just how central some of South Africa's raw materials were to the Japanese economy. They also suggest the enormously complex political ramifications of what was, in reality, a rather simple economic relationship between the two countries.

NOTES

1 The investment ban imposed by the Japanese government on Japanese investment in South Africa supposedly kept Japan effectively out of government and public corporation procurements. In relation to this the *Financial Mail* (Japan Survey), November 1980, p. 54, wrote that: 'Japanese businessmen estimated in 1980 that they may lose around $1 billion (combined) a year in government and semi-government business.' They also estimated that South Africa, on the other hand, might be missing out on anything from $5 billion to $10 billion that Japan would have invested in its mining, agriculture and manufacturing industries.

2 *Financial Mail* (Japan Survey), 12 November 1976, pp. 71–72. The 4 February 1977 issue of the *Financial Mail*, p. 297, carried a statement qualifying what the General Manager of Mistui & Co. said in a previous publication: 'Mr. Kumagai tells the Financial Mail (FM) that what he wished to convey – and thought he had conveyed – was that Mitsui would only like to invest in South Africa under more favorable political circumstances.'

3 'Japan's Men in Johannesburg', *Financial Mail* (Japan Survey), 21 November 1980, p. 57.

4 Stuart Jones, and André Müller, *The South African Economy, 1910–1990*, Basingstoke, Macmillan, 1992, p. 221.

5 The South African Party ruled South Africa from 1910 to 1924, first under Louis Botha, and from 1919 under J.C. Smuts. The party was defeated in the 1924 election by a pact between J. B. M. Hertzog's National Party and the Labor Party. Hertzog's National Party won an absolute majority in the 1929 election but he retained Labor in government. The pact ended in 1933.

6 Union of South Africa, *Arrangement with the Japanese Government, Prime Minister's Office 8 October 1930*, PM. 38/15; Morikawa Jun 'The Myth and Reality of Japan's Relations with Colonial Africa, 1885–1960', *Journal of African Studies*, vol. 11, no. 1, Spring, 1985, p. 43.

7 Morikawa, 'The Myth and Reality of Japan's Relations with Colonial Africa', p. 43.

8 Kitagawa Katsuhiko, 'Senzenki nihon no ryōji hōkoku ni mirareru afurika keizai jijō chōsa no kenkyū – gaimushō tsūshōkyoku [tsūshō-kōhō] o chūshin toshite' *Afurika kenkyū*, vol. 35, 1989.

9 Jones and Müller, *The South African Economy, 1910–1990*, p. 116.

10 *Weekly Cape Times and Farmers' Record*, 25 August 1916, p. 14.

11 Henry Birchenough 'Some Effects of the War Upon British and German Trade in South Africa', *Journal of South African Society*, vol. xi, no. lv, 1915, p. 233; 'Germany's Trade with South Africa: The Problem of its Exclusion', *Weekly Cape Times and Farmers' Record*, 4 February 1916, p. 7.

12 Henry Birchenough, 'Some Effects of the War Upon British and German Trade in South Africa', p. 232.

13 Kitagawa, 'Senzenki nihon no ryōji hōkoku ni mirareru afurika keizai jijō chōsa no kenkyū', pp. 57–58.

14 'South Africa's Demand For Toys: Japan a Keen Rival; Prospects of Local Effort', *Weekly Cape Times and Farmers' Record*, 14 January 1916, p. 17.

15 Kitagawa, 'Senzenki nihon no ryōji hōkoku ni mirareru afurika keizai jijō chōsa no kenkyū', pp. 59–60.

16 Ibid., p. 57.

17 'Japan and South Africa: The Wool Trade', *Weekly Cape Times and Farmers' Record*, 12 May 1916, p. 13

18 Jones and Müller, *The South African Economy, 1910–1990*, p. 116.

19 Ibid., p. 120; Kitagawa, 'Senzenki nihon no ryōji hōkoku ni mirareru afurika keizai jijō chōsa no kenkyū', p. 60.

20 Ibid.

21 'South Africa's Demand for Toys', *Weekly Cape Times and Farmers' Record*, 14 January 1916, p. 17.

22 Greta Bloomhill, 'The Japanese Trade Menace: The Story of How Japan Invaded the African Market', *African Observer*, 1936, vol. 4, no. 4, p. 42.

23 Jones and Müller, *The South African Economy, 1910–1990*, p. 218.

24 Ibid., p. 348.

25 Ibid., p. 344.

26 Hanns Maull, *Raw Materials, Energy and Western Security*, London, Macmillan 1984, p. 13.

27 Japan External Trade Organization, *Foreign Trade of Japan*, Tokyo, JETRO, 1974.

28 Japan External Trade Organization, *White Paper on International Trade*, Tokyo, 1980, pp. 269–70.

29 'Japan Survey' (supplement to) *Financial Mail*, 21 November 1980, p. 53

30 *Financial Mail* (Japan Survey), 12 November 1976, p. 10.

31 Japan External Trade Organization, *White Paper on International Trade*, Tokyo, 1978, p. 225.

32 Ibid.

33 Japan External Trade Organization, *White Paper on International Trade*, Tokyo, 1988, p. 389.

34 Japan External Trade Organization, *White Paper on External Trade*, Tokyo, 1987.

35 *Financial Mail*, 14 September 1990, p. 106.

36 *Mainichi Daily News*, 18 June 1989.

37 'The Year of the Tiger', *Financial Mail*, 4 January 1974, p. 23.

38 This was followed by non-ferrous metal scrap ($50.8 mn.), non-ferrous metals ($5.7 mn.), wool ($50.4 mn.), iron ore ($39.8 mn.), non-metallic mineral ores ($35.7 mn.), and iron and steel products ($32.6 mn.).

39 Japan External Trade Organization, *White Paper on International Trade*, Tokyo, 1976.

40 Ibid.

41 Japan External Trade Organization, *White Paper on International Trade*, Tokyo, 1981, p. 389.

42 Japan External Trade Organization, *White Paper on International Trade*, Tokyo, 1988, p. 389.

43 Yoshida Masao, 'Nihon no keizai enjo ni okeru afurika', in Suzuki Nagatoshi, (ed.), *Nihon no keizai kyōryoku no ashidori*, Tokyo, Ajia keizai shuppankai, 1989.

44 ISCOR was established in 1928, as South Africa's first parastatal organization.

45 *Financial Mail* (Japan Survey), 12 November 1976, p. 12.

46 Kitazawa Yōko, 'Aparutoheito e no nihon no katan – nihon minami afurika keizai kankei chōsa hōkoku', *Ajia taiheiyō shiryō sentā*, 1975, pp. 25–28; 'Iron Ore Bonanza', *Financial Mail*, 11 January 1974, p. 79; 'Iscor, Beware' *Financial Mail*, 18 February 1972, p. 417.

47 *Financial Mail*, 26 September 1986, pp. 30–33.

48 Kitazawa Yōko, 'Aparutoheito e no nihon no katan', pp. 81–82.

49 *Financial Mail* (Japan Survey), 12 November 1976, p. 10. See also Raymond Vernon and Brian Levy, 'State-owned Enterprises in the World Economy: The Case of Iron Ore', in Leroy P. Jones, et al., (eds.), *Public Enterprise in Less-developed Countries*, Cambridge, Cambridge University Press, 1982, p. 172.

50 *Financial Mail*, 30 May 1974, p. 848; *Financial Mail*, 12 November 1976, p. 12; Kitazawa Yōko, 'Aparutoheito e no nihon no katan'.

51 'Mining Survey', (supplement to) *Financial Mail*, 30 October 1981.

52 W. C. J. van Rensburg and D.A. Pretorius, *South Africa's Strategic Minerals: Pieces on a Continental Chess Board* (ed. Helen Glen), Johannesburg, Valiant, 1977, p. 48.

53 'Growing Reliance on South Africa', (supplement to) *Financial Mail*, 30 October 1981, p. 7.

54 Hanns Maull, 'South Africa's Minerals: The Achilles Heel of Western Economic Security?', *International Affairs*, no. 4, Autumn, 1986, p. 619.

55 Naikaku kanbō naikaku shingishitsu, *Kokusai kokka nihon no sōgō anzen hoshō seisaku*, (Heiwa mondai kenkyūkai hōkokusho), Tokyo, Ōkurasho insatsukyoku, 1985, pp. 59–60.

56 'Growing Reliance on South Africa', *Financial Mail*, 30 October 1981, p. 7.

57 Van Rensburg and Pretorius, *South Africa's Strategic Minerals*, pp. 126–132.

58 Maull, *Raw Materials, Energy and Western Security*, pp. 290–308.

59 Barbara Rogers and Brian Bolton, *Sanctions Against South Africa: Exploding The Myths*, Manchester, Manchester Free Press, 1981; Maull, *Raw Materials, Energy and Western Security*; Richard Payne, *The Non-Superpowers' South Africa Policies: Interests and Strategies*, Princeton, Princeton University Press, 1991, Chapter 1.

60 Maull, *Raw Materials, Energy and Western Security*, p. 203.

61 Ibid.

62 Naikaku kanbō naikaku shingishitsu, *Kokusai kokka nihon no sōgo anzen hoshō seisaku*, p. 59.

63 Ibid., pp. 196–197.

64 Ibid., p. 200.

65 Ibid., p. 60.

66 Phillip Crowson, *Minerals Handbook, 1987–88: Statistics and Analysis of the World's Mineral Industry*, Basingstoke, Macmillan, 1987, p. 310.

67 Ibid., pp. 314–315.

68 'South Africa's Platinum Hold', *Financial Mail* (Mining Survey), 30 October 1981, pp. 36–38.

69 Ibid., p. 37.

70 Maull, *Raw Materials, Energy and Western Security*, p. 249. See also Sir Albert

Robinson, 'Rustenburg Platinum Holdings Limited: Chairman's Review', *Financial Mail*, 4 February 1977, pp. 274–275.

71 Crowson, *Minerals Handbook, 1987–88*, p. 210.

72 This includes Atok Platinum Mines, Potgietersrust Platinum, Union Platinum and Waterval Rustenburg Platinum.

73 Crowson, *Minerals Handbook, 1987–88*, p. 214, says that most ores and concentrates imported into the UK for refining were from South Africa, whose importance was thus much greater in world trade than Table 3.14 suggests.

74 *Mainichi Daily News*, 18 June 1989.

75 Maull, *Raw Materials, Energy and Western Security* , p. 189.

76 Ibid., p. 59. Maull, however, argues that the South African share in the Japanese import figures might have been exaggerated, since Japanese companies had contracted for huge imports of uranium from Australia.

77 Crowson, *Minerals Handbook, 1987–88*, p. 307.

78 Robert Pfaltzgraff Jr., *Energy Issues and Alliance Relationship: The United States, Western Europe and Japan*, Cambridge, Institute for Foreign Policy Analysis, Inc., 1990, pp. 61–62.

79 Maull, *Raw Materials, Energy and Western Security*, p. 59.

80 Naikaku kanbō naikaku shingishitsu, *Sōgo anzen hoshō senryaku* (Ohira sōri no seisaku kenkyukai hōkokusho–5), Tokyo, Ōkurasho insatsukyoku (3rd edition), 1985, p. 65.

81 According to 1985–1986 figures, Canada produced 31.3 percent of the West's uranium, while the USA and South Africa produced 13 percent each. In addition, Namibia and Niger produced 9.5 percent and 8.7 percent, respectively. See Crowson, *Minerals Handbook, 1987–88*, p. 305.

82 'Agreement Between the Government of the Republic of South Africa and the Government of Japan to Place Source Material Transferred from South Africa to Japan Under the Safeguards of the International Atomic Energy Agency', *Republic of South Africa Treaty Series*, no. 4/1962, Vienna, 20 June, 1962.

83 Crowson, *Minerals Handbook, 1988–89*, pp. 332, 335.

84 Ibid. p. 119.

4 Japanese investment in Nigeria
Ignoring the resource potential

As shown in the previous chapter, the value of South Africa to Japan was based on the fact that it possessed natural resources that were essential for its economic security; and the straightforward calculation of state interests as determined by the old-fashioned analysis of cost and benefit. But the importance of South Africa to Japan was further underlined by the fact that there was no alternative country in sub-Saharan Africa to provide Japan with the 'services' that it became dependent on Pretoria for. Nigeria had the potential to do so, if only because it is one of the world's major oil producing countries. Interestingly, however, that potential was hardly tested by Japan and its team of 'corporate interests', although some Japanese firms did set up commercial operations in Nigeria. The questions to start this chapter off with are: What were the inducements to Japanese investors in Nigeria; and what deterred potential investors from investing in Nigeria? Before searching for answers to these questions one very important point needs to be made clear, and it is that Japanese investments in Nigeria were hardly raw materials-oriented. Implicit in this fact is an obvious truth; Japan's dependence on external sources for almost all her raw material requirements hardly contributed to Japanese investment interests in Nigeria. On the basis of these rather resounding facts, which shall be adequately confirmed in the course of the discussion, and given the abundance of raw materials in Nigeria, including crude oil, a rather lucrative, if not a 'strategic' resource, this analysis shall go to strengthen the contention that Japan had no significant resource interests (in sub-Saharan Africa) outside South Africa, during the period under review.

Thus, as argued in Chapter 1, Japanese investments in Nigeria did not reflect the pattern of foreign direct investment in sub-Saharan Africa and the international division of labor that the latter was based on. Nor did they conform to the pattern of Japanese direct investment that Kojima Kiyoshi suggests obtains in the developing countries. This is not to say, however, that none of the Japanese investors in Nigeria took resource availability into consideration when deciding to set up there. As will be shown, some of the textile firms, and indeed the equity holders in the Japan Petroleum Company (Nigeria) Ltd., saw Nigeria's cotton and crude oil, respectively, as an incentive. And a few of the firms mentioned 'abundant labor' as an incentive for investing in Nigeria. However, the most attractive incentive for most of the firms was the availability of good market prospects. In other words, while most theoretical explanations of foreign direct investment (FDI) emphasize explanations which are independent of the macro-economic policy and performance of the recipient country, this study shows it was instead the macro-economic management of Nigeria that contributed immensely to the lack of Japanese interest in investing in Nigeria. Of great importance to this analysis, therefore, is the argument that Japanese investment was based largely on expected gains from access to Nigeria's large market. This further explicates the argument that, despite Japan's anxieties about access to secure strategic materials, or probably because of it, the country has not shown any real interest in Nigeria's oil. Nor has it shown any interest in other raw materials under Nigeria's possession which may be relevant to Japan's economic security.

A PROFILE OF JAPANESE (GLOBAL) FDI

Japan's global FDI increased from $33.4 bn. in 1987 to $47.0 bn. in 1988, and registered 1,492 and 6,076 cases of investments, respectively; with the increase in 1988 recording the highest growth since 1984. In 1988, for example, on the basis of balance of payments, Japan's FDI exceeded that of the US stock and emerged as the biggest in the world. In terms of the regional breakdown of its FDI, North America accounted for 48 percent of the total, which translated into $22.3 bn.; Europe took $9.1 bn. worth of it, of which the UK and Germany received $3.9bn. and $409 mn., respectively. Japan's FDI in Asia did not increase much for the fiscal year 1988, even though the cases of new equity acquisitions in the manufacturing sector in four ASEAN countries (Thailand, Malaysia, the Philippines and Indonesia) were a great improvement, at $1.36 bn., over the previous year's investment of $704 mn. The overall amount towards investment in the four countries in 1988 was $1.96 bn. The share of Japanese investments in the NICS' manufacturing sector was $776 mn. compared to its overall investment of $3.2 bn. in these countries. The Latin American[1] states received $6.4 bn. of investments from Japan in 1988, up from $4.8 bn. the previous year. Oceania attracted $2.65 bn.[2] worth of Japanese investment that year compared to $1.4 bn. in 1987 and $992 mn. in 1986.

In fiscal 1988, Africa, too, experienced what, on the surface, was a large increase in Japanese investments at $653 mn. compared to $272 mn. the previous year. The expansion of Japanese investment in the 1980s should be seen within the context of the high appreciation of the yen in the latter part of the decade. In reality, however, the huge inflation of the exchange value of the yen had almost no effect on the country's investment in sub-. Saharan Africa. By industry, transportation accounted for over 80 percent of the total. In effect, $547 mn. of those investments were in shipping in Liberia, primarily to take advantage of the country's flag of convenience. Thus, as in previous years, there was very little investment in the manufacturing and other sectors. By country, therefore, Liberia alone received 95.8 percent of the total value of Japanese investments in the region.[3] Effectively, Africa was noted among Japan's foreign direct investors as the slowest in attracting investments, except for the Middle East. The cumulative total of Japanese investments in Africa from 1951–1990 was $5.8 bn., compared to $3.4 bn. for the Middle East.[4]

JAPANESE FDI IN SUB-SAHARAN AFRICA

The structure of Japanese investment in Africa seems to have changed with time, which presumably also reflected the pattern of changes in the structure of the Japanese economy itself. Excluding 'investment' in shipping (in Liberia), Figure 4.1 indicates that from 1976–1980, other sectors (mostly raw material exploration) accounted for a large share of the number of cases of investment in the region. This must have been a result of the oil crisis of 1973–1974, to which Japanese policy makers reacted by diversifying their sources of raw material investments and imports, as part of their comprehensive (economic) security policy. As Figure 4.1 demonstrates, however, the structure was different in 1971–1975, with more cases of equity participation in the manufacturing sector. The period before that was even more biased towards manufacturing, while the latter part of the 1980s show a lack of interest in all areas, except in shipping-related ventures in Liberia. One other observable development of the Japanese industrial policy, from the latter part of the 1980s onwards, was the extent to which the importance of raw materials to the economy was de-emphasized.

Japan's global investments in resource (development) nevertheless expanded phenomenally from the 1960s onwards. As the figures in Table 4.1 show, however, Africa did not attract much investment from Japan in this sector, compared to Japanese investments in other regions, even though the Japanese government had explicitly indicated, in 1974, a strong interest in Africa's raw materials.[5] At the end of the 1988 fiscal year, North America had 622 cases of resource (raw materials) development investments from Japan, compared to 519 for Latin America and 879 for Asia. The Middle East and Europe had 23 and 39 cases respectively,

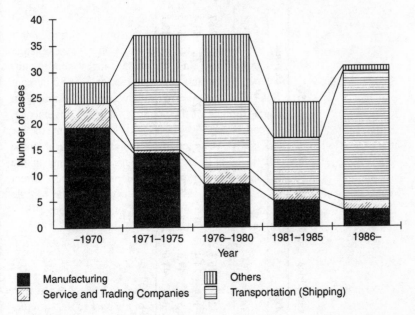

Figure 4.1 Japanese investments in Africa: number of cases and changes in types of investment

Source: Satō and Ishizaki, *Afurika repōto*, no. 12, March, 1991

while Africa and Oceania's share stood at 231 and 599, respectively. In terms of the value of these investments in percentage terms Europe had 7.1 percent of global Japanese investment in the resource development sector, compared to 4.3 percent for Africa. Oceania had 13.1 percent. It is also worth mentioning that while Africa accounted for over 14 percent of Japan's overall investment in the fisheries industry, its mining ventures in the region accounted for only 4.2 percent of Japan's global mining investments. Its investment operations in agriculture and forestry stood at a mere 0.7 percent of its global operations.

It should be emphasized that, in this study, the so-called Japanese 'ventures' in Liberia are not considered as investments because every single one of those 'ventures' (valued at US$4.8 bn., see Table 4.3, cumulative at the end of 1990, out of a total of US$5.8 bn. for Africa for the same period) were to do with Japanese ships that used the Liberian flag of convenience.[6] John Cantwell warns us that 'it is unclear to what extent this investment is simply a matter of legal convenience'; and suggests that, 'without further evidence on the involvement of Japanese firms in Liberia, it is wise to keep an open mind on just how important the role that they

Table 4.1 Japan's FDI in raw materials development in the major regions and Africa, fiscal 1988 (unit: cases, $ mn., %)

Industry	North America			Latin America			Asia			Africa			Oceania		
	No. of cases	Amt.	%	No. of cases	Amt.	%	No. of cases	Amt.	%	No. of cases	Amt.	%	No. of cases	Amt.	%
Agriculture and forestry	210	354	33.6	242	190	18.0	387	277	26.3	13	7	0.7	236	218	20.7
Fisheries	94	156	24.7	125	146	23.1	259	154	24.4	90	94	14.9	123	72	11.4
Mining	318	1,647	11.8	152	1,557	11.2	233	6,912	49.6	128	579	4.2	240	1,758	12.6
TOTAL	622	2,157	13.8	519	1,893	12.1	879	7,343	47.6	231	680	4.3	599	2,048	13.1

Source: Compiled from Satake Takanori, 'Trends in Japan's Direct Investment', 1991, p. 30

play is'.[7] The fact that Japanese investments (especially in manufacturing) in sub-Saharan Africa were concentrated in Nigeria (see Table 4.2) also has to be emphasized. This is partly because, in addition to a number of underlying strengths for the development of the manufacturing sector, Nigeria had a large enough internal market (if we go by population size alone) to enable a number of industries to achieve some economies of scale in production. And, in addition to its relatively vibrant and dynamic private capital and a growing cadre of active local entrepreneurs,[8] it is also endowed with a diversity of raw materials and abundant energy resources[9] that would provide a sound basis for a variety of manufacturing processes. Apart from petroleum, Nigeria's other mineral resources include coal, iron ore, tin, uranium, phosphates, limestone, lead, zinc, colombite, marble, gold and gas. In short, outside South Africa, Nigeria is one of the most attractive markets for raw materials in the sub-Saharan African region.

Nevertheless, Japanese investors showed relatively little interest in investing on a wider scale in Nigeria. In short, Japanese investments in Nigeria were hardly determined by the availability of raw materials in the country, contrary to the popular perception about Japanese economic interests in Africa. Of the forty firms with Japanese equity in Nigeria mentioned in Tōyō keizai's annual publication, for example, only four were identified as attracted by the availability of raw materials.[10]

It should be stressed that Japanese investors found certain periods in the development of the Nigerian economy more attractive for investment than others. The assumption here is that when the Nigerian economy gave positive signals to Japanese firms they did not hesitate to establish viable investment ventures in the country. On the whole, however, Japanese firms did not find the economic climate in Africa worth investing in, primarily for macro-economic reasons.

At a consultation meeting between the Keidanren and UN officials on the question of Africa's primary products, for example, the former made it absolutely clear that while Japan was being pressured by the African countries to buy more of their primary resources, these resources were of poor quality. They stressed that the primary reason for Japan's few imports of Africa's primary resources was because they were simply not competitive.[11] The Keidanren also seemingly ignored assurances from the head of the Africa Development Bank who, in 1989, led a delegation of African business executives to Tokyo and implored the Japanese to invest in the 'radically changing raw-materials rich' African economies.[12] The World Bank's request along the same lines to Tokyo[13] did not attract any positive responses either. Suffice to say that, on the whole, Japanese investors were not attracted to Africa's resources except for the 'strategic resources' in South Africa and a few others in certain countries like Zaire, and Niger[14].

Table 4.2 Year and number of cases of investment in sub-Saharan Africa

Country	Total	1969	1970–1979	1980
Senegal	3	–	3	–
Sierra Leone	1	1	–	–
Liberia	128	1	66	34
Cote d'Ivoire	5	-	4	1
Ghana	3	1	2	–
Burkina Faso	1	–	–	1
Nigeria	40	7	23	9
Niger	1	–	–	–
Cameroon	4	–	–	3
Gabon	2	–	2	–
Congo	1	–	–	1
Zaire	6	–	6	–
Ethiopia	3	2	1	–
Kenya	7	2	4	1
Uganda	2	2	–	–
Tanzania	7	6	1	–
Mozambique	1	–	2	–
Madagascar	4	1	1	1
Mauritius	2	–	2	–
Zimbabwe	1	–	–	1
Zambia	3	–	3	–
Swaziland	2	–	2	–

Note: Some cases and their year of investment cannot be accounted for
Source: Tōyō keizai, *Kaigai shinshutsu kigyō Sōran*, 1986, pp. 11, 438–40

Japanese business executives insist that there were problems with Nigeria's oil as well as other commodities. As far as Nigeria's oil is concerned, however, the problem could not have been quality. In fact, Nigerian oil was known for its low sulphur, which made it competitive because it is ecologically less hazardous. However, Japan could obtain low-sulphur oil from Indonesia as well, and at a cheaper price. It is not surprising, therefore, that Japanese oil imports from Nigeria were said to be more expensive because of high freight cost, obviously due to the huge geographical distance between the two countries. In effect, Nigeria's primary products, as those of most of the African states, were not deemed competitive.

THE NIGERIAN ECONOMY AND FDI

Oil and mining stood out as the leading sectors in Nigeria, accounting for 30.5 percent and 16.2 percent of FDI stock in 1978, respectively.[15] Yet import-substituting industrialization had proceeded well in the country, to the extent that manufacturing activities were responsible for 31.6 percent of FDI stock in 1978, above the African average. Indeed, this was fuelled by the massive oil revenues and the government's identification, through its Third National Development Plan (1975–1980),[16] of rapid industrialization as a priority in the country's future economic development. Thus, Nigeria's manufacturing sector expanded rapidly at an average rate of about 12 percent per annum, between 1973 and 1982.[17] These developments were a direct result of the dramatic change in the price of oil in 1973–1974 and 1979, resulting in the huge transfer of wealth to Nigeria. Since oil revenues accrued to the government, public expenditure increased greatly, as did the international capital market's attraction to the country.

The share of oil in the country's GDP rose astronomically after 1973, accounting for 90 percent of the country's foreign exchange earnings.[18] The huge oil revenues improved Nigeria's terms of trade immensely, becoming 'virtually synonymous with the price of oil deflated by the import price index'.[19] Meanwhile, the absorption (public and private investment and consumption) rate of the country remained high, exceeding GDP and national disposable income. But government spending was biased towards non-tradables like construction, services and capital-intensive investments. Brian Pinto notes that 'with government spending concentrated in urban centres and on nontradables, mobile labor moved from the agriculture to the services and construction sectors in the cities'.[20] In short, there was a reallocation of resources in the non-oil sectors of the economy. In addition the 'overvaluation of the Naira . . . and rising costs of agricultural labor made current production and new investment'[21] in the agricultural sector (export crop and of cotton, for example) 'unattractive'.

The effect was that tradable outputs, as in agriculture, fell; a clear indication of 'Dutch disease'.[22] From the 1970s to the early 1980s there was a 50 percent drop in Nigeria's cocoa exports, due to low profitability. This resulted in a drop in its position in world production from about 16 percent in the pre-oil-boom years to 8 percent in the mid-1980s. Between 1970 and 1982 the annual production of Nigeria's groundnuts, cotton and rubber (three of its major agricultural commodities) fell by 64 percent, 65, and 29 percent, respectively.[23] 'Cotton production', for example, 'declined drastically from 80,400 tons in 1977 to 21,600 tons in 1982 and then to 9,700 tons in 1986'.[24] Cocoa was all that was left of agricultural exports; accounting for about three-fourths of the exports of the country's agricultural sector, in the mid-1980s. The agricultural sector, we should note, accounted for only 2 percent to 3.5 percent of national export value.[25] The point to stress here is that while Nigeria used to be a net agricultural exporter, it spent more on import of agricultural products than it earned from agricultural exports in the boom years, and a great part of the 1980s. For example, food imports rose from a base of less than US$1 per capita in the early 1970s to over US$30 per capita by 1981.

The high domestic inflation and the appreciation of the Naira during the above period all exacerbated production costs for industry. According to a World Bank report:

> By the late 1970s, a clear picture of the structure of Nigeria's manufacturing sector had emerged. The sector was characterized by low value-added, high production costs, high geographical concentration (mainly around Lagos and to a lesser extent the Kaduna and Kano Axis), high dependence on imported raw materials, hardly any production for export, and low levels of foreign investment.[26]

Since the oil glut in 1982, the government's immediate reaction was to 'intensify rationing of foreign exchange'. In effect, 'rather than let the Naira depreciate in an attempt to restore equilibrium, it was decided to amend the import licensing system'.[27] Thus, in 1982, a foreign exchange budget constraint and a priority allocation formula were imposed on the issuing of licenses. This led eventually, in 1984, to the scrapping of the open general licensing system which allowed for the importation of almost any item and goods prior to 1981. In addition, the government reintroduced, in 1982, the system of advance import deposits for all goods.[28]

The further rationing of foreign exchange on the official market inevitably ushered into existence a growing premium on foreign exchange on the parallel (illegal) market, which then became the standard determinant, either explicitly or implicitly, of the marginal cost of foreign exchange. As Nigeria's terms of trade continued to worsen (in conjunction with the decline of the real price of oil) the government initiated fiscal austerity measures in 1984 which reduced the growth rate of the nominal money. This was because the measures greatly reduced the deficit.[29] By 1986, the Naira had been cut loose to find its value first in a two-tiered and then a single foreign exchange market. In the process, the official exchange rate depreciated faster (as the value of the Naira plummeted), thus making the parallel market premium grow. Pinto argues that:

> The rising parallel market premium may be taken as an indicator of inconsistency between fiscal and exchange rate policy, resulting in foreign exchange rationing. This may be exacerbated by a fall in the price of oil, and hence revenues, which in the absence of further reductions in government spending, would lead to a higher inflation tax.[30]

He further argues, quite rightly, that the 'inconsistency between fiscal and exchange rate policy makes it impossible for investors to use the real exchange rate as a signal for decisions about resource allocation', a point stressed by both Mr. Yamamoto Yoshimichi, Managing Director of MBK (Nigeria) Limited and Mr. Hidaka, Managing Director of JGC (Nigeria) Ltd.[31] Pinto attributes this partly to a 'measurement problem': the official nominal exchange rate is likely to become increasingly irrelevant as the parallel market premium expands. In that respect 'the prices of traded goods are more likely to reflect the parallel exchange rate'.[32]

The presence of a dislocated official foreign exchange system and the lack of proper measures to narrow the difference between the official and the parallel rate took their toll on the credibility of the country's macro-economic policies and heightened the potentials of business risk. This point was stressed by all the Japanese business executives interviewed for this research. In effect, a high premium would be a serious disincentive for foreign investors who may not want to solicit the parallel channels. Yet 'going through the official channels would imply a significant tax on such investments when the premium is high'.[33] In addition, most investors did not want to deal with the bureaucratic nightmare that it entailed. Nor did they want to invest in a worsening climate of political instability. This point was echoed by the Director of JETRO (Lagos), Mr. Ayoola, in his assessment of the investment climate of Nigeria. Astute and potential investors have therefore assumed a 'wait-and-see' attitude with respect to investing in Nigeria.

Meanwhile, manufacturing production trends in the private sector, from the mid-1970s to 1990, largely reflected the biases in the incentive structure. Import-intensive consumer goods and light-assembly industries, under high government protection, grew rapidly at the expense of local resource-based industries, even though the former contributed relatively little value-added to the economy. The indicators show that,

> the share of food and textile products in manufacturing output fell from 51 percent in 1973/74 to 36 percent in 1977/78, while the share of durable goods which have low value added rose from 7 percent to 19 percent during the period. Within durable goods, the share of transport equipment which had a ratio of value added to gross output of only 0.16 rose from about one tenth of one percent to 11 percent during 1971/72–1977/78.[34]

A survey of manufacturing enterprises by the Nigerian government in 1984 showed that by the early 1980s domestic value-added was only 14 percent of the value of gross output, and over two-thirds of raw materials were imported.[35] However, certain sectors of the manufacturing industry seemed to be recovering, the report noted. The textile industry, by all standards, showed the biggest recovery from 1986 onwards, after a huge decline by about 68 percent between 1980 and 1986. Production in the sector more than doubled from 1986 to 1988 with synthetic fabrics, followed by cotton products, showing the greatest increase.[36] This industry was one of the sectors which received the first set of Japanese investments in Nigeria.

The intermediate goods industry on the whole was not doing well; its share in value-added having fallen from 29 percent to 19 percent in 1971/1972 and 1984 respectively. In terms of contribution to employment, by 1984 it had declined to 18 percent from 24 percent in 1971/1972. Chemicals and paints, leather tanning and finishing, tyres and tubes, sawmills and wood products, building materials (like iron rods and roofing sheets) and metal products formed a major part of production in this sector. On the other hand, building materials showed mixed performance, with the production of cement, paints and tiles increasing slightly. At the same time, the production of PVC pipes and iron rods, an area which Japanese investors were particularly interested in, rose relatively sharply, while production of roofing materials declined substantially.[37]

SPECIFIC CASES OF CONSTRAINTS ON FDI IN NIGERIA

In a survey of 233 West German firms, Keith Marsden and Therese Belot make the point that 'the level of foreign private investment in Africa is affected by barriers to entry and the potential investor's perception of the prevailing business environment'.[38] Specifically, they note difficulty in dealing with government authorities (bureaucracy) as the most important individual constraint. Conditions regarding the ownership and return (transfer) of capital; the regulations governing local participation, financing conditions and return of the profits; restrictions on the supply of raw materials and intermediates (import restrictions, cash deposits, customs and compulsory use of local products both for production and plant investment) were all noted as individual constraints on investors. And there was great concern about Nigeria's unstable fiscal and monetary policies.

The question of ownership and return of capital, and indeed financing conditions, not to mention the return of profits, were seen as extremely troublesome. More specifically, the constantly changing policy in relation to local equity participation, and the murkiness of the indigenization policy as a whole, was emphasized as a major hindrance to foreign investment. In 1984, for example, the federal government approved a plan for the joint production of electrical equipment between UAC of Nigeria and the Matsushita Electric Company of Japan. The project, however, fell through[39] because of uncertainty about aspects of the indigenization decree. 'Were the companies that sold equity to Nigerians under the decree to be treated as foreign or Nigerian companies for purposes of fresh investment?', was the pertinent issue here, as Tom Forrest suggests. Obviously, as he points out, 'to treat them as foreign companies would involve a dilution of foreign equity'.[40]

On the question of repatriation of profits, the Director of Chiyoda (Nigeria) Ltd., for example, noted that 'in the last 3–4 years it has been very difficult to realize profits in foreign currency, much more repatriate the parent company's share of dividends because conversion of the Naira into foreign currency was very difficult, in view of the lack of foreign exchange and government controls over it'.[41] The problem of corruption was another sore point of the African political economy that was mentioned as a hindrance to foreign investment in the continent. The 'institutionalized' nature of bribery, as a way of circumventing red tape 'becomes a millstone when failure to pay causes a firm to seize up',[42] Marsden and Belot point out. Incidentally, the points raised by these authors are as relevant to the political economy of any of the countries on the continent as they are to Nigeria. The general image of the Nigerian business class as corrupt and interested only in quick returns, and uncertainty about whether legal and contractual rights would be respected in what is perceived as a corrupt social set up[43] were always mentioned as a major concern for foreign investors.

The industries surveyed by Marsden and Belot also expressed concern about dangers in relation to nationalization of firms, since it was a common practice for most African countries. Yanaihara Katsu, in his seminal paper on Japanese overseas enterprises in Africa, makes note of the problems of indigenization that Japanese companies faced in Nigeria in the early 1970s.[44] His point is underlined by Mr. Shiozuka, President of a Japanese Consortium of nine leading Japanese textile firms (the Overseas Spinning Investment Company) who, during a visit to Nigeria in 1971, expressed concern about the difficulties of 'Nigerianization' for Japanese firms in the country.[45] And although in recent years many African governments have seemingly liberalized their economies to a considerable degree, Paul Collier points out that 'surveys of actual and potential investors identify the perceived risk of policy reversal as the most potent deterrent to foreign investment'.[46] He further reiterates the point that foreign investment is low in Africa as a whole partly because 'the stated intentions of governments are not sufficiently credible'.[47]

All the firms that are surveyed in this study also complained about the lack of proper (updated) statistical information on the Nigerian economy and basic information about the industrial structure of the country. At a meeting in 1990 between friendship associations of the two countries involving important business representatives, the Japanese delegation expressed a number of grievances. For example, the delegation pointed out that:

> it is after in-depth study of the markets . . . to determine needs, volumes etc. that Japan would be in a position to formulate policies and long-term strategies highlighting specific criteria under which Japanese investment could be attracted in certain areas.[48]

Needless to say, rational investment decisions can be made only when managers receive adequate information on the effects of their decisions, in the form of market-determined prices and indeed long-term security of their investments. It has to be noted that this is indeed an important aspect of Japan's CNS strategy, which stresses the importance of dependability, especially for sources of raw materials.

Capacity utilization in industries was another area of great concern to Japanese investors in the country. Mr. Yamamoto Yoshimichi of MBK (Nigeria) Ltd. stressed that this problem, which was obviously a result of the poor performance of the economy as a whole, was a major hindrance to attracting Japanese investors. At the meeting mentioned above, the delegation for instance expressed deep concern about the fact that capacity utilization in industries (1988/1989) ran between only 38 percent and 42 percent. However, the delegation was informed by its Nigerian counterpart that this applied mainly to firms that relied on foreign raw materials, with the attendant overhead cost operating at such level because of the depreciating rate of the Naira. The fact remains, however, that most of the major firms fell under this category, because of the lack of adequate local raw materials and technology. Another important factor that attracted a great deal of complaint was the lack of decent infrastructure (electricity, water, roads), which was mentioned as a serious drawback to the Nigerian economy. In view of the problems identified above, it is not surprising that the foreign investment climate in Nigeria remained rather discouraging. Net foreign investment in Nigeria for the period from 1978–1980, for example, represented less than 1 percent of total domestic investment.[49]

CASES OF JAPANESE EQUITY PARTICIPATION IN NIGERIA

According to 1992 figures, the period from 1951 to 1990 saw ninety-three cases of actual Japanese investments in Nigeria. In value terms, these amounted cumulatively to $159 mn.[50], as shown in Table 4.3, representing a mere 0.1 percent of Japanese overseas investments during the period.

Table 4.3 The size of Japanese major investments in sub-Saharan Africa ($1 mn.)

Country	1989		1990		1951–90		
	No. of cases	Amt.	No. of cases	Amt.	No. of cases	Amt.	%
Nigeria	1	1	2	1	93	159	0.1
Zambia	–	–	–	–	17	142	0.0
Zaire	–	–	–	–	56	282	0.1
Liberia	72	643	50	531	930	4,832	1.6
Others	15	27	18	19	362	411	0.1
TOTAL	88	671	70	551	1,458	5,826	1.9

Source: Tōyō keizai, *Kaigai shinshutsu kigyō sōran*, 1992, p. 121

Most of Japan's investments in Nigeria were in the manufacturing sector, producing tradables as in consumer goods like textiles. The textile industry alone employed 8,659 of the 10,568 workers[51] in the firms with Japanese equity in Nigeria. Metal-working industries producing iron rods and roofing sheets and other intermediate goods provided the next-highest level of employment among the manufacturing firms with Japanese equity holdings. This sub-sector provided employment for approximately 1,226 people. Investment in the fishing industry provided employment for another 241 workers, and involved only one venture. In the capital goods sub-sector, finally, transportation attracted the highest investment, in the form of import-substitution companies that assembled mostly motorcycles and sold spare parts. In 1990 only two such ventures with Japanese equity participation existed.

It is important to note that 'Japanese enterprises in Africa have parent companies, sometimes multiple, in Japan'; and that while in some cases the firms themselves were locally established corporations the Japanese staff in the firms were, in most cases, short-term 'transfers' from the parent companies. The pattern of behavior of Japanese firms in Nigeria underlines Yanaihara's argument that Japanese firms in Africa assumed a 'temporary character', in the sense that they either faded away by going bankrupt, or transferred the venture to the cooperating local company.[52] The 'temporary character' of the Japanese firms may, however, be attributable to the lack of sustainable growth of the African economies, and the fact that these economies were unable to sustain the firms. But, as already pointed out, there were a host of other factors that drove these firms away.

The overall picture of Japanese investments in Nigeria in the period was indeed very poor. This, as stated earlier, was a reflection of the extent of Japanese investment interests in Africa as a whole. In the latter part of the

1960s, and most certainly in the 1970s, however, the climate of opinion in Japan seemed to support extending some forms of investment in Nigeria.[53] Between 1962 and 1971 Nigeria had ten Japanese firms[54] established in different parts of the country. Almost as a continuation of its successful exports of textile commodities in the 1930s,[55] by 1958 Japan was the leading exporter of textile products to Nigeria; and by 1961 it was far ahead of its major contenders. With respect to cotton piece goods, for example, in the same year Japan exported £12.9 mn. worth of goods, compared to the UK, with the second-highest level of exports, at £4.1 mn.[56] Peter Kilby also notes that 'as a result of Japanese textiles being highly competitive with local production'[57] and due to the huge balance of payments constantly in favor of Japan in 1965 Nigeria invoked Article 35 of the GATT proceedings against Japan.[58] Kilby tells us that before the invocation of the above principle, in December 1963, the Tafawa Balewa administration informed the Japanese Ambassador to Nigeria 'that if his country could not manage to purchase more of Nigeria's exports, a total embargo might be placed on Japanese goods'.[59]

The level of diatribe against Japan over the question of the lopsided trade relationship was phenomenal. The then Commissioner for Communications, Alhaji Aminu Kano, for example, castigated Japan, according to the *Sunday Post,* for 'sapping our economy and retiring to sit on the fence at the time when Nigeria needed her financial aid most'. The Commissioner is further quoted as saying that 'it is time we expose Japan' for what it is.[60] And the Deputy Permanent Secretary to the Federal Ministry of Trade, Mr. G. N. O. Safia, was also reported to have 'deplored the practice of Japanese ships discharging their goods in Nigeria and leaving our ports in ballast, whereas it would have been more profitable to both countries if the boats took some Nigerian products with them back to Japan'.[61] Thus, the issue of the lopsided trade balance was debated extensively by the Nigerian press in the latter part of the 1960s and early 1970s,[62] and was to re-emerge in the 1980s. The indications, however, were that Japan made attempts to ameliorate the problem, including setting up investments in Nigeria, albeit without expanding its imports from the country.

These investments[63] were either solely Japanese-owned or jointly owned with indigenous companies/entrepreneurs and another foreign investor, in accordance with the Nigerian Enterprises Promotion Decree 1972, amended in 1977 to involve Nigerians in ownership. The decree was subsequently relaxed (in the latter part of the 1980s). It may be appropriate to note that the investments were set up, with the huge backing of the Japanese government,[64] to produce locally those commodities that were being heavily imported from Japan. Suffice to say that by 1975 the Nigerian government had found it necessary to withdraw the invocation of

Article 35 of the GATT proceedings against Japan, 'in recognition of', as the government put it, 'the genuine efforts on the part of the Government of Japan to improve its trade relations with Nigeria'.[65] It may be said that the invocation of Article 35 was withdrawn primarily because of the increasing Japanese investments in Nigeria at the time. It may now be worth looking at, in order of importance, the main sectors of Japanese investment in the country, some of which will be dealt with in detail. The investments included ventures in the construction sector (some of which were turnkey projects) and certainly ventures in the services (mostly trading companies) sector. As already noted, Japanese FDI almost invariably necessitates the presence of a trading company, as an inevitable adjunct of the investment equation.

The textile firms

At the time of writing, there were only three major Japanese investments in the primary sector, all of which were involved in textile production. They were Arewa Textiles Ltd., Afprint (Nigeria) Ltd., and Northern Textile Manufactures. Arewa Textiles Ltd., which was established in 1965, started with a production capacity of 10 mn. yards of grey and bleached cloth. It was 'undertaken as part of a move to protect the overseas market of its sponsors' – Kaigai Bōseki Tōshi (Overseas Spinning Investment Company). This was a consortium of ten leading Japanese spinning firms.[66] Within five years of establishment, Arewa Textiles Ltd. embarked on two phases of expansion at a total cost of £3.5 mn. In 1969 it had fifty-one Japanese technicians and nine administrative staff. It is worth noting that at the time the firm was set up Japan was supplying 'from half to two-thirds of all Nigeria's textiles'.[67] The indications then were that prospects, in Nigeria as a market, were good.

In tune with the policy of 'Nigerianization', Arewa Textiles was a joint venture involving the above consortium of Japanese spinners – which held 44 percent of the equity. The local investors had (according to 1992 indicators) 40 percent equity participation in the firm. The remaining equity was held by other foreign firms.[68] Arewa Textiles, with an investment capital of N (naira) 80 mn., was by far the largest Japanese investment in Nigeria, according to 1990 indicators, and employed 2,759 workers, nineteen of whom, including the General Manager, were Japanese. The financial position of the firm was said to be favorable, with 1986 figures showing annual sales of N63 mn.[69] This is an indication that the country was a good market for textile products. It seems also to support the Nigerian government's survey (mentioned earlier), which noted that the textile sector showed the biggest signs of recovery between

1986–1988. But the firm was also attracted by the availability of natural resources in the country.

The two other textile firms, Afprint (Nigeria) Ltd. and Northern Textile Manufactures, were set up in 1961 and 1962 and had only 5.6 percent and 9.11 percent Japanese equity holdings, respectively, by 1990 indicators. The size of the shares of the Japanese equity holders changed over the years. In 1980, Nishizawa had 7.4 percent of Afprint's $5.75 mn. capital investment. The firm then had a workforce of 1,000. By 1982 its capital investment had been hugely increased to $14.3 mn., of which Nishizawa's equity participation had been reduced to 5.6 percent. The firm was by then employing 2,000 people. The figures had not changed by 1986. The indications are that Afprint was attracted to Nigeria by the availability of resources, and the potential huge market.

Nishizawa also had 12.8 percent of Northern Textile Manufactures' $710,000 investment equity in 1980. The firm then employed a work-force of 800. By 1982 the firm's investment capital had increased to $2.68 mn., of which Nishizawa's share holdings had fallen to 11.6 percent. The firm's work-force had by then increased to 1,500. The figures were the same by 1986. The firm, which produced blankets, was attracted to Nigeria by the same factors that attracted Afprint. Unlike the latter, however, it exported some of its products to Japan.

The intermediary sector

The intermediate goods producing sector with Japanese equity share-holdings was concentrated mainly in the metal, steel and wire manufacturing industries. These were set up, primarily, to take advantage of public sector-led growth – through infrastructural developments – which created a huge market for the construction sector especially in the 1970s, and early 1980s. The share of this sector's value-added to the economy declined heavily in the mid-1980s, however. It fell from 29 percent in 1971/72 to 19 percent in 1984, as noted earlier. The firms in this sector with Japanese equity holdings are discussed below.

Galvanizing Industries Ltd. was set up in 1964 and had an investment capital of N5 mn., twice the figure for 1980. This was split up between Itōchū Shōji (24 percent), Yodogawa Seikōjo (12 percent), and CFAO and others (64 percent). It produced galvanized zinc plates and iron for local consumption, and provided employment for 119 people, only one of whom, the Managing Director, was Japanese.[70] In 1980, it had a work-force of 504. This fell dramatically in two years to 282, and subsequently went down to 264 by 1986. The venture was attracted by the Nigerian government's protection for infant industries.

Pioneer Metal Products Co. Ltd., on the other hand, is said to have recorded an annual (June 1991) turnover of over N13 mn., and was in good standing financially. It registered a higher turnover in 1980 (N19 mn.) and 1982 (N16.5 mn.). The firm's equity of N3.1 mn. was shared among three Japanese investors, NKK (19.1 percent), Marubeni (19.1 percent), G.H. Katō Shōkai (2.7 percent), Peterson Zochonis, and some local investors (59.1 percent).[71] Its l:ne of production, from 1964 when it was established, was mainly galvanized zinc plates. It was also responsible for the marketing of its products. Its work-force of 622 in 1980 was down to 165 by 1982; and stood, with a Japanese Managing Director, at 130 in 1990. The company produced for the local market, but was also attracted by the government's protection (in the form of corporate tax and import tax reductions and exemptions) policy for such small investors.

Rolled Steel Products Ltd., the only one of these firms not located in the industrial estate in Ikeja, was the smallest of the five metal firms with Japanese equity participation. Its N2.5 mn. investment capital was split between Kawatetsu Shōji (10 percent) and Colanda Investments (50 percent), with the remaining 40 percent equity belonging to a third party. Its work-force of forty in 1980 increased to 100 in 1982, but had subsequently decreased to sixty-one by 1990. Two of its employees (in 1990) were dispatched from Japan, and the head of the firm, Mr. C.J. Shah, was of Indian origin. Set up in 1978, its annual sales for 1989[72] were worth N33.1 mn. The primary attraction of Nigeria to Japanese investors was the protection provided by the government, presumably in the form of tax reductions or exemptions. It was also attracted by the potential huge market and the availability of a big and cheap labor force.

Continental Iron and Steel Co. (Nigeria) Ltd. was established in 1979, and had an equity capital of N3.5 mn., divided between Shokuei Seikō (11.43 percent), Nisshō Iwai (8.57 percent) and local entrepreneurs (80 percent).[73] Its equity capital was N2.6 mn. in 1980. The Japanese shares increased from 9.13 percent and 6.84 percent, respectively, in 1980. The firm's 140-strong work-force, which was a huge reduction from 500 in the early 1980s, and 220 in 1986, was primarily involved in the production of iron rods (*marubō*). The company was established to expand its share of the Nigerian market, and also to make good use of the local labor force. It seemed, however, barely to be surviving financially by the latter part of the 1980s in the face of the economic recession the country was suffering and its concomitant effects on the construction sector. Its financial standing was said to be in equilibrium.[74]

The last of the metal manufacturing companies in this section of our survey is the Standard Industrial Development Co., Ltd., which was established in 1977 and had an investment capital of N3 mn. The figure was only one-third of that amount in 1979. The structure of equity participation involved Mitsubishi Shōji (17.3 percent), Kantō Seikōjo (10.2 percent), John Holt and Co., and local entrepreneurs (72.5 percent). With an annual sales (1991 figures) of N59 mn.,[75] a significant increase on its N20 mn. sales in 1981, it seemed to be doing relatively well in the latter part of the 1980s. Nevertheless, its work-force shrank from 177 in 1982 to just seventy-two in 1986, and then to forty-six according to 1993 indicators. The firm had one Japanese employee, and the main reason it was attracted to Nigeria was the potentially huge market.

The production function of the Nigeria Wire and Cable Co. Ltd., in Ibadan, classified it as being part of the intermediate goods-producing sector. It was a manufacturer of different kinds of electric and cable wires, for local consumption, and it was set up in 1977 to take advantage of the construction boom of the 1970s. The firm had an equity value of N4 mn. and employed 177 workers, compared to 200 in 1986, 270 in 1982 and 241 in 1980. Its investment capital was, however, much smaller at N2.8 mn. in 1980. Despite the significant level of Japanese equity participation in this firm (42 percent), it was headed by, presumably, an employee of the local participant, Mr. K. Agoro. The 42-percent Japanese investment was split between Sumitomo Denki Kōkyo (28 percent) and Sumitomo Shōji (14 percent). The remaining 58 percent equity belonged to the local participant, Odu'a Investment Company Ltd. Previously, in 1979, the Japanese shares were 60 percent in 1979, split 40 percent and 20 percent, respectively, between the two firms. The venture was set up with the view to expanding its share of the local market. The company was said to be financially stable in 1990.

The only other manufacturing firms in Nigeria with Japanese equity holding (in 1990) were the Yamaha Manufacturing (Nigeria) Ltd., and Honda Manufacturing (Nigeria) Ltd. The former started operating in 1981, and had an investment capital of N5 mn., shared between Yamaha Motors (17.5 percent), MBK Nigeria Ltd. (17.5 percent), John Holt Ltd. (25 percent) and local entrepreneurs (40 percent). Its investment capital in 1982 was down to a mere N870,500. The firm simply assembled motorbikes and imported spare parts for sale. It was headed by a local Indian entrepreneur, and had a staff of ninety,[76] which was a dramatic increase over its work-force of twenty-five in 1982. It was set up (in Lagos) to expand its share of the Nigerian market and to benefit from the government's protection policy in favor of infant firms. Its annual sales (1986 figures) were N7.58 mn.

Honda Manufacturing (Nigeria) Ltd. produced various autoparts, and assembled motorbikes, also mainly for local consumption. Set up in 1981, it had an investment capital of N4.5 mn., split between Honda Giken

Kōgyō (30 percent) and local entrepreneurs (70 percent).[77] It had a work-force of 300 in 1986. As with those mentioned above, Honda was established with the objective of expanding its share of the local market. The firm was headed by Chief S. Ade John. There is no information about its domestic added value.

The other area in which Japan had sustained investment was the fishing industry; even though its investment in this sub-sector was in only one venture, Osadjare Fishing Company Ltd.[78] Japan's equity participation in this company was said to have started in April, 1974. Taiyō Gyogyō held 30 percent of the company's equity capital of N1 mn., and provided for the management of deep-sea trawlers and shrimpers. The remaining equity belonged to Cafad Ltd. (Ibru Sea Food), a local company. The company specialized in the trawl fishing of prawns and shrimps, and the processing of seafood (frozen fish), in addition to being responsible for the marketing of its produce. The venture (according to 1990 indicators) employed a work-force of 241, eight of whom, including the Managing Director, were Japanese. In 1986 it had fifty-one Japanese employees, out of a work-force of 264, which was still less than its 1980 work-force of 382. The venture was set up because of the abundance of fish in Nigerian waters. It is important to reiterate the fact that this venture was also set up primarily because of the potential market opportunities provided by Nigeria, and not because of the need for raw materials.

The construction sector

Another 'popular' target area for Japanese investments was the area of non-tradables, as in the construction sector, which included turnkey projects, telecommunications and electrical, and water works. Writing in 1984, the *Guardian* (Nigerian newspaper) noted that 'though Japanese involvement in the construction industry in Nigeria dates back just one decade, their impact has become very significant and all-embracing'.[79] Since this sector has no real relevance to the argument concerning Japan's resource needs and Japan's CNS plan, this analysis will not be concerned with a detailed appraisal of the sector. Suffice to say that there were seven (1992 indicators) of such Japanese ventures in Nigeria, compared with six in 1986. These firms, as the ones mentioned above, were primarily 'Nigerianized' Japanese companies, some of whom were located in Nigeria with a firm backing from the Japanese government. The latter's provision of financial assistance through the Export–Import Bank of Japan and other sources towards certain aid projects ensured, in many cases, that the project was undertaken by a Japanese company or companies.

This was an aspect of the international 'aid enterprise', of which Japan was no exception. In the Japanese case, the process involved the identification of a project by a Japanese trading, engineering or construction company in a country like Nigeria, and helping the latter's government to obtain financial assistance towards the project from the Japanese government. Thus, a number of the trading companies were engaged in some construction projects as in the case of MBK Nigeria Ltd., Marubeni, C. Itoh and Nisshō Iwai (Nigeria) Ltd. Some of these functioned only as system organizers or promoters, meaning they primarily arranged for the financing of the project from the Export–Import Bank of Japan. It needs to be pointed out that Japanese (private) commercial banks did not provide funding towards such projects in Nigeria.

Each of the construction firms was set up in response to the booming economy of the 1970s, when the resources from the sale of oil made Nigeria a viable economic entity. In the event, these firms have remained the most precarious among Japanese investors in the face of the ever-worsening Nigerian economy. Not surprisingly, the sector makes no real financial commitments (by way of investments) in the country. Thus, Taisei (West Africa) Ltd., which was set up in 1979, made a capital investment to the tune of N400,000, while Nija Water Development and Construction Co. had an equity value of N120,000 (according to 1992/ 1993 indicators). The latter's 1986 investment capital, for example, was a mere N10,000. Nevertheless, some of these construction firms have been involved in major projects. For example, Chiyoda (Nigeria) Ltd.'s first project was the construction of the Port Harcourt Oil Refinery, a project which, at its peak, provided employment for about 4,000 local workers and involved 500 experts from Japan and the Philippines. And together with Marubeni (Trading Company) and Spibat of France, JGC (Nigeria) Ltd. was involved in a contract worth $12 mn. and an additional N52 mn. for the construction of the Bonny Export Terminal.

Japanese trading/service companies in Nigeria

According to 1992 statistical data, there were nine Japanese trading companies[80] with offices in Nigeria. Because of the definition of FDI chosen for this study, which includes NFI (new forms of investment), these ventures have also been accepted in this study as Japanese foreign investments in Nigeria. It has to be stressed that the equity capital invested in these trading companies was negligible. The fact that the companies provided very little added value towards the Nigerian economy also has to be emphasized, since some of these firms had been operating in Nigeria for over two decades. Essentially, they were concerned with exports of

Japanese goods to Nigeria, and contributed very little in terms of the promotion of Nigerian exports to Japan or third countries. This fact disputes Kojima's trade-oriented theory of Japanese direct investment in developing countries. It also questions Buckley's point supporting what he refers to as 'the market access which the links with a Japanese distribution network brings'.[81] Their functional responsibilities also included monitoring the performance of the Nigerian economy and supplying their Japanese clients with the information. A number of them were equity participants in other ventures as well, as noted earlier.

While these trading companies contributed very little in terms of the promotion of Nigerian exports, it must be noted that, since these enterprises were primarily interested in making profits, it is conceivable that if Nigeria had products which were highly competitive they would not have hesitated to find markets for them in either Japan or a third country.[82] Mr. Yamamoto, the Managing Director of MBK, noted, for example, that the company was looking into the possibilities of prospecting for natural gas in Nigeria. The impression is, however, that the availability of exportable items alone was not good enough.[83] As noted earlier, there were no exports of Nigerian oil to Japan; and this is supposedly attributable to the fact that Nigeria's oil was not competitive, as has been already argued. It is interesting, however, to note that some of the trading companies had actually proposed to trade with Nigeria on barter: providing Japanese goods in exchange for oil. This proposal was, understandably, wholly rejected by the Nigerian authorities,[84] since the gains from oil exports had first to be realized in foreign exchange. The above proposal, needless to say, was indicative of the fact that the Japanese were simply not interested in Nigeria's oil, but rather more interested in how best to market Japanese products in the country. Nor did they find Nigeria's other raw materials worth investing in. Another point to stress here, then, is that, on the whole, the service-related companies have been doing rather badly in Nigeria since the mid-1980s.

The survey of the firms above shows, as illustrated in Table 4.4, that the main attraction that drew them to Nigeria was the availability of good local market prospects. Approximately thirty-two of the forty firms that existed in 1986 mentioned this factor as the main incentive for investing in Nigeria, even though some of these firms must have also been attracted by the potential of third-country exports. This study, however, shows that few of the firms actually engaged in sales outside Nigeria. Northern Textile Manufacturing, according to the survey, was the only firm that engaged in exports to Japan, as illustrated in Table 4.4. The second-most important attraction to the firms was the protection given by the Nigerian government to small industries through corporate tax reductions and exemptions. A

Table 4.4 Stated reasons (by Japanese firms) for investing in specific African countries

Country	Raw* materials, resources	Raw** materials	Cheap labor	Govt*** protection	Local, third-country sales	Collection of data	Royalty	Trade+ friction	Local market	Exports to Japan
Nigeria	4	–	3	10	20	7	2	1	12	1
Cote d' Ivoire	2	–	1	3	1	–	–	–	3	–
Liberia	1	–	5	–	8	–	1	–	–	2
Kenya	–	–	1	3	3	–	–	–	2	–
Tanzania	1	1	1	4	4	–	1	–	4	–

Notes: * To secure raw materials and resources
** Raw materials abundant for local production
*** Corporate tax reductions and exemptions
+ To circumvent trade barriers

Note: The figures do not necessarily match the actual no. of cases of Japanese investments in these countries (some firms stated more than one reason)
Source: Tōyō keizai, Kaigai shinshutsu kigyo sōran, 1986, p. 9

number of the construction firms were attracted by that. This was followed by 'collection of data', mostly by trading companies who, among others, supplied their clients with information about the country's macro-economic situation. Table 4.4 also clearly supports the argument that Japanese investments in Nigeria were hardly resource-oriented. As can be seen, only four firms mentioned raw materials/resources (which included cheap labor) as an incentive for investing in Nigeria; and none of the firms were attracted because of abundant raw materials for local production.

SAMPLE CASES OF JAPANESE DIVESTMENTS FROM NIGERIA

In view of the very few firms in Nigeria currently with Japanese equity participation, it would have to be admitted that the country was not very successful at sustaining most of the Japanese investments that it had attracted over the past thirty years or so. As noted earlier, between 1951 and 1990 there were ninety-three cases of Japanese equity participation in Nigeria. However, by 1992 there were only twenty-three. This means that of the forty firms (see Table 4.2, p. 110) with Japanese equity that existed in 1986, seventeen (42.5 percent) had divested by 1992 (see Table 4.5), showing a high divestment rate in the latter part of the 1980s as Nigeria's capital accumulation rate and resource allocation continued to deteriorate rapidly. Even firms that were established as late as the first part of the 1980s had a high divestment rate. Of the nine firms established between 1980 and 1986, three (33 percent) had divested by the end of the decade. This contrasts with the low level of divestment in the early part of the decade. Of the thirty-four firms existing by 1980, only three divested between 1980 and 1986. The following is a description of a sample of the firms (starting with the textiles sector) who lost their Japanese equity participants.

The textile firms

In 1970, Teijin Ltd. of Osaka, in collaboration with a Japanese trading firm, C. Itoh and Co. Ltd., and CFAO (Nigeria) Ltd. established a joint venture to manufacture synthetic fabrics. The resulting firm, Nigeria Teijin Textile Ltd., was the first synthetic textile factory in the whole of West Africa. Starting with an initial production target of about 4.8 mn. square yards of blended synthetic suiting, it had the objective of marketing its products in the whole region, and did manage to extend its sales, for example, to Ghana, where its brand name 'Teijin Tetoron' was popular. It recorded a sales value of $12.9 mn. in 1978. Established with £1.1 mn. as its initial investment capital, Nigeria Teijin Textile Ltd. started with a staff

Table 4.5 A selection of cases of Japanese investments in and divestment from Nigeria, 1961–1992

Firm involved	Year firm established	1980	1986	1992
Afprint (Nigeria) Ltd.	1961	*	*	D
Northern Textile Manufactures	1962	*	*	D
Galvanizing Industries Ltd.	1964	*	*	*
Pioneer Metal Products Co. Ltd.	1964	*	*	*
Arewa Textiles Ltd.	1965	*	*	*
Sanyo (Nigeria) Ltd.	1969	*	*	D
Nichimen Co. (Nigeria) Ltd.	1969	*	*	*
Nishizawa (Nigeria) Ltd.	1969	*	*	*
Bhojsons Industries Ltd.	1970	*	*	D
Japan Petroleum Co. (Nigeria) Ltd.	1970	*	*	D
Toyo Menka Kaisha (Nigeria) Ltd.	1970	*	*	*
Woollen & Synthetic Textile Mfg. Ltd.	1970	*	D	
Nigeria Teijin Textiles Ltd.	1970	*	D	
Ninetco Ltd.	1971	*	D	
General Cotton Mill Ltd.	1973	*	*	D
Nigerian Wire Industries Ltd.	1974	*	*	D
Nigerian Wire & Cable Co. Ltd.	1974	*	*	*
Osadjere Fishing Co. Ltd.	1974	*	*	*
Zaria Industries Ltd.	1975	*	*	D
Metal Box Toyo Glass (Nigeria) Ltd.	1975	*	*	*
Elson (Nigeria) Ltd.	1977	*	D	
Metcome (Nigeria) Ltd.	1977	*	*	D
MELCO (Nigeria) Ltd.	1977	*	*	D
Standard Industrial Development Co. Ltd.	1977	*	*	*
Rolled Steel Products Ltd.	1978	*	*	*
C. Itoh Co. (Nigeria) Ltd.	1978	*	*	D
Sumitomo Shōji Kaisha (Nigeria) Ltd.	1978	*	*	*
MBK (Nigeria) Ltd.	1978	*	*	*
SEI (Nigeria) Ltd.	1978	*	*	*
Continental Iron and Steel Co. Ltd.	1979	*	*	*
Sumalco Ltd.	1979	*	*	*
Taisei (West Africa) Ltd.	1979	*	*	*
Nissho Iwai (Nigeria) Ltd.	1979	*	*	*
Marubeni (Nigeria) Ltd.	1979	*	*	D
Fujikura (Nigeria) Ltd.	1979	*	*	D
Nigerian Textile Products Ltd.	1980	*	*	D
NEC (Nigeria) Ltd.	1981		*	*

Table 4.5 Continued

Firm involved	Year firm established	1980	1986	1992
Honda Manufacturing (Nigeria) Ltd.	1981		*	*
Yamaha Manufacturing (Nigeria) Ltd.	1981		*	*
Fire Equity and General Insurance Co. Ltd.	1983		*	*
Chiyoda (Nigeria) Ltd.	1983		*	*
Toda Construction (Nigeria) Ltd.	1983		*	D
Nija Water Development and Construction Co. Ltd.	1983		*	*
Panasonic (Nigeria) Ltd.	1983		*	D
JGC (Nigeria) Ltd.	?		*	*
Mitsubishi Shoji Kaisha (Nigeria) Ltd.	?		*	*
Itochu (Nigeria) Ltd.	1991			*

Notes: *   Firm operating
      ?   Year established unknown
      D   Divestment (firm not operating): firm divested anywhere between 1980–1985 and 1986–1991

of 800 locals, five technical experts and twenty-one supervisors from Japan. By 1978, its work-force had increased to 1,080, of whom only twelve were dispatched from Japan. A comment to the effect that, 'we have every reason to believe that the quality of our products will be equal, or even superior, to those imported from Japan, because, apart from using the same quality of raw yarns, the factory's facilities would be identical with those in Japan', by the General Manager, Mr. Ichikawa,[85] suggests that the firm was trying to circumvent the problem of 'trade friction' between Japan and Nigeria. However, the firm seems either to have lost its Japanese investments between 1980 and 1982 or must have gone out of business during that period.

Nigerian Textile Products Ltd. was established in 1980 with an investment capital of N1.5 mn. to manufacture textile and lace products. Saibō, the Japanese investor, held 20 percent of the firm's equity. With a work-force of 120 the firm registered sales value of N700,000 for 1981; producing 1.2 mn. metres of textile and 120,000 metres of lace. The firm's investment was premised on two main objectives. The first of these was to offset the trade friction between Japan and Nigeria which was making it difficult for free exports of Japanese goods to Nigeria. This reaffirms the fact that Saibō's participation in this venture was primarily due to the attraction of the huge local market. The second reason for this investment was the protection the Nigerian government gave infant industries, in the form of corporate tax reductions and exemptions, at the time. The firm was, however, in deficit by 1982, and must have lost its Japanese investments before 1985.

Bhojsons Industries Ltd., was established in November 1970 with an investment capital of N4.2 mn., of which 10.6 percent belonged to two Japanese participants. It had a work-force of 670 (according to 1980 and 1986 figures). In 1978, it registered a sale value of $2.3 mn., compared to N16.4 mn. and N24.5 mn. for 1982 and 1984, respectively. The firm either lost its Japanese participation or went out of business somewhere in the latter part of the 1980s.

General Cotton Mill Ltd. had 17.8 percent Japanese equity. With a capital of N8.4 mn. in 1980, the venture had a work-force of 2,100 and manufactured polyester and other textile goods. The venture was set up in 1973 because of the big local market, the abundant labor force and the protection given such firms by the Nigerian government. The firm must have lost its Japanese investments in the latter part of the 1980s. Another textile company that lost its Japanese equity was the Woollen and Synthetic Manufacturing Ltd. Seventeen percent of its N800,000 investment capital belonged to Kurare (11 percent) and Marubeni (6 percent). The venture was established in 1970, and had a work-force of 300 in 1980. This was down to 276 by 1982. Its products were targeted at the local market.

The intermediate sector and others

Metcome (Nigeria) Ltd. was established in 1977 with 20 percent Japanese (Nichimen) equity. The firm manufactured and sold metal products. In 1983–1985 it registered an annual sales of N17 mn., compared to over N24 mn. in 1981. Its workforce, which increased from sixty-three in 1979 to 159 in 1981, was 104 in 1986. Nichimen, the Japanese investor, was attracted by the available labor force and local market, but seemingly left the venture in the latter part of the 1980s.

Fujikura Cableworks (Nigeria) Ltd. was set up in 1979. With a work-force of 150 and 120 in 1979 and 1986 respectively, it manufactured electric and cable wires. Two Japanese investors controlled 40 percent of the firm's investment capital of N300,000 in 1986. Its annual sales figure for 1984 was N2.7 mn., compared to N6.5 mn. in 1981. The Nigerian government's protection for infant industries was a crucial incentive to the Japanese investors, although by the latter part of the 1980s they had pulled out of the venture.

Nigerian Wire Industries Ltd. was established in 1973. In 1982, it had an investment capital of N3.7 mn., compared to N2.5 mn. in 1980, and had a work-force of 400 and 700, respectively. By 1986, however, its work-force was down to 225, while maintaining its 1981 investment capital. This may prove that the overvaluation of the naira increased the cost of industrial labor and supervisory personnel, as mentioned in the analysis of the Nigerian economy earlier.[86] Mitsui Bussan had 30 percent of the shares in 1980. This went down by 10 percent between 1982 and 1986. Mitsui Bussan must have pulled out of the venture in the latter part of the 1980s.

Ninetco Ltd., which manufactured fishing nets for the local market, was particularly attracted by the availability of cheap labor. Established in 1971, its Japanese shareholders were Hirata Bōsekikō and Itōchū Shōji, who had 11.25 percent and 10 percent, respectively, of the venture's N1.2mn. investment capital. CFAO held 38 percent of the remaining shares, with 40 percent belonging to local entrepreneurs. The venture must have lost its Japanese equity holders before 1985.

Sanyō (Nigeria) Ltd. was set up in 1969, to manufacture household electrical equipment for the local market and to expand this market. It had a work-force of 482 in 1980. This went up to 540 by 1982 but was subsequently down to 405 by 1986. The firm's Japanese shareholders were Sanyō Denki (20 percent) and Marubeni (the trading company, 20 percent) who, in 1986, had 20 percent and 10 percent, respectively, of the venture's N2 mn. investment capital. The venture must have lost its Japanese shares in the latter part of the 1980s.

Elson (Nigeria) Ltd. manufactured and sold polythene. Two Japanese firms held 40 percent of the venture's N600,000 capital investment. Established in 1977, it employed a work-force of 40 in 1981, but must have lost its Japanese investors before 1985.

CMB Tōyō Glass Co. Nigeria Ltd., had only 6 percent Japanese equity holdings (belonging to Tōyō Glass of Japan), compared to 40 percent for Nigerian shareholders and 54 percent for the Metal Box of Britain. Nevertheless, the Japanese involvement in this venture 'guaranteed technical training facilities for the shop floor and technical management'.[87] The firm was noted as one of the most intensive users of local raw materials (which made up about 85 percent of total production need) to meet an average production value of N 40 mn. The venture was set up in 1975. In 1980, the firm's investment capital stood at N8.5 mn., and it had a work-force of 1,164. By 1986, however, its work-force had been drastically reduced to 674 (of whom five were Japanese), even though the firm's investment capital was twice the size it had been in 1980. The firm lost its Japanese shareholder in 1991.[88]

Japan Petroleum Co. (Nigeria) Ltd. was (according to our findings) the only Japanese investment that was established just for the purposes of prospecting for raw materials in Nigeria. It was set up in 1970 with an investment capital of ¥270,000, all of which belonged to a 'Nigerianized' Japanese firm, Nigeria Sekiyu Kaihatsu. Its work-force in 1986 was twenty-one. As with most of the above cases of divestment, it must have pulled out in the latter part of the 1980s.

Melco (Nigeria) Ltd., the last of our sample of cases, was established in 1977 (as a trading company), with a view to expanding the sales of Mitsubishi Electric's heavy electric machines in Nigeria. The latter firm and Mitsubishi Shōji (the trading company) had 25 percent and 15 percent, respectively, of the venture's N100,000 (1986) capital investment. The firm must have pulled out in the latter part of the 1980s.

One particular discernible pattern of our sample of divested firms is that almost all of them were set up in the 1970s. The exceptions were Nigerian Textile Products Ltd. which was established in 1980, and Sanyō (Nigeria) Ltd., which was set up in 1969. Of the fourteen firms, eight were set up in the early 1970s. This suggests that the boom years of the 1970s, especially the early period, with its huge oil revenues and the giant market it turned Nigeria into, attracted a significant amount of Japanese investments. The fact that all these divestments (with the exception of the case of Tōyō Glass) took place in the 1980s is also instructive. By 1981, the Nigerian economy had hit rock bottom, and it remained depressed into the latter part of the decade. Of particular importance, too, is the fact that from 1986 onwards the official exchange rate of the naira depreciated very fast in tune with government attempts to let the currency find its value in an open market. Realizing profits in any of the major foreign currencies, therefore, became extremely difficult for all the firms, since they were primarily dependent on the local market. This affected repatriation of profits very badly. Why Tōyō Glass lost its Japanese equity in 1991 is difficult to say, since the firm was seemingly doing very well.[89] It is also instructive that almost all the firms that divested were in the manufacturing sector. Only one – Japan Petroleum Co. (Nigeria) Ltd. – was involved in the extraction of raw materials. Five of those in the manufacturing sector were involved in the production of textile goods, while seven were in the intermediate sector. The remaining firm (Melco Nigeria Ltd.) was a trading company.

CONCLUSION

As demonstrated above, Japanese investments in Nigeria were hardly resource-oriented, and therefore cannot be explained by the neo-classical international trade theory of differences in factor endowments. In effect, the fact that Japan is essentially an importer of raw materials hardly contributes to Japanese investment interests in Nigeria; and the Japanese policy since the early 1970s of diversifying its sources for raw materials imports, especially energy, did not change the situation, at least with respect to Nigeria. Indeed, Japan did not import any crude oil from Nigeria after 1981, and imported very little of it in the 1970s. The point to stress here is that most of the firms with Japanese equity holdings with reasonable added value to the Nigerian economy were in the manufacturing sector, and were attracted, particularly, by Nigeria's huge market potential in the 1960s and 1970s. This reaffirms the point made earlier that the popular idea that Japan was interested primarily in the raw materials in Africa was grossly exaggerated.

Overall, Japanese equity participation in Nigeria suggests that the 'push factor' for those investments was the market, and the potential expansion of the market. It has to be noted, for example, that the establishment of the textile firms in the 1960s, in particular, was designed to circumvent the ban that the Balewa administration imposed on the imports of Japanese textile products which were extremely competitive in Nigeria, to the point of destabilizing local textile production. Table 4.4 (p. 126) does not account for these because it is based on recent data, while most of the firms which invested in Nigeria for the above reason did so in the 1960s and conceivably divested before the data was compiled. The construction companies, as pointed out, were primarily set up because of the construction boom of the 1970s. In view of all this, and the fact that hardly any of the manufacturing firms identified in this study were engaged in the promotion of exports (except Nigeria Teijin Textiles Ltd., Nigeria Wire Industries, and the Northern Textile Manufacturing which seemingly exported blankets to Japan), it has been argued that Kojima's trade-oriented theory of Japanese direct investment in developing countries is not applicable in our case. This may be attributable to the fact that, indeed, the entrepreneurial efforts of the Japanese were yet to be exerted in Nigeria. As already noted, from 1951 to 1990, Nigeria was the setting for only ninety-three Japan-related ventures, while there were only twenty-three such ventures from twenty-two Japanese firms in Nigeria, according to 1990 indicators. Most importantly, however, the case of Japanese FDI in Nigeria fails to sustain Kojima's argument that Japanese investment in a developing country endowed with natural resources would automatically reflect Japan's resource requirements. As the discussion above has shown in full, this contention cannot be sustained in the case of Japanese FDI in Nigeria. In effect, the argument is flawed. This indeed reflects on the question of Japan's CNS and how one interprets it in relation, specifically, to Nigeria.

The simplest way to interpret it is to note that the abundance of oil in Nigeria was not seen by Japanese policy makers and business executives as being relevant to Japan's national security. The alternative argument may be that because Japan was obsessed with perfecting its resource security it decided not to invest in resource procurement in a country with a rather erratic political and economic system, so as not to be dependent on a supplier who may not deliver the goods on time or who may use the goods as a political tool, as in the case of the Arab oil exporting countries in the 1970s.

The paucity of Japanese investments in Nigeria is explained through the argument that the prevailing pattern of the host country's economic structure and performance largely determines how much FDI it will receive and sustain. The poor performance of the Nigerian economy, especially from the 1980s, was largely responsible for the lack of enthusiasm on the part of potential Japanese investors. The dislocated official foreign exchange system and the lack of proper measures to counteract the growth and importance of the parallel market to the economy made most Japanese investors, as well as potential investors, lose faith in whatever fiscal and monetary policies the Nigerian government initiated. The inability of the firms to repatriate dividends was a major concern, not to mention the fact that most of these ventures were hardly making any profits, as shown by the sales of the firms surveyed above.

As has also been mentioned, labor productivity (measured by value added per worker) continued to decline from the 1970s onwards, due in part to the underutilization of capacity, infrastructure problems, and technical and managerial deficiencies. The lack of confidence in the macro-economic management skills of the country's ruling elite, and the depreciation of the naira, effectively translated into divestments, especially in the 1980s. The rate at which the firms divested in that decade was a reflection of the rather poor state of the market for consumer products, and indeed for non-tradables. Overall, the survey of firms (both those that divested and those that stayed) has shown a cautious and steadily declining interest of Japanese investors in the country. In the majority of cases, shareholders participated with a small and, indeed, decreasing share of equity. Even those firms doing very well, such as the textile firms, were gradually pulling out in the 1980s.

Yanaihara's point about Japanese firms in Africa being temporary in nature is, seemingly, a fact that reflects the state of the African economies, rather than indicating that Japanese firms are that way by design. It is merely a result of the fact that the economies in which the firms were located in sub-Saharan Africa were unable to sustain them. And as long as the Nigerian economy remained as it was, Japanese firms were bound to maintain their 'temporary character' in it.

On the whole, the analysis shows that Japanese investment interests in Nigeria (as demonstrated by this case study) were determined more by the prospects of expanding the investor's share of the local market than by any interest in raw materials, and therefore were not positively relevant to Japan's conception of its CNS policy.

NOTES

1 Most of Japan's investments in this region were concentrated in the finance and insurance sectors, in tax havens.

2 A large percentage of these investments were located in the real estate sector, while a sizeable amount of it was also in the automobile industry through joint ventures with US car makers in Australia.

3 Japan External Trade Organization, *White Paper on FDI – Foreign Direct Investment Promoting Restructuring of Economy Worldwide Summary*, Tokyo, March, 1991, p. 1

4 Ministry of Finance, *Annual Report of International Affairs*, Tokyo, 1991.

5 Gaimushō, *Wagakuni gaikō no kinkyō, 1973*, vol. 2, Tokyo, 1974.

6 Satō Yurie and Ishizaki Eriko, 'Afurika to nihon', *Afurika repōto*, Tokyo, Ajia keizai kenkyūjo, No. 12, 1991, p. 17.

7 John Cantwell, 'Foreign Multinationals and Industrial Development in Africa', in Peter Buckley and Jeremy Clegg (eds.), *Multinational Enterprises in Less Developed Countries*, London, Macmillan, 1991, p. 196.

8 Tom Forrest points out that 'in terms of scale of individual enterprises, the degree of corporate organization and the size and diversity of investment, Nigerian private capital has advanced well beyond African enterprise in Kenya, the Ivory Coast, Zimbabwe, and other sub-Saharan African countries'. See Tom Forrest, 'The Advance of African Capital: The Growth of Nigerian Private Enterprises', *Ld'A – QEH Development Studies Working Papers*, no. 24, 1990.

9 Of the mineral resources mentioned in the text (coal, tin ore, colombite, crude oil and natural gas), few had entered, or had (at the time of writing) the potentials for entering the mainstream of international market transactions. Coal was mined primarily for domestic consumption, and by the 1980s tin ore production in particular had lost its importance as a competitive mineral commodity on the international market. The same goes for columbite. The country's natural gas was only 3 percent of the world reserve. Crude oil, therefore, was the only resource with much value on the international market and, undoubtedly, had been the mainstay of the Nigerian economy since the early 1970s. There seemed, however, to be a certain amount of Japanese interest in the exploration of natural gas in Nigeria.

10 Tōyō keizia, *Kaigai shinshutsu kigyō sōran*, Tokyo, Shinpōsha, 1986, pp. 438–440.

11 'Furēzā kokuren ichiji sanhin mondai senmon gurūpu iinchō to kondan, *Keidanren shūhō*, No. 1967, 4 September, 1989.

12 'Afurika keizai seminā o kaisai', *Keidanren shūhō*, no. 1939, February, 1989.

13 Edward V.K. Jaycox (Vice-President, Africa Region, The World Bank), 'Japan's Role in African Development: Challenges and Opportunities', keynote address to the Africa Symposium, Keidanren kaikan, Tokyo, 27–28 October 1988.

14 1986 indicators show that Japanese firms were prospecting for oil and other raw materials in Zaire from 1973 and 1971, respectively. A Japanese company, Kaigai uran shigen kaihatsu, had (according to 1986 indicators) 25 percent

equity of a firm prospecting for uranium in Niger. The investment was set up in 1974. See Tōyō keizai, *Kaigai shinshutsu kigyō sōran*, 1986, p. 440; Tōyō keizai, *kaigai shinshutsu kigyō sōran*, 1993, p. 1031.

15 Cantwell, 'Foreign Multinationals and Industrial Development in Africa, p. 197.

16 Tom Forrest, however, thinks that the existence of a large literature on plans in Nigeria give a totally false impression of the importance of planning in the Nigerian economy. He insists that there has never been a planning mechanism in Nigeria. Tom Forrest, *Politics and Economic Development in Nigeria*, San Franscisco, Westview Press, 1993, p. 141.

17 World Bank, *Nigeria, Industrial Sector Report: Restructuring Policies for Competitiveness and Export Growth, Vol. II: Main Report*, Washington DC., 13 July 1990, p. 1.

18 Ibid.

19 Brian Pinto, 'Nigeria During and After the Oil Boom: A Policy Comparison with Indonesia', *The World Bank Economic Review*, vol. 1, 1987, p. 420.

20 Ibid. p. 422.

21 Gavin Williams, 'The World Bank in Rural Nigeria, Revisited: A Review of the World Bank's Nigeria: Agricultural Sector Review 1987', *Review of African Political Economy*, no. 43, 1988, p. 43.

22 This can occur due to a rise in the real wage in terms of tradables and a fall in terms of non-tradables. Forrest, *Politics and Economic Development in Nigeria*, pp. 183–87, however, argues that the issue of agrarian stagnation and crisis in Nigeria during this period was grossly exaggerated. In his review of the World Bank's (1987) report *Nigeria: Agricultural Sector Review, Vol. I, Main Report*, Williams, 'The World Bank in Rural Nigeria, Revisited', shows how seriously flawed are some of the methods and arguments used by the World Bank.

23 R. A. Akindele, 'The Domestic Structure and National Resources Profile of Nigeria's External Trade', in R. A. Akindele and Ate E. Bassey (eds.), *Nigeria's Economic Relations with the Major Developed Market-economy Countries, 1960–1985*, Lagos, The Nigerian Institute of International Affairs, 1988, p. 62.

24 Gavin Williams, 'The World Bank in Rural Nigeria, Revisited', p. 46.

25 Bukar Bukarambe, 'Nigeria's Economic Relations with Japan: The Direct and Indirect', in Akindele and Bassey (eds.), *Nigeria's Economic Relations*, p. 266.

26 Ibid.

27 Pinto, 'Nigeria During and After the Oil Boom', p. 438.

28 Ibid., pp. 438–439.

29 Ibid., p. 439.

30 Ibid., p. 441.

31 Interview with Mr. T. Hidaka, in Lagos, 22 August 1991.

32 Pinto 'Nigeria During and After the Oil Boom', p. 441.

33 Ibid.

34 World Bank, *Nigeria, Industrial Sector Report*, 1990, p. 3.

35 Ibid. p. 4.

36 It is interesting to note that the industry's revival coincided with the revival (since 1986) of cotton production in Nigeria after over a decade of decline. 'Nigerian cotton', as Williams, 'The World Bank in Rural Nigeria, Revisited', footnote 4, tells us, 'was mainly consumed by the Nigerian Textile Industry'.

37 World Bank, *Nigeria: Industrial Sector Report*, 1990, p. 22.

38 Keith Marsden and Theresa Belot, *Private Enterprise in Africa: Creating a Better Environment, World Bank Discussion Paper, No. 17*, Washington D.C., 1988, p. 16.

39 The 1986 publication of Tōyō Keizai, *Kaigiai shinshutsu kigyō sōran*, stated that the venture had been put on hold (*kyūgyō chū*). See also 'UAC, Japanese Firm in Joint Venture', *Daily Times*, 3 May, 1984, p. 2.

40 Forrest, *Politics and Economic Development in Nigeria*, p. 177.

41 Interview with Mr. Ishihara Kenichi, in Lagos, 20 August 1991.

42 Marsden and Belot, *Private Enterprise in Africa: Creating a Better Environment, World Bank Discussion Paper, No. 17*, Washington D.C., 1988, p. 19.

43 Ibid.

44 Yanaihara Katsu, 'Japanese Overseas Enterprises in Developing Countries Under Indigenization Policy: The African Case', *Japanese Economic Studies*, vol. 4, no. 1, 1975.

45 'Japanese Industrialists in Nigeria Praised', *New Nation*, 7 June 1971, p. 18.

46 Paul Collier, 'The Role of the African State in Building Agencies of Restraint', Nigeria–Japan Association mimeograph of the Centre for the Study of African Economies, Oxford, 1995, p. 2.

47 Ibid.

48 Nigeria–Japan Association, Notes on the first meeting of the members of Nigeria–Japan Association and the Delegation of Japan–Nigeria Association, Lagos, 4 October 1990, p. 2.

49 Marsden and Belot, *Private Enterprise in Africa*, p. 16.

50 Exchange rate value of (Nigerian Pounds (NP)/naira (N) to the $US: 1961–1970, US$1= NP 2.80; 1971, US$1= NP 3.04; 1973, US$1= N 1.52; 1974–1980, US $1= N 1.26–1.36; 1985, US $1= N 1.09; 1986, US $1= N4.05; 1987, US$1= N5.87; 1988–1991, US$1 = N7.20–14.10.

51 Tōyō keizai, *Kaigai shinshutsu kigyō sōran*, 1992, p. 40.

52 Yanaihara, 'Japanese Overseas Enterprises in Developing Countries', pp. 27–28.

53 In 1969, Mr. Hara of the Export–Import Bank of Japan announced in Lagos a loan of $10 mn. that the Japanese government was to make to Nigeria, to be paid back in eighteen years. He also 'disclosed that [the] bank had decided to invest large sums of money in some industrial establishments in Nigeria.' See *Morning Post*, 16 June 1969, p. 3.

54 James Talabi, 'On Japan and Nigeria', *Daily Times*, 11 August 1979, p. 3. Mr. Talabi was employed at the Japanese Embassy, Lagos.

55 As noted in Chapter 2, heavy import quotas and tax were imposed on Japanese exports to West Africa by the British colonial governments of the region in the early 1930s. See Kweku Ampiah, 'British Commercial Policies Against Japanese Expansionism in East and West Africa, 1932–1935', *The International Journal of African Historical Studies*, vol. 23, no. 4, 1990.

56 Peter Kilby, *Industrialization in an Open Economy: Nigeria, 1945–1966*, London, Cambridge University Press, 1969, p. 110.

57 Ibid., p. 112.

58 Akindele, 'The Domestic Structure and National Resources Profile of Nigeria's External Trade'.

59 Kilby, *Industrialization in an Open Economy*, p. 112.

60 *Sunday Post*, 18 February 1968, p. 1.

61 'Nigeria Angry', *Sunday Times*, 19 March 1967.
62 'Trade with Japan to Improve Fast', *Morning Post*, 28 July 1969, p. 3; 'Ban on Jap[anese] Goods Won't Be Lifted Till . . .' *Daily Sketch*, 27 June 1970; 'Trade Not Aid', *Daily Times*, 17 December 1971, p. 3; 'Growth of Industrial Ties with the Japanese', *Daily Times*, 8 January 1972, p. 14. This was a response from the Japanese Embassy: 'Japan Out to Correct Trade Imbalance with Nigeria', *Morning Post*, 21 December 1971, p. 16; 'Japan May Buy Nigerian Oil', *Daily Sketch*, 4 October 1972.
63 See Table 4.5 (p. 128) for a list of some of the ventures.
64 Kilby, *Industrialization in an Open Economy*, (footnote 1) p. 115.
65 Federal Ministry of Information, 'Nigeria Reconciles with Japan', *News Release*, No. 1145, Lagos, 8 October 1975.
66 Kilby, *Industrialization in an Open Economy*, p. 115.
67 Ibid., p. 111.
68 Tōyō keizai, *Kaigai shishutsu kigyō sōran*, 1992, p. 1000.
69 Ibid.
70 Tōyō keizai, *Kaigai shinshutsu kigyo sōran*, 1992, p. 1000.
71 Ibid.
72 Ibid.
73 Tōyō keizai, *Kaigai shinshutsu kigyō sōran*, 1986; Tōyō keizai, *Kaigai shinshutsu kigyō sōran*, 1993.
74 Ibid.
75 Ibid.
76 Tōyō keizai, *Kaigai shinshutsu kigyō sōran*, 1991, p. 1001.
77 Ibid.
78 Ibid.
79 *Guardian*, 13 November 1984, p. 15.
80 The trading companies in Nigeria at the time of writing were Nichimen Co. (Nigeria) Ltd., Nishizawa (Nigeria) Ltd., Tōmen (Nigeria) Ltd., Nissho Iwai (Nigeria) Ltd., Marubeni (Nigeria) Ltd., Sumitomo Shōji Kaisha (Nigeria) Ltd., MBK (Nigeria)Ltd., Mitsubishi Shōji Kaisha (Nigeria) Ltd., and NEC (Nigeria) Ltd. The first two companies started operating in 1969. The third company was set up in 1970. The rest were either established in the late 1970s or the early 1980s. These firms were all subsidiaries of their parent companies in Japan. They were set up as local entities ('Nigerianized' Japanese outfits) for the purposes of circumventing the Nigerian Enterprises Promotion Decree, 1977, which classified certain ventures (with small-scale equity) as businesses exclusively reserved for 100-percent Nigerian ownership. The only other venture in the service industry with Japanese equity participation was the Fire Equity and General Insurance Co. Ltd., which was set up in 1983. Japanese participation in this venture was obviously designed to attract the Japanese firms operating in Nigeria, and to take advantage of the government's protection policy in favor of small firms. Mitsui Kaijō Kasai Hoken held 15 percent of the company's ¥2 mn. (up 100 percent from 1986) investment capital. The company employed nineteen (compared to eight in 1986) workers in 1992. In 1990 it had an annual turnover of over N15 mn.
81 Peter J. Buckley, 'A Critical View of Theories of the Multinational Enterprise', in Peter J. Buckley and M. Casson, *The Economic Theory of Multinational Enterprise*, London, Macmillan, 1985, p. 17.

82 Interview with Mr. Yamamoto Yoshimichi, Managing Director, MBK (Nigeria) Ltd., in Lagos, in August 1991.
83 Interview with Mr. Iida Yōsuke, Senior Staff, Energy and Chemical Project Department, Marubeni Corporation. The interview took place in Lagos, in August 1991.
84 Interview with Mr. Yamamoto Yoshimichi, in Lagos, in August 1991.
85 *Nigeria–Japan Economic Newsletter*, Lagos, January, 1970.
86 World Bank, *Nigeria, Industrial Sector Report*, p. 3.
87 *Guardian*, 13 November 1984, p. 7.
88 *Financial Times*, 1 April 1993, p. vii.
89 Ibid.

5   Voting for economic security
Japan and the apartheid debate at the UNGA

In order to preserve and rationalize its dependence on South Africa for the strategic resources discussed in the previous chapters, the UNGA, ironically, served as a very useful conduit for Japan's policy makers. Not least because the UN, despite its faults and weaknesses, embodies procedures to which nation-states may increasingly repair in matters of profound importance to them. Yet, like most diplomats at the UNGA, Japan's representatives unfailingly pledged their country's support to the international community's efforts to abolish apartheid. And they continually made reference, from the moment of Japan's admission to the United Nations in 1956, to Japan's request in 1919 at the League of Nations for the inclusion of a racial equality clause in the League's Charter as proof of Japan's committed position against apartheid. As Mr. Nishibori, Japanese representative at the 35th Session of the General Assembly in 1980, said at that session, for example 'the people and the government of Japan whole-heartedly support the principle of racial equality which "we" argued for, to no avail, in 1919'. And, like his predecessors, he stated that Japan 'vehemently oppose[s] South Africa's policies of apartheid because they are nothing more than blatant, institutionalized racial discrimination, depriving the overwhelming majority of people in South Africa of their fundamental human rights and dignity'.[1] That Japan opposed apartheid in principle is unquestionable, not least because it in principle allowed for discrimination against Japanese nationals.

To some observers, however, the quoted position of the Japanese government was simply part of Japan's exhibitionist – rather than completely engaged – diplomacy.[2] In essence, it was merely rhetorical. Some of these observers[3] maintained that Japan failed to translate its words into deeds. In his analysis of Japan's voting behavior in the UNGA on 'issues of colonial and human rights', for example, Matsumoto Saburō concludes that Japan's performance isolated it within the Afro-Asian bloc.[4] Using a total of 143 roll-call votes selected from seven General Assemblies between the eleventh assembly of December 1956, and the seventeenth, in 1962, Matsumoto's study identifies Japan as often being pro-American and anti-Soviet; and somewhere in between in its relationship with India and the United Arab Republic.

On the other hand, Ogata Sadako, a veteran diplomat and an academic, and Saitō Shizuō,[5] point out that from 1960 to 1985 Japan voted with the non-aligned countries more often than it did with the USA.[6] Ogata further argues that 'there seemed to be no direct link between Japan's relations with the US and its global agenda in the United Nations'; even though she acknowledges that 'the interests of Tokyo and Washington largely overlap[ped]'.[7] In a similar vein, Saitō contends, for example, that 'Japan . . . maintained an independent stance with regard to the issue of South Africa', and identifies Japan as a moderating force in its diplomacy at the UN.[8] He attributes this voluntary role as a moderator partly to the 'wish to ensure stable supplies of natural resources and markets for Japan's exports'. The different arguments and propositions highlighted above alone suggest that it is time to look at Japan's votes at the UNGA on apartheid issues, and attempt to answer the questions they present. By defining the specific issue areas within the apartheid debate and looking at them individually, this study attempts to move beyond general statements (such as those above) regarding Japan's position on apartheid, and should allow us to establish that the Japanese attitude on this issue was far more complicated than is commonly assumed. But it also throws light on Japan's determination to ensure its economic and ultimately national security interests.

Indeed, a detailed investigation of Japan's voting behavior at the UN General Assembly in relation to apartheid issues is of the essence, particularly on the question of how Japan's voting reflected on its interest in the strategic resources under South Africa's control. But before the reasons behind Japan's voting behavior can be properly assessed, it is necessary to trace the evolution of the apartheid debate at the UNGA and to develop a quantitative analysis of Japan's votes on apartheid-related issues. The key question is: how far were Japan's votes on the apartheid issue influenced by questions pertaining to its economic interests?

A brief mention of the methodology used for the quantitative analysis is also warranted here. At a general level, Japan's votes on the above issue are compared with those of the USA, Norway and Sweden (Western countries), on the one hand, and the voting pattern of the selected AA (Afro-Asian) countries, on the other. The Asian states selected for the study are India, Pakistan and the Philippines, whereas the African states are represented by the members of the FLA (Frontline States of Southern

Africa). Essentially, Japan's votes on the chosen issue area(s) are analyzed with the view to answering two main questions. First, did Japan vote with the African states more often than with the USA, the leading opponent of anti-apartheid proposals at the General Assembly?[9] Second, what was the incidence of Japan's voting with the African states as compared with its incidence of voting with the USA, and the three Asian states selected for our study? The crucial subject-matter for investigation that runs through the two questions is whether Japan in fact fulfilled its promise to 'vehemently oppose' apartheid in support of the overwhelming majority of people in South Africa, as one of its UN representatives put it.[10] To answer this question, Japan's voting behavior in relation to roll call and recorded votes on apartheid resolutions in the General Assembly from 1973 to 1986 is examined. The total of 108 votes examined are selected from the UNGA's Plenary Meetings.[11]

In relation to the Asian states selected for the study, it is important to note that their ideological orientations differed within the context of the Cold War, as demonstrated by their relations with the superpowers, the USA and the USSR. India was a professed non-aligned country. Pakistan and the Philippines on the other hand, like Japan, were close allies of the USA. However, Japan's vote is compared with those of Norway and Sweden, because these are the Northern European countries often referred to as demonstrating a similar political outlook to that of Japan at the UN.

As for the African states, the FLS is used as a representative sample of the OAU (Organization of African Unity) because they comprise a smaller number of countries and are therefore easily manageable for this analysis. Most important, however, is the fact that the 'diplomatic work of the OAU in Southern Africa [was] undertaken by the FLS . . . and the fact that at the UN Africa follow[ed] the guidelines laid down by the OAU which delegated policy-making to the frontline states'.[12] The FLS was a political alliance comprising Tanzania, Zambia, Botswana, Mozambique, Angola and Zimbabwe.

Finally, the cases of Pakistan and the Philippines are used to show that alliance with the USA, especially in relation to the East–West divisions, did not necessarily affect the satellite states' voting behavior on apartheid issues.[13] Thus, despite their ideological orientation, which was similar to Japan's (Tokyo and Manila had common defense arrangements with Washington), as pointed out in the discussion on the Bandung conference in Chapter 2, they voted very differently from Japan, and indeed from the USA, on the issues examined here. It should be further established, through more discussion of the literature on bloc politics, that a variety of factors influence the voting pattern of states at the UNGA.

METHODOLOGY

The votes selected in the attempts to answer the above questions were analyzed in three issue areas: 1) political; 2) economic; 3) cultural. These are further broken down into sub-issue areas. In developing an index to measure the degree of voting agreement between Japan and the countries mentioned above it was useful to adopt and apply the 'Z score of agreement' (ZSA) used by Trong R. Chai in his study of Chinese voting in the General Assembly.[14]

What the ZSA of a country does, it is important to mention, is to show the degree of agreement in voting between Japan and that country. It cannot indicate, however, whether Japan supported that country, or vice versa. And it also manifests another humbling truth at this point in the development of voting analysis: it says nothing that can be reliable about the motivations or reasons for the two countries voting together. In the second section of the chapter an attempt is made to make up for this shortcoming through an examination of statements by Japanese representatives at the UNGA. A short exploration of the discussion on bloc politics will be useful at this stage.

BLOC POLITICS AT THE UNITED NATIONS GENERAL ASSEMBLY

According to Thomas Hovet 'by the very nature of the United Nations Organization bloc politics has assumed an emphatic role in the conduct of the General Assembly as an inevitable feature of representative political body'.[15] He defines a bloc/group broadly as 'any political group of states operating as units in the General Assembly – ranging from those with formal organizations and binding commitment to those with no organization and only with like areas of interest'.[16] The need to establish a consensus on major issues of importance to their individual states is what brings the members of the UNGA to the idea of participating in bloc politics. Hovet identifies different categories of pressure groups within the body politic of the General Assembly: blocs, caucusing groups, geographical distribution groups, regional organizational groups, common interest groups, and temporary groups.[17]

He perceives a bloc as comprising a group of states that meet regularly, and the members of which are bound in their votes in the UNGA by the caucus decision. According to this definition, however, the only existing true bloc during the period under review was the Soviet bloc. Arend Lijphart, on the other hand, argues that all the non-caucusing blocs and groups can quite justifiably be called blocs.[18] Thus, although the FLS did not always vote the same way, it is, nevertheless, considered as a bloc in this study; without forgetting of course that its members were in reality members of the African bloc, and therefore members of the Afro-Asian bloc. The complex nature of bloc politics in international organizations will be examined more closely in the course of this analysis. Suffice to say, analysts of the theories of international politics as already alluded to in the introductory chapter, suggest racial, economic, geographic and military variables, among others, at work in influencing voting patterns of states at the GA.[19]

This multidimensional conflict process in the UNGA is perfectly illustrated by Conor Cruise O'Brien's exposé on Assembly (bloc) politics in *To Katanga and Back*. As he points out,

> Most of the small countries have to exercise considerable discretion in the way they vote, because of their ties – very often coercive ties – with this or that power. [Yet] . . . Apart from genuine satellites, like Bulgaria and El Salvador, there are other cases where reasonably safe predictions may be made, but on the basis of a more complex calculus. Thus Pakistan, say, likes, as a member of CENTO, to vote with the West, but is also sensitive to Afro-Asian opinion, particularly sensitive to opinion in Moslem countries and strong on self-determination . . . A Western canvasser can therefore safely count on Pakistan's vote in a direct East– West controversy . . . but must make separate calculations if relevant racial, religious or colonial factors are involved. For example, in a colonialist issue, where the Moslem factor tells on the colonialist side (Cyprus), or where the Kashmir issue comes into play (Goa), the West may reasonably expect Pakistan's support. On the other hand, on a straight racial issue (apartheid), or an issue where a Western power is, or has been, in conflict with Moslem population . . . Pakistan will be indistinguishable from the most anti-colonialist Afro-Asians. On issues where both anti-colonialism and the cold war are involved . . . accurate prediction of a Pakistan vote becomes impossible.[20]

In short, 'agreement in voting may be caused either by similar attitudes or by group pressure and loyalty'.[21]

It may be helpful then to look at some activities of the AA group, in an attempt to understand at least some aspects of the convoluted politics in the Assembly. This group is, incidentally, a good guide to understanding bloc politics, given its size and its enormous diversity, not to mention its lack of orthodoxy. The AA group meets regularly to consult on substantive issues and related procedural matters before the sessions of the Assembly. The meetings are, however, confined to those issues on which the majority of the group has a common view, to avoid escalating divisions within the group. Hovet notes that the real function of the AA is to bring its members together formally so that those having special interests in common can consult conveniently.[22] In this sense, the AA group might be considered to have certain factions which operate within it; 'factions which are not hard and fast but represent poles within the group'.[23] To substantiate the above point Hovet informs us that in the 11th, 12th, and the 13th Sessions, India and Japan operated 'as polar states within the group'; and that Japan appeared to be closer to Thailand, the Philippines and some of the Middle Eastern states.[24]

Lijphart's work substantiates this. His analysis of voting alignments on colonial issues at the UNGA show, among other things, that among the non-Arab Asian members of the AA caucusing group, the degree of voting cohesion varies. The indices of agreement that he derived using quantitative analysis shows that 'Laos and Turkey were only marginal members'. Ceylon [Sri Lanka], India, and Nepal on the other hand were part of a small voting bloc with a 90-percent cohesion. Lijphart's findings further show that the AA group also included two voting blocs at the 80-percent level (one composed of the three states above plus Afghanistan, Burma, Iran and Indonesia). The other composed of Japan, the Philippines and Thailand. There was also an overlapping voting bloc at the 70-percent level.[25] Suffice to say, the ideological link between Japan and the Philippines, for example, has been reasonably assessed in the discussion on the Bandung conference.

As noted in that discussion, the historical background of the AA group reveals that the group evolved out of the Bandung conference of 1955. Thus, it comprises most of the world's poorer and less developed countries in Asia and Africa, many of which share bitter recollections of colonialism and are determined to create better life chances for their people's in a world dominated by what they see as powerful countries with further imperialist intentions. Yet the cohesion of the AA group was far from complete, obviously because of the polarized nature of world politics at the time. An examination of the development of the apartheid debate at the UNGA should help clarify some of the conflicting trends as represented by the different groupings.

THE EVOLUTION OF THE APARTHEID DEBATE AT THE UNGA

The first complaint against the Union of South Africa on this issue was made by India in 1946, when, at the very first session of the UNGA, the Indian representative initiated the debate on how South Africa was officially discriminating against its 285,000 citizens of Indian origin. It may be useful to note at this stage that to traverse the evolution and development of the fight against apartheid at the UNGA, from its early stages to the mid-1980s, Mohammed El-Khawas' seminal paper concerning the opening of the apartheid debate and the phases that it went through cannot be ignored.[26] It is also important that the study draws on the work of N.M. Stultz work which builds on El-Khawas' by analysing the issues beyond 1960, where the latter ends his study, to 1984.[27]

The apartheid debate, as the term is used here, refers to the efforts of the UNGA first to coax and later to coerce the government of South Africa to abolish 'its use of legal, institutionalized segregation by race in order to organize society by a racial-ethnic hierarchy at every level'.[28] Merle Lipton identifies four defining idiosyncratic features of apartheid that distinguished it from other forms of discriminatory practices:

> First, it [was] the hierarchical ordering of the whole social, economic and political structure of South African society on the basis of statutorily defined race ... Secondly, apartheid involves systematic political and economic discrimination against all blacks, but particularly against Africans. Thirdly, it involved segregation of the races not only politically and economically but also socially, particularly in housing and social services, including education and health care. Fourthly, apartheid [was] the legalization and institutionalization of this hierarchical discriminatory and segregated system.[29]

These invariably provided the moral justification for the overwhelming international campaign against apartheid.

Historians and social scientists agree that a strong determinant and supporter of the above system was capitalism, but most essential is the fact that the triumvirate of economics, politics and ideology operated together in making apartheid effective and meaningful to those whose interests it served. In view of this, Ali Khan contends that 'the struggle against apartheid must also have economic, political and ideological dimensions'.[30] How much of each of these recipes was to be enforced in an assessment of the problem is difficult to say, but an attempt will be made here to see which of the three was the most divisive of the Assembly members in the struggle against apartheid in the UN; and consequently which of these Japan was more inclined to support. As has been noted several times already, it was the economic factor that prevailed decisively on Japan's votes, especially on the question of comprehensive sanctions against South Africa.

For several years after the initial introduction of the apartheid debate until 1952, the Assembly's handling of the matter was restricted to the question of discrimination against people of Indian origin. The debate was, however, subsequently broadened, and featured in every UN session except the 19th in 1964. That, in a way, confirmed the 'Afro-Asian tendency to regard the UN not so much as an organization primarily designed to ensure peace and security – as the big powers intended it to be – but as an organization which should be primarily concerned with human rights at large'.[31] In that event, apartheid, needless to say, became the most emotionally charged single issue in the politics of the UN.

The dynamism of the international political climate of the 1960s brought with it persistent inquiry into the domestic affairs of the Republic of South Africa and diatribe against it. The Security Council passed Resolution 134 on 1 April 1960, condemning apartheid for the first time, in response to the Sharpville massacre of 21 March 1960, where sixty-seven Africans were shot and several hundred demonstrators were wounded by the South African police. Resolution 134 stipulated that the situation in South Africa was one that led to international friction, and if continued might endanger international peace and security. It also demanded that the government of South Africa initiate measures to bring about racial harmony in the country.

At the 50th Plenary Meeting of the General Assembly on 8 December 1946, when the first vote on South Africa's racial policy took place, South Africa argued that the UN had no legal right to debate the matter. With the support of the USA, seven European or other Commonwealth states, and six Latin American countries, it almost defeated the resolution, since substantively important questions at the UNGA must be approved by a two-thirds' majority. The argument of those against the resolution was that the UN had no authority to intervene in matters which were essentially within the domestic jurisdiction of any state. When, on 5 December 1952, the competency issue came up again, this time even the USA, together with forty-four other states, voted in favor of it against six states, including South Africa. From then on the question of UN jurisdiction over apartheid remained settled, even though it crept up again in November 1959.

El-Khawas points out that from 1946 to 1960 the evolution of the apartheid issue at the UNGA went through two main phases. The first of these was the establishment of the UNGA's competence, politically, to consider South Africa's domestic policy of racial discrimination. The second was the Assembly's success in discrediting the strategy of compromise (with South Africa) as the only appropriate means of influencing Pretoria on the race question; leading to the Assembly's adoption of coercion as an instrument to prevail on Pretoria to change its racist laws. An examination of the Assembly's early declarations in relation to apartheid, compared to declarations on the topic in the 1970s and 1980s, shows that the tone of the early declarations 'was in retrospect remarkably civil reflecting a feeling that the issue might be resolved through conciliation'.[32] What is crucial to note here is that the change in the UNGA's attitude did not in any way result in a change of heart on the part of Pretoria; it remained obstinate and showed no signs of compromise.

As noted, it was the events in Sharpville, resulting in the enactment of Security Council Resolution 134, which condemned apartheid as a threat to international peace and security. In conjunction with this event was the sudden increase in the early 1960s in the representation of Africa[33] in the UN. These two factors dramatically altered the relaxed nature of the debate on apartheid in the UNGA; increasing the pressure on the world body to attempt, without compromising, to resolve the situation in South Africa. In essence, the African states demonstrated, without pulling any punches, their dissatisfaction with the UN's approach to resolving the problem. El-Khawas quotes Collet Michel (Guinea's representative to the UN) as saying: 'The UN could not continue . . . to content itself with the annual adoption of moderate resolutions which were not carried out'.[34] The message of the African states was that the Western states' supposition that apartheid could not be ended, or significantly modified, except with the active cooperation of the South African government was unacceptable. In fact, the African states perceived this argument as an excuse to do nothing about the problem.

Worse still, the newly independent states saw the Western states as collaborators with South Africa's racial discrimination policy, and so pointed out in GA Resolution 1761 (XVII) in 1962 that 'the actions of some of the member states indirectly provide encouragement to the Government of South Africa to perpetuate its policy of racial segregation'. In the same resolution the Assembly strongly denounced 'the continued and total disregard by the Government of South Africa of its obligations under the Charter of the United Nations'. With time the Assembly's language became stronger and more offensive, as El-Khawas and Stultz point out. In Resolution 36/6 I, enacted in 1976, the Assembly stated that the 'situation in South Africa constitutes a grave threat to international peace and security'; and proclaimed that the 'racist regime of South Africa is illegitimate and has no right to represent the people of South Africa'. In the same breath it accused France, the UK and the USA of using their veto power in the Security Council to 'protect the racist regime of South Africa'.

By 1977, in Resolution 32/105 J, the Assembly, without mincing words, reaffirmed the legitimacy of the struggle of the national liberation movement in South Africa against the regime. It declared that 'the national liberation movement has an inalienable right to continue its struggle for the seizure of power by all available . . . means . . . including armed struggle'. In contrast to earlier resolutions in the 1950s – which 'regretted' the Union government's refusal to cooperate with the United Nations to end apartheid, 'invited' that government to reconsider its position and 'called' upon Pretoria to recognize its obligations as a member of the UN – the Assembly had become substantially radicalized, and certainly anxious to deal with the problem of injustice and racial discrimination in the international scheme of things. As will be shown later in this analysis, Japan remained consistently opposed to the Assembly's support for armed struggle by the liberation movements against Pretoria.

The confrontational approach adopted by the Assembly came with certain coercive measures that its sponsors hoped, with proper support, would force Pretoria to respond positively to international demands. The coercive measures included political and economic sanctions designed to isolate South Africa. For example, a motion tabled by the African states in the Special Political Committee (April 1961) appealed to the member states to break diplomatic relations with South Africa, close their ports to its vessels, forbid their own ships from entering South African ports, boycott all South African goods, cease exporting to South Africa and refuse landing rights to South Africa. The motion, however, failed to obtain the required two-thirds support, with only forty-two states in favor, thirty-four against and twenty-one abstentions. In Resolution 1761 (XVII)[35] of 1962, however, the Assembly, in addition to all the above demands, specifically exhorted the members not to export any form of arms and ammunition to South Africa. This resolution passed with sixty-seven votes in favor, sixteen against and twenty-three abstentions.

These developments clearly exposed the philosophical and ideological division within the world body. As El-Khawas notes 'between 1960 and 1962 the Assembly remained divided on the new turn of events'.[36] The Assembly was extremely divided on all votes taken on these African proposals and up to one-third of the delegates of the developing countries – mainly Asian – failed to vote in favor of punitive measures against South Africa when it had to vote on the above-mentioned Special Political Committee motion for sanctions; especially on the operative paragraph specifying the sanctions. Thus, the resolution was withdrawn, and was subsequently passed in the UNGA without the proposal for sanctions. According to El-Khawas, however, the Asian states were fundamentally in agreement with their African colleagues, but (at this point) only differed in their choice of strategy. They showed their hesitation by simply abstaining from voting, although Japan and Turkey voted against the proposals. This suggests that since the early 1960s the economic motive, especially in the area of raw materials procurement, was the driving-force behind Japan's attitude to the apartheid question.

In fact, the Assembly remained divided even after 1962 on the question of punitive measures. However, the post-1962 division was essentially between the Western countries (including Japan) and a few Third World countries on the one hand, and the Afro-Asian countries and the socialist states, on the other. It was Resolution 1761 (XVII) that highlighted Afro-Asian solidarity, and by so doing exposed the 'hard-core' opponents of sanctions. 'These included all but two of South Africa's ten highest ranking trading partners, in order of importance (1961 figures): the UK, USA, Japan, France, Belgium, the Netherlands, Canada, and Australia. (The missing trading partners were West Germany, which would not become a member of the UN until 1973, and Italy, which abstained).'[37] The other hard-core opponents of sanctions were Spain, Portugal, Turkey, Luxembourg, Greece, New Zealand, Ireland and, of course, South Africa. It is therefore not surprising at all that, referring to a report of the Special Committee, Mr. Ackah, the Guinean representative at the UNGA in 1965, stated that 'the primary responsibility for the failure of the UN's efforts must be borne by the major trading partners of South Africa, including several permanent members of the Security Council'.[38]

The report revealed a variety of activities between the Western countries and South Africa, including military assistance from France, Italy, the UK and the USA, and further disclosed, surprisingly, that Japan was contemplating the sale of arms to the South African government. It also set forth an accusation to the effect that, between 1959 and 1964, West Germany had increased its trade with Pretoria by 69 percent, Italy by 83 percent, and Japan by 182 percent. The Guinean delegation 'was particularly shocked by such a selfish attitude on the part of Japan, which aspired to represent the Afro-Asian states on the Security Council',[39] and Mr. Ackah warned Japan that its attitude towards the people of South Africa would not be forgotten.

Speaking for most of the African states, the Guinean representative stated clearly that South Africa's disrespectful attitude towards the Assembly's resolutions was due to its conviction that its main trading partners had no respect for the resolutions. This was confirmed by South Africa's Prime Minister H. F. Verwoerd, in a statement to the effect that the resolutions calling for sanctions caused no great concern in South Africa, 'since so many of the countries who really count do not want to let themselves in for this kind of foolishness'.[40]

Since the 1970s, the UN's records showed a dramatic increase in UNGA resolutions dealing exclusively with apartheid. Whereas there was a total of fourteen such resolutions considered by the UNGA from 1963 through to the end of 1969, the number of such resolutions jumped to seven in 1970 alone. And throughout the 1970s, the number of resolutions focused exclusively on apartheid was 105. From the standpoint of those proposing these resolutions, therefore, the 1970s marked a real change in their overt confrontationist legislative strategy against Pretoria.[41] And since that period the goal of the Assembly had been to isolate South Africa. This is demonstrated in its major resolutions with respect to South Africa which, over the years, called for:

- an end to military and nuclear collaboration;
- comprehensive economic sanctions;
- an oil embargo;
- effective mandatory sanctions;
- a world conference on sanctions;
- a sports boycott;
- an end to foreign investments in South Africa;
- curtailing the activities of transnational corporations;
- a cultural boycott, and so on.

Obviously, these did not all elicit the same level of dissent. The voting records show that the least popular were resolutions asking the members to implement comprehensive or economic sanctions against South Africa; whereas more directly focused resolutions proposing boycotts on military and nuclear collaboration, sports boycotts or general ones about information on apartheid were the most popular.

By observing voting trends at the Assembly on four main recurrent proposals – (1) foreign investments in the Republic, (2) economic collaboration with the country, (3) nuclear (for instance nuclear/military) collaboration between South Africa and the West, and (4) oil sales to South Africa – Stultz concludes that from the early 1970s to 1984 there was no great change in the level of UNGA dissension on key issues of South African policy. 'And such changes as did occur, limited as it was, were generally towards the majority positions on these matters'.[42] His principal finding is that 'to 1984 at least, key votes in the General Assembly on South Africa exhibited an essential continuity in support levels over several decades more clearly than they did a growing unanimity of opinion, with one important exception or qualification.'[43]

The indications are that from 1969 onwards there was an increase in the number of states prepared openly to oppose sanctions against South Africa. All this points to the fact that from 1962 (the year that ushered in a reduction in the number of countries opposing sanctions) to 1984 the net result on the key question of comprehensive economic sanctions against Pretoria was the shift of just one vote (Turkey) from among the 'hard-core' opponents of sanctions to 'favorable', and four others (Australia, Spain, Greece and New Zealand) into the abstention column.[44] It is important to stress here that Japan was not among these countries. The indicators, however, show that although not one of South Africa's ten most important trading partners was prepared to support comprehensive economic sanctions against it, in 1983 four of these (Japan, Belgium, the Netherlands and Sweden) were prepared to endorse a cessation of foreign investments in South Africa.[45] Indeed, by 1968, the Japanese government had officially imposed a ban on direct investment in South Africa by Japanese firms, and had even made a show of enlarging the parameters of the ban in 1974. This could be interpreted to mean that, with the oil crisis of 1973 and the growing Japanese awareness of the political implications of trade, Japan's policy makers saw it as strategically appropriate to give signals of support to the AA on the apartheid question, so as to prevent further victimization from members of the group. In essence, the imposition of the investment ban might have been designed to prevent further crises in relation to Japan's oil imports from the Arab states, and indeed with regard to its overall resource imports from the developing countries.

It is important to note that, on many of the substantive issues mentioned above, most of South Africa's trading partners with serious reservations about various proposed anti-apartheid resolutions adopted what Stultz refers to as the 'decision rule', which was common for some years after 1962. It simply entailed voting 'against such resolutions in the General Assembly only when that vote could count', that is, make a difference in determining the legislative outcome; 'otherwise abstain'.[46] The findings in this study show that, at least as far as apartheid issues were concerned, Japan abstained frequently.

At this juncture it may be useful to look at Urano Tatsuo's tabulation of roll call votes at the General Assembly, with specific reference to apartheid issues.[47] This may serve as a good introduction to the findings of this study, based on the analysis of the 108 roll call votes. Urano demonstrates (see Table 5.1) that Japan – like the Northern European countries – had a strong tendency to support anti-apartheid resolutions, compared to the rest of the industrialized states. He further shows that Japan's votes were more supportive of the majority decision than, for example, the UK and the USA's. Between 1961 and 1965, for example, Japan supported 77.8 percent of the UNGA's anti-apartheid resolutions compared to 66.7 percent for the USA, and 44.4 percent for the UK; while Norway and Sweden voted for 77.8 percent and 66.7 percent respectively. All these countries, including Japan, however, fell short of the 90.2 percent average support rate that such resolutions had during the above period. India, Pakistan, the Philippines, Tanzania, Zambia, Nigeria and Ghana are just a few of the Afro-Asian states who supported each of the resolutions they voted on.[48]

Table 5.1 Votes of selected countries on apartheid issues: yes, no and abstain (every 5 years, 1946–1985)

Country		46–50	51–55	56–60	61–65	66–70	71–75	76–80	81–85
Japan	Yes	–	–	100.0	77.8	46.2	67.6	49.3	38.5
	No	–	–	0.0	11.1	0.0	2.7	4.2	13.5
	Abstain	–	–	0.0	11.1	53.8	29.7	46.5	48.1
US	Yes	0.0	22.2	87.5	66.7	23.1	21.6	9.9	1.9
	No	0.0	11.1	0.0	11.1	30.8	27.0	53.5	86.5
	Abstain	0.0	66.7	12.5	22.2	46.2	51.4	36.6	11.5
Norway	Yes	0.0	22.2	100.0	77.8	53.8	75.7	59.2	51.9
	No	0.0	11.1	0.0	0.0	15.4	5.4	8.5	17.3
	Abstain	0.0	66.7	0.0	22.2	30.8	18.9	32.4	30.8
Sweden	Yes	0.0	22.2	100.0	66.7	53.8	75.7	60.6	53.8
	No	0.0	33.3	0.0	0.0	15.4	2.7	7.0	7.7
	Abstain	0.0	44.4	0.0	33.3	30.8	21.6	32.4	38.5
Tanzania	Yes	–	–	–	100.0	100.0	100.0	100.0	100.0
	No	–	–	–	0.0	0.0	0.0	0.0	0.0
	Abstain	–	–	–	0.0	0.0	0.0	0.0	0.0
Zambia	Yes	–	–	–	100.0	100.0	100.0	100.0	100.0
	No	–	–	–	0.0	0.0	0.0	0.0	0.0
	Abstain	–	–	–	0.0	0.0	0.0	0.0	0.0
India	Yes	0.0	88.9	100.0	100.0	100.0	100.0	98.6	100.0
	No	0.0	0.0	0.0	0.0	0.0	0.0	0.0	0.0
	Abstain	0.0	11.1	0.0	0.0	0.0	0.0	1.4	0.0
Pakistan	Yes	0.0	100.0	100.0	92.3	100.0	100.0	100.0	100.0
	No	0.0	0.0	0.0	0.0	0.0	0.0	0.0	0.0
	Abstain	0.0	0.0	0.0	7.7	0.0	0.0	0.0	0.0
Philippines	Yes	0.0	88.9	100.0	100.0	100.0	100.0	100.0	100.0
	No	0.0	0.0	0.0	0.0	0.0	0.0	0.0	0.0
	Abstain	0.0	11.9	0.0	0.0	0.0	0.0	0.0	0.0

Source: compiled from Urano, *Kokusai shakai no henyo to kokuren tōhyō kōdō*, 1989

As the resolutions became more controversial with time, and also increased in number, the gap between Japan's votes in support of the majority decision, on the one hand, and in support of the US decision, on the other, widened. But Japan's voting record also shows a definite drift away from that of Norway and indeed the African states, obviously because it was agreeing with the majority less, especially as resolutions that infringed on its economic security became popular with the majority group. Between 1971 and 1975, for example, Japan voted in favor of 67.6

percent of the Assembly's anti-apartheid resolutions, compared to 100 percent support by Tanzania, India, Pakistan, Zambia and the Philippines. Norway, the USA and the UK supported 75.7 percent, 21.6 percent and 13.5 percent, respectively, although the average support rate for the majority position was 90 percent. Between 1981 and 1985, however, Japan's support for the majority position fell to 38.5 percent, compared to 1.9 percent for the USA, and the UK, and 51.9 percent for Norway. In effect, contrary to Urano's analysis, Japan was drifting away from his sample of the Northern European voting behavior as it drifted even further away from the USA, even though, generally, Japan's voting record was closer to that of the two Northern European states. Because of the general nature of Urano's voting analysis, it is difficult to establish, on the basis of his data, the specific aspects, and indeed determinants, of Japan's position in the evolving apartheid debate. It may be relevant to add, however, that by 1981 the CNS strategy had been formally institutionalized as an essential point of reference for the economic security of the nation; with particular emphasis on the procurement of strategic resources.

Another factor that made Japan stand out as an Afro-Asian state in terms of voting patterns at the UNGA was its marked tendency to abstain from voting. Between 1966 and 1970, 1971 and 1975, 1976 and 1980 and 1981 and 1985, Japan abstained from voting on 53.8 percent, 27.7 percent, 46.5 percent and 48.1 percent, respectively, of the resolutions passed at the Assembly. The USA, for the same period, abstained from voting on 46.2 percent, 51.4 percent, 36.6 percent and 11.5 percent, respectively, of the resolutions. The average abstention rate during the period was 13.7 percent, 7.7 percent, 10.5 percent and 8.4 percent, respectively. The only period that Pakistan, for example, abstained from voting was between 1966 and 1970; and it abstained from voting on only 7.7 percent of the resolutions passed during the period. Neither India, the Philippines, Tanzania nor Zambia abstained from voting at all during the period. Thus, the more controversial the resolutions, the more Japan abstained from voting. It was noted earlier that from the mid-1960s onwards the anti-apartheid resolutions became more radicalized as a result of the phenomenal increase of African representation at the UNGA. An interesting finding in Urano's work, however, is the low abstention rate displayed by Japan in the period 1971 to 1975, contrasting with a move in the opposite direction by the USA.

This may be suggestive of the fact that Japan was capable of manifesting a contrary position to that of the USA when it felt its national economic security interests were threatened by international developments, as in the case of the oil crisis in the early 1970s, when Japan was forced to confront the political ramifications of its trade relations. It may now be appropriate to try and answer the questions that were raised earlier in the discussion, in relation to how Japan voted on specific issues raised in the 108 anti-apartheid resolutions selected for this analysis.

FINDINGS

Table 5.2 compares the West, Africa and Asia on the mean ZSA with Japan. A comparison is made of each of the three issue areas dealt with in the UNGA during the 1973 period to 1986, when the anti-apartheid debate had already gathered a more radical and sympathetic majority in the Assembly. As can be observed from this table, every ZSA value in column 1 (for the West), except for the cultural value, was higher than its corresponding values in other columns. This is an indication that Japan was more supportive of the West on political and economic issues than it was of either of the other two geographical areas. On cultural matters, however, Japan was less supportive of the West and more supportive of the AA group of nations. At a general level, then, these results confirm Japan's ambivalent position between blocs. Most importantly, however, it highlights the importance of South Africa to Japan, economically; since, as we have already argued, Japan's so-called support for the 'West' cannot be accounted for on the basis of ideological affinity. In other words, Japan's perceived support for the West may be seen as the result of the overlapping (as Ogata puts it) economic interests between Japan and the advanced economies of the West.

Table 5.2 also shows that the African states had a higher voting agreement ($-.08$) with Japan than did the Asian states ($-.18$) on political and economic issues. This, in essence, means that the Asian states were more supportive of the majority position on these issues than the African states. This result is primarily due to Botswana's tendency to agree more

Table 5.2 Comparison of the West and the Afro-Asian group of countries on the mean ZSA with Japan in 1973–1986, by issue

Issue	West	Africa (FLS)	Asia
1 Political	.68	−.11	−.19
2 Economic	.45	.02	−.16
3 Cultural	−.46	.20	.26
1–2	.64	−.08	−.18
1–3	.52	−.05	−.14

Note: Western countries: The USA, Norway, and Sweden; Africa: frontline states; and Asia: India, Pakistan and the Philippines.

with Japan, and to vote differently from the majority position. On a few occasions when it first joined the Assembly, Zimbabwe also voted differently from the majority. Thus, on economic issues the Asian countries were pretty much in disagreement with Japan with a mean ZSA of −.16, compared with .02 for the African states. Their voting agreement with Japan on political issues was also less, at −.19 compared with −.11 for the African states. A reminder that, according to the methodology adopted for this study the ZSA − the more a country voted with Japan the higher that country's mean ZSA would be. The less its voting agreement with Japan, therefore, the less its mean ZSA.

As is observable from Table 5.2, the average ZSA for the West on the three issue areas for the period 1973 to 1986 was far higher (.52) than that of the Asian (−.14) and African groups (.05). It is even higher, at .64, if cultural issues are excluded. This shows that, on the whole, Japan was in far less agreement with the AA states on the issues that mattered most to the majority of the Assembly's voters.

Table 5.3 shows that the three Western states − Norway (.86), Sweden (.79) and the USA (−.04) − had a higher voting agreement with Japan than all the other countries, except Botswana (.34), which had a higher voting score with Japan than the USA. The level of voting disagreement between the USA and Japan is illuminating for this discussion. Indeed, at a very general level, it supports the argument made by Ogata and others[49] that there was hardly a direct link between Japan's relations with the USA

Table 5.3 Comparison of our selected countries on the mean ZSA with Japan, 1973–1986

Country	ZSA	Rank
Japan	1.50	
India	−.13	5
Pakistan	−.14	6
Philippines	−.13	5
Tanzania	−.13	5
Botswana	.34	3
Zambia	.14	6
Mozambique	−.16	8
Zimbabwe	−.13	5
Angola	−.15	7
United States	−.04	4
Sweden	.79	2
Norway	.82	1

and its position on the apartheid issue. A breakdown of the problem into sub-issue areas, however, makes this argument rather less convincing.

The average ZSA of the individual African (except Botswana) and Asian states are highly negative. At a mean ZSA of −.13, −.14, −.16 and −.14 for Tanzania, Zambia, Mozambique and Pakistan, respectively, the study shows that there was a huge gap of agreement between Japan and the AA states on the apartheid issue. Earlier in the discussion it was pointed out that Pakistan, as well as the Philippines, had the same ideological orientation as Japan within the context of the Cold War and therefore, like Japan, had strong relations with the USA. This, however, is not reflected in the voting behavior of these satellite states, in the sense that both Pakistan and the Philippines were more committed to the AA bloc's position on the apartheid issue than they were likely to be on the US position on it, a confirmation of Cruise O'Brien's prediction about the voting behavior of 'satellite' states.[50] And the high mean ZSA attained by our two Northern European (Norway .82, Sweden .79) states also attests to the fact that Japan had a higher agreement with the Northern European states at the UN on this issue than it did with the USA.

Table 5.4 shows the mean ZSA of the three Western states by issue and sub-issue area. Japan's mean ZSA for all the issues also appears for the

Table 5.4 Comparison of three Western states on the mean ZSA with Japan, 1973–1986, by issue

Issue	No.of votes	Japan	USA	Norway	Sweden
1 Political issues:					
A: Arms embargo and military collaboration	10	1.43	−.68	.62	.61
B: Sanctions	12	2.32	1.83	1.09	1.01
C: S.A.'s relations with Israel	11	1.28	.67	1.09	1.09
D: Others	45	1.46	−.29	.99	1.03
A–D	78	1.56	.11	.96	.97
2 Economic issues:					
A: Investments	8	.88	−.91	−.13	−.13
B: Others	11	2.22	1.56	.76	.51
A–B	19	1.73	.65	.43	.27
3 Cultural issues:	11	.69	−2.28	.44	.44
1–2	97	1.60	.22	.86	.83
1–3	108	1.50	−.04	.82	.79

purposes of easy comparison and convenience. Several interesting points emerge from this. As already pointed out, the USA attained the lowest mean ZSA among the Western countries because its level of voting disagreement with Japan was the highest in this group. Viewed at in terms of specific issues, however, the USA had the highest voting agreement with Japan in certain areas. Its mean ZSA for economic issues (A–B) was .65 compared to .43 and .27 for Norway and Sweden, respectively. Equally on 'others' (which include oil embargo, economic collaboration with South Africa, etc.) the US voting agreement with Japan was the highest: a mean value of 1.56 compared to .76 and .51 for Norway and Sweden, respectively. This is not surprising at all since, for example in the 1980s, Japanese ships continued to supply South Africa with oil,[51] against the position of the majority.

On investments, however, Japan agreed more with the Northern European countries than with the USA. This seems to support Tokyo's official position against Japanese investments in South Africa. On cultural issues as well, Norway and Sweden scored a high agreement with Japan (.69) at .44 mean ZSA each. The USA on the other hand had a mean ZSA of −2.28.

The question of sanctions, as must be explained, entailed among other things, proposals for the curtailment of economic relations with South Africa. The two most important sub-issues (arms embargo and military collaboration, and sanctions) under political issues present us with results showing that on sanctions the USA attained a very high voting agreement with Japan, at 1.83. Japan's negative reaction to resolutions demanding sanctions, as mentioned several times already, is attributable to its overzealous concern for its economic security which, to repeat the point, was dependent on some of the strategic resources under South Africa's control. With respect to the other sub-issue, however, the USA scored a low mean ZSA of −.68 compared to .62 and .61 for Norway and Sweden, respectively. As to the question of South Africa's relations with Israel, the Northern European countries had a higher voting agreement with Japan at a mean ZSA of 1.09 each, compared to the US, mean ZSA of .67.

Under the category 'others' (including resolutions on the 'situation in South Africa', acts of aggression by South Africa against African states, etc) under political issues, Norway and Sweden once again had a higher mean ZSA value (.99 and 1.03 respectively) than the USA (−.29). It is important to note, however, that Japan's mean ZSA of 2.32 on sanctions was extreme, meaning that a very small number of Assembly members supported the Japanese position. The same goes for 'others' under Economic issues. Japan's mean ZSA of .69 for cultural issues, on the other hand, indicates that a very small number of countries opposed the Japanese position on this.

JAPAN'S VERBAL RESPONSES TO THE APARTHEID ISSUE: AN ATTEMPT AT EXPLAINING JAPAN'S VOTES

The methodology which concentrates primarily on analyzing roll-call votes and compares the coincidence of voting between states leaves many problems unresolved, as can be seen from the above analysis. For example, the statistical findings do not tell us the reasons why Japan voted for, against or abstained from voting on, a resolution. Nor, for example, do these statistical findings tell us why Japan voted in the same way as or differently from any other country. The idea in this section, therefore, is to try and make up for some of these inadequacies by looking at Japan's explanations for some of its votes at the Plenary Session, the Special Political Committee, the Fourth Committee and the Third Committee of the General Assembly. It is hoped that the explanations will provide some insight into what motivated Japan's representatives to vote the way they did.

This approach itself has its own problems, in the sense that there are no comprehensive verbatim reports on every single vote that a state casts, and particularly for Japan, it is very difficult to find what could be considered a comprehensive explanation of its votes, since there was what may pass as a culture of silence within the Gaimushō on Japan's voting pattern at the United Nations.[52] Nor did the Japanese media say much about Japan's votes at the UN during the period under study. Thus, this part of the discussion is mostly dependent on UN sources, which provide nothing more than the pronouncements delegates made at the meetings. It should also be noted that most of the explanations provided here are in relation to abstentions, since a great number of the 'votes' examined here were abstentions. This was, in a sense, another of Japan's recurring patterns of behavior at the UNGA, a pattern that emerged whenever it was faced with a controversial issue. Apparently, the Liberal Democratic Party government(s) applied this as a strategy to mitigate the [domestic] opposition parties' criticism of the government as a lackey of US diplomacy.[53] This corroborates Stultz's view concerning tactical voting noted earlier in the discussion that states normally 'vote[d] against such resolutions in the General Assembly only when that vote could count . . . *otherwise [they] abstain[ed]*'.[54] Thus, where a definite 'no' was not crucial, Japan abstained from voting on many of the sanctions resolutions. It is, however, fair also to note Saitō's observation that, 'at one point Japan was so lacking in direction in its UN policy that it often abstained from voting on major issues'.[55] This pattern of voting behavior, however, goes to confirm the importance of the methodological point that those abstaining against the pressure of a sizeable majority were more likely to vote 'no'. It may also be appropriate to state that, while this study itself looks at the period from

1973 to 1986, the verbatim reports used here go back to the 1960s. Earlier reports are used so as to provide us with an idea of Japan's responses to the apartheid debate in the heat of decolonization.

In all, Japan emphasized three main themes as part of its diplomatic rhetoric towards the resolution of the problem of apartheid. The most important of these concerned Japan's position on sanctions against South Africa. As already demonstrated, Japan was determinedly opposed to sanctions. In other words, sanctions against South Africa might have been detrimental to Japan's economic, and national, security. What is also imperative to note on this issue, therefore, is that although Japan, to all intents and purposes, was opposed to sanctions, it responded to criticism of this position with a standard claim to the effect that if sanctions were imposed by the Security Council it would not hesitate to support them. This rhetoric, it may be argued, was conveniently correlated to the knowledge that a Security Council imposed sanctions on South Africa in the middle of the Cold War was clearly out of the question, since neither the UK nor the USA would have supported it.

The second most important piece of rhetoric of the Japanese diplomacy at the time was the message that the problem in South Africa should be resolved through peaceful means. This effectively meant, and this was clearly spelt out by Japan's representatives at the UNGA, that Japan was opposed to armed struggle against the minority regime; an idea which had gained immense popularity among the AA group of states by the latter part of the 1960s. Japan's primary concern here was that such an action would amount to political instability in a region that served as one of the world's most important repositories for rare metals. Thus, a war situation in South Africa was seen as an outcome potentially detrimental to Japan's economic security and one that would close off access to the strategic resources, as noted in the PPRC report mentioned in Chapter 1.

The third theme, which should be mentioned in passing, is one that evokes Japan's own history as a second-class citizen of the global community, as it were. This refers to the request by Japan for the inclusion of a 'racial equality clause' in the League of Nations' Charter in 1919. Japan's representatives at the UN chanted this theme like a mantra, evidently in an attempt to redeem their country from the aura of ambivalence, and unpopularity with the AA states, that Japan was cloaked in on the issue of apartheid. In other words, Japan's post-war policy makers seemingly repackaged the 1919 appeal for a racial equality clause, giving it universal resonance to fit the new political climate of the post-war period. Thus, in 1976, for example, Mr. Abe Shintarō, representing Japan at the Plenary Meeting recounted how as early as 1919 . . . Japan attempted, though unsuccessfully, to have a clause proclaiming racial equality included in the Covenant of the League of Nations. Thus, our position on racial discrimination is based not on some abstract intellectual understanding, but on the fact that our bitter experience has made us profoundly sensitive to this problem. This experience, moreover, had led us to feel intense repulsion and indignation against the practice of apartheid in Southern Africa.[56]

The points raised above are meant to highlight, in relation to the two thresholds that El-Khawas identifies in his analysis of the development of the debate on apartheid at the General Assembly, the fact that, as a member of the AA group, Japan was a special case, if not a deviant one, for not advancing its position against apartheid to that of supporting sanctions against South Africa. As noted earlier, by the early 1960s there was a movement within the Assembly to substitute coercive sanctions for the bankrupt efforts at persuasion and conciliation. And although a number of the Asian states felt uncomfortable with the coercive approach initially, by 1962 they had been won over by the African states. Japan, however, refused to be 'coopted', for a variety of reasons, some of which were identified earlier. The following is an examination of some of the explanations for Japan's votes in relation to the first two pieces of rhetoric mentioned above.

Japan's appeal for a peaceful solution to apartheid

In 1967, the Japanese representative at the 22nd Session of the Plenary Meeting 'appealed to the minority regimes in Southern Africa to face the fact that basic justice demands the abolition of racial discrimination'. He made it quite plain, however, that Japan could not support 'the end justifies the means' approach adopted by the liberation movements in Southern Africa in their struggle for independence and majority rule. In his attempt to negate the importance of force as a means to resolving the problem of inequality, he recommended 'understanding, patience, and cooperation' of all countries as the appropriate means to resolving the problem.[57] This supposedly principled position against armed struggle was repeated in 1969 at the 24th Session of the Special Political Committee (SPC).[58]

At the meeting of the SPC in 1970, Ogata Sadako, representing Japan at the Assembly meetings, explained that her delegation abstained from voting on draft resolution A/L 3/L.1800/Rev.1 (on racial discrimination) because it was identical to those of the SPC and the Fourth Committee. The real reason for abstaining in this case, however, was to demonstrate the fact that Japan was uncomfortable with the fact that the Third Committee had been turned into a purely political forum that agitated for a radical resolution to the South African problem. However, she stated, as most of her predecessors did whenever they abstained from voting, that abstaining from voting on the draft resolution 'should not be taken to indicate a negative attitude towards the elimination of racial discrimination, particularly apartheid'. The delegation, however, voted for draft resolution A/C.3/L.1799/Rev.1 because its 'proposed legislative, educational and social measures were all encompassing and conducive to the elimination of racial discrimination on a *long term basis*' (emphasis added). The implied message here, it seems, was that Japan, since it attached the greatest importance to the strict observance of the principle of peaceful settlement of international disputes as set out in the Charter of the UN,[59] could not support armed struggle as a means to terminating apartheid. For example, explaining Japan's votes at the 26th Session of the SPC in 1971, Mr. Akatani said that his delegation abstained from voting on draft resolution A/SPC/L. 214/Rev.1 because it suggested that the victims of apartheid could use armed struggle against the state. In other words, Japan's support strategy for resolving the problem of apartheid amounted to a negotiated process, and was eminently out of tune with the position adopted by the AA member states by the 1970s.

Thus, at the 1971 session, Mr. Akatani reconfirmed[60] Japan's support for international pressure on Pretoria to abolish apartheid, as long as it was conducted through 'peaceful, practical and realistic' means. And in 1973, Mr. Otaka, leading the Japanese delegation at the 28th Session of the SPC, explained that his delegation voted in favor of draft resolution A/SPC/L.265 (Activities of the International Conference of Trade Union against Apartheid)[61] because it considered trade union action against apartheid, which it saw as less of a radical approach, as an important aspect of the negotiation process. He noted that the delegation was pleased with the activities of the Conference. To reaffirm this position, at the 31st Session of the Plenary Meetings in 1976, Mr. Kanazawa explained[62] that his delegation abstained in the vote on draft resolution A/31/L.13 (Situation in South Africa) because, among other things, they did not believe that the situation in South Africa constituted a threat to international peace and security. The delegation may have also been concerned that the draft resolution could lead to an uprising in South Africa, something that the Japanese had made plain would not get their support. Thus, faced with a similar situation in December 1979, Mr. Murata representing the Japanese delegation at the Plenary Meeting, reiterated Japan's position of not supporting 'the view that holds the legitimacy of the Government of South Africa in doubt and considers that the problem of apartheid should be resolved in the context of decolonization'. He further reiterated Japan's principled position against endorsing 'the notion of a UN encouraging armed struggle of any kind . . . by anybody' against the South African regime. When the issue raised its head again in 1981 at the Plenary Meeting Mr. Nishibori further reaffirmed Japan's position against armed struggle against the South African government.[63]

In defence of trade and opposition to sanctions

By the mid-1960s the world community was becoming aware of the extent of Japan's trade relations with South Africa. Thus, while Japanese delegates were making such laudable statements about their experiences with racism and commitment against the minority regime of South Africa, those with whom they purported to sympathize, ironically, accused Japan of supporting apartheid. In one instance, the Guinean delegate (Mr. Ackah) berated Japan for expanding trade with South Africa at the expense of the victims of apartheid. The Japanese representative's response to this accusation was simply that since Japan 'was geographically a small nation and . . . its natural resources were very poor . . . Foreign trade represented a life-line for Japan's 100 million people'. In view of that, Japan 'had endeavoured to trade as widely as possible throughout the world'. [64] Thus, he tried to explain an aspect of Japan's strategy for economic security. In essence, the Japanese delegation did not deny the allegations levelled against their country, even though they claimed them to be exaggerated. Mr. Mitsui (the representative) then went on to make it clear that, until lawful and effective measures involving sanctions were implemented by the Security Council against Pretoria, Japan would continue to trade with it. This meant, in effect, that South Africa was a country (with natural resources) that Japan could not afford to ignore in pursuance of its wider economic interests. But it also suggests that Japanese policy makers were convinced that the Security Council would not impose comprehensive sanctions against Pretoria. Again in 1966, Mr. Takahashi, representing Japan at the SPC, deplored South Africa's continued defiance of UN decisions. Like his predecessors, he stated unequivocally that apartheid was 'the most virulent form of racial discrimination in the modern world', and he reiterated Japan's promise to cooperate fully[65] with the international community if the Security Council imposed sanctions on Pretoria. The point made earlier that reference to Security Council-imposed sanctions (in the knowledge that it would not happen) was part of Japan's diplomatic rhetoric, ought to be reiterated here.

Thus, at the 24th Session of the Third Committee in 1969, Mrs. Kume explained why she, and her delegation, felt obliged to abstain from voting on the Committee's adoption of the text of the Economic and Social Council which, among other things, appealed to the committee members to impose obligatory sanctions on South Africa. As Mrs. Kume put it, 'had serious doubts about whether the committee was competent [enough] to deal with the matters covered in the draft resolution'. She also made it very clear, in defense of her vote, that in her opinion, 'only the Security Council was entitled to impose obligatory sanctions'.[66]

Following this pattern of behavior, at the 26th Session of the SPC in 1971, Mr. Akatani had to defend his country against the Committee's criticism of Japan's expanding trade with South Africa. He stressed that Japan had no diplomatic relations with South Africa, and no direct investments in the country; correctly pointing out that it (officially) had a policy of discouraging any investments in South Africa. He then proceeded to confirm[67] Japan's support for international pressure on Pretoria to abolish apartheid, as long as it was conducted through 'peaceful, practical and realistic' means, suggesting, in effect, that sanctions against South Africa were not a feasible approach to solving the country's problem. There was, thus, nothing inconsistent about Mr. Otaka's speech in 1974[68] when he defended Japan's trade with South Africa in the face of harsh criticisms from some Assembly members. In an attempt to temper these criticisms, he made the case that Japan had refrained from adopting any measures to increase trade with South Africa.

The delegation at the 1976 Plenary Meetings also abstained from voting on draft resolution A/31/L.12 which dealt with the question of economic collaboration with South Africa; and among others recommended sanctions against Pretoria. Mr. Kanazawa, the leader of the delegation, explained that they abstained because they found difficulty in accepting some paragraphs in the resolution. The following year at the Plenary Meetings Mr. Okazaki, among other things, tried to elicit the sympathy of the Assembly members by making reference to the fact that Japan had voluntarily imposed a strict ban on direct investment in South Africa upon itself. But he also implicitly lamented the fact that:

> of special importance to Japan is trade that is supported by, and combined with, direct investment in resource rich areas such as Southern Africa. Therefore, the ban on investment in South Africa was significantly limiting the scope of Japan's activities in its search for the necessary natural resources,

and indeed its economic security. Mr. Okazaki, however, claimed that he was not complaining about these significant sacrifices that his country was making in the common cause of mankind.[69] When, at the 69th meeting of the same session, the representative from Gabon accused Japan of investing in South Africa, Mr. Okazaki denied it, saying that he did 'not believe that there [was] a single Japanese investor active in South Africa'.[70]

Three years later, in 1980, Japanese delegates were still playing the '1919 racial equality' card while giving signals that they might change their ambivalent position on the South African question. At the 35th Session Plenary Meetings, Mr. Nishibori (Japan's chief representative) repeated the fact that, although the proposal for racial equality was an appeal for justice, it was rejected by the League of Nations. He then went on to enumerate Japan's contribution to the struggle against apartheid, and called on the international community to continue on the path of peaceful resolution of the South African problem. He deplored the non-cooperative attitude of Pretoria towards the world body's efforts, going as far as to state that 'if the Government of South Africa continued to defy such efforts . . . Japan for its part will be forced in the future to reconsider its position regarding the solution of the problem in South Africa'.[71] It is tempting to speculate that the Japanese delegation, in this rare move, was suggesting a possible approval of the application of coercive measures, already adopted by the AA bloc, as a means of resolving the apartheid issue. By 1981, however, this rhetoric had been toned down, to reflect Japan's position against armed struggle. It is also important to reiterate the point that 1981 was the year that the CNS strategy was initiated. Thus, in 1981, Mr. Nishibori spoke at the Plenary Meetings, and again condemned apartheid, pledging that 'Japan is making every possible effort to reduce [its] dependence on imports, particularly of natural resources from South Africa'. He did not make any reference to the veiled threats he made earlier in 1980.[72] The following year Mr. Hirashima, leading the delegation,[73] also noted that the delegation could not vote for A/37/ L.19, which called for comprehensive and mandatory sanctions against South Africa, because they did not believe that such a measure would constitute an effective and expeditious means of achieving a peaceful solution to apartheid. They also viewed the draft resolution as an attempt to deprive the Security Council of its responsibility: the authority to impose such sanctions.

A number of points made by Mr. Osanai Takashi (First Secretary to the UN Japan Mission)[74] should neatly summarize the above discussion. Mr. Osanai did note that Japan's attitude towards some of the anti-apartheid resolutions were lukewarm, if not cold. However, he attributed this attitude to the following factors, in order:

1 Japan doubted the effectiveness of comprehensive mandatory sanctions in resolving the problem of racial discrimination in South Africa. As a result, Tokyo did not support such resolutions.

2 Japan, in principle, opposed armed struggle as a means of resolving the problem in South Africa and thus did not support resolutions designed to legitimize such causes.

He then made a less relevant point about what he referred to as 'name-calling', which, he said, also contributed to Japan's lukewarm attitude towards the apartheid debate:

3 The vicious accusations against certain countries (including Japan), for supposedly supporting apartheid, in many of the anti-apartheid resolutions.

He pointed out that Japan saw this behavior as counter-productive to the business of finding a solution to the apartheid problem.

The analyses above confirm Mr. Osanai's explanation of the situation, but they also reveal something rather fundamental about Japan's concern for its economic security, and indeed its overall national security. They show that South Africa, to all intents and purposes, was important to Japanese industries because of the rare metals it possessed. This is demonstrated in Japan's negative attitude to sanctions, and indeed towards all radical measures, including armed struggle against the minority regime. As has been argued above, such radical actions against South Africa could have amounted to Japan losing access to the strategic materials crucial for its CNS strategy.

CONCLUSION

In the above discussion of anti-apartheid issues and the voting behavior of the selected sample of countries, Japan, despite its race and 'geographical placement' in Asia, is identified as a deviant case within the AA community. The AA group itself saw it as a 'heretic'. This may be explained by reference to Jack Vincent's point that there is a causal relationship between a country's votes and the level of its economic development. Japan's industries, needless to say, were dependent on South Africa for resources that they needed in order to keep them in active productive competition and to sustain the country's industrial growth. Thus, economic development might be viewed as something fundamental to the attitudes, operations and outcomes at the UN. On that premise, it is not surprising, then, even if politically incorrect, that Japanese delegates were consistent in not accepting measures designed to compel South Africa to renounce apartheid, above all when this might involve the application of economic sanctions. Thus, as proven by the findings in this study, Japan's voting agreement with the USA, the leading opponent of anti-apartheid resolutions, was highest on sanctions. Its voting agreement with the USA on 'others' (under 'economic' measures, and involving very sensitive trade matters) was equally high.

On the basis of the findings presented in this chapter, therefore, it could be said that specific issue areas in which Japan consistently voted with the USA, have clearly been identified, calling into question some of the central arguments put forward by Ogata and others. The results of the findings are no less significant in light of the sensitivity of the issue areas in question, embracing the core themes of economic relations in general and sanctions in particular. Equally important, however, is the fact that the study discloses the national economic security interest at the core of Japanese foreign policy. In view of this, it could be concluded that, at the general level, Japan's South Africa policy at the UN was not consistent. Considered in its specific aspects, however, the consistency of the Japanese position was striking, not least because it intimately correlated with established parameters of its immobilist foreign policy and its evolving national security interests.

NOTES

1 United Nations, *Official Records of the General Assembly – 35th Session, Plenary Meeting*, November 1980, p. 983.
2 Morikawa Jun, 'The Anatomy of Japan's South African Policies', *The Journal of Modern African Studies*, 1984, vol. 22; Morikawa Jun, 'The Myth and Reality of Japan's Relations with Colonial Africa, 1885–1960', *Journal of African Studies*, vol. 11, no. 1, Spring, 1985; Morikawa Jun, *Minami afurika to nihon: kankei no rekishi, kōzō, kadai*, Tokyo, Dōbunkan, 1988.
3 Richard Payne, *The Non-Superpowers' South Africa Policies: Interests and Strategies*, Princeton, Princeton University Press, 1990; Hayashi Kōji, 'A Half-hearted Anti-apartheid Policy', *Japan Quarterly*, July–September, 1989.
4 Matsumoto Saburō, 'Japan's Voting in the United Nations', in Itoh Hiroshi (ed.), *Japanese Politics – An Inside View: Readings from Japan*, Ithaca and London, Cornell University Press, 1973, p. 42.
5 Formerly Japan's Ambassador to the United Nations.
6 Ogata Sadako, 'The United Nations and Japanese Diplomacy', *Japan Review of International Affairs*, Fall/Winter, 1990; Ogata Sadako, 'Japan's United Nations Policy in the 1980s', *Asian Survey*, vol. xxvii, no. 9, September, 1987; Saitō Shizuo, 'The Evolution of Japan's United Nations Policy', *Japan Review of International Affairs*, Fall/Winter, 1989; Urano Tatsuo, *Kokusai shakai no henyō to kokuren tōhyō kōdō, 1946–85*, Tokyo, kokusai chīki shiryo sentā, 1989.
7 Ogata, 'The United Nations and Japanese Diplomacy', p. 156.
8 Saito, 'The Evolution of Japan's United Nations Policy', p. 193.
9 According to James Gbeho, Ghana's permanent representative to the UN, the African states 'singles out the US . . . in anti-South African resolutions for good reason', because it actively supported Pretoria. See J. de St. Jorre, 'The African Group: A New Political Realism', *Africa Report*, March–April, 1985, p. 79.

10 United Nations, *Official Records of the General Assembly – 35th Session, Plenary Meetings,* 11 November 1980.

11 Plenary votes are the final votes for the record and are generally cast after individual members have presumably given much thought to how they would like to vote on an issue. This sample of votes is an adjusted gross number of roll-call votes. Excluded from the analysis were show of hands and other non-recorded votes, unanimous votes (defined as all members voting one way), near-unanimous votes, votes on amendments to resolutions and votes on the Bantustans. Roll-call votes will be considered near-unanimous if they are within five single shifts of complete agreement. See Hayward A. Alker Jr. and Bruce Russet, *World Politics in the General Assembly,* New Haven, Yale University Press, 1965, p. 26. As the authors put it, 'statistically such votes inform us of few or no policy differences, and they tend to have few high inter-correlation with other roll-calls evidencing greater divisions . . . Virtually unanimous agreements may represent a considerable achievement in the building of consensus, but they are not useful in describing voting dimensions'.

12 Nathan Shamuyarira, *Liberation Movements in Southern Africa, The Eighth Annual Hans Wolff Memorial Lecture, 14 April, 1977,* Africa Studies Program, Indiana University, Bloomington, Indiana, 1978, p. 18; J. de St. Jorre, 'The African Group', p. 78.

13 B. W. Tomlin, 'Measurement Validation: Lessons from the Use and Misuse of the UN General Assembly Roll Call Votes', *International Organization,* vol. 39, no. 1, Winter, 1985, p. 202.

14 Trong R. Chai, 'Chinese Policy toward the Third World and the Super-powers in the United Nations General Assembly, 1971–77: A Voting Analysis', *International Organization,* vol. 33, no. 3, Summer, 1979. See Appendix I for an explanation of the methodology.

15 Thomas Hovet Jr., *Bloc Politics in the United Nations,* Cambridge, Mass., Harvard University Press, 1960, p. 9.

16 Ibid., p. 13.

17 Ibid., p. 30–31.

18 Arend Lijphart, 'The Analysis of Bloc Voting in the General Assembly: A Critique and a Proposal', *The American Political Science Review,* vol. lvii, no. 4, 1963, pp. 904–913.

19 Hayward R. Alker Jr., 'Dimensions of Conflict in the General Assembly', *The American Political Science Review,* vol. lviii, no. 3, September, 1964, p. 164.

20 Conor C. O'Brien, *To Katanga and Back,* London, Hutchinson, 1966, p. 17–18.

21 Lijphart, 'The Analysis of Bloc Voting in the General Assembly', p. 904.

22 Hovet, *Bloc Politics in the United Nations,* p. 85.

23 Ibid., p. 85.

24 Ibid.

25 Lijphart, 'The Analysis of Bloc Voting in the General Assembly', p. 912.

26 Mohammed El-Khawas, 'The Third-World Stance on Apartheid: The United Nations Record', *The Journal of Modern African Studies,* vol. 9, no. 3, October, 1971.

27 N. M. Stultz, 'The Apartheid Issue at the General Assembly: Stalemate or Gathering Storm?', *African Affairs,* vol. 86, no. 342, January, 1987.

28 Ali H. Khan, *The Political Economy of Apartheid,* London, Lynne Rienner, 1989, p. 5.

29 Merle Lipton, *Capitalism and Apartheid: South Africa, 1910–1986*, Aldershot, Wildwood House Ltd, 1986, pp. 14–16.

30 Khan, *The Political Economy of Apartheid*, p. 11.

31 Ali Mazrui, 'The United Nations and Some African Political Attitudes', *International Organization*, vol. xviii, 1964, p. 508.

32 N. M. Stultz, 'The Apartheid Issue at the General Assembly', p. 29.

33 Seventeen new members were admitted to the UN. Fourteen of these were admitted on the same day, 20 September 1960. Sixteen of the total were newly independent sub-Saharan African states. By 1962, six more states from the region had joined the organization. In a space of two years, therefore, the African membership of the UNGA increased from nine to thirty-three (excluding South Africa). The African group registered the second largest caucusing group after the Afro-Asian group, in which it actually constituted the majority.

34 El-Khawas, 'The Third-World Stance on Apartheid', p. 446.

35 The resolution was a reaffirmation of the appeal in 1961 for member states, (a) to break off diplomatic relations with the government of the Republic of South Africa; (b) to close their ports to all vessels flying the South African flag; (c) to enact legislation prohibiting their ships from entering South African ports; and (d) to boycott South African goods and refrain from exporting goods, including all arms and ammunitions, to South Africa.

36 El Khawas, 'The Third-World Stance on Apartheid,' p. 447.

37 Stultz, 'The Apartheid Issue at the General Assembly', p. 33.

38 United Nations, *Official Records of the General Assembly – Special Political Committee, 469th Meeting*, 29 November 1965, pp. 2–3.

39 Ibid. p. 3

40 El-Khawas, 'The Third-World Stance on Apartheid', p. 450.

41 Stultz, 'The Apartheid Issue at the General Assembly', p. 34.

42 Ibid., p. 41.

43 Ibid.

44 Ibid., p. 42.

45 Ibid.

46 Ibid., p. 35.

47 Urano, *Kokusai shakai no henyō to kokuren tōhyō kōdō, 1946–85*.

48 Nine resolutions were passed during the five-year period, of which Ghana, Pakistan, Tanzania, and Zambia voted on eight. The rest of the countries mentioned above voted on all nine resolutions.

49 Ogata, 'The United Nations and Japanese Diplomacy', p. 156; Saito, The Evolution of Japan's United Nations Policy', p. 193.

50 O'Brien, *To Katanga and Back*, pp. 17–18.

51 United Nations, *Report of the Intergovernmental Group to Monitor the Supply of Oil and Petroleum Products to South Africa, Supplement No.44* (A/44/44), 31 October 1989.

52 Hayashi Yōko, 'Hōgan ḥōdō kara dakkyaku o: nihon no minami afurika hōdō o furikaete', *Shimbun kenkyū*, no. 482, September, 1992.

53 Saitō, 'The Evolution of Japan's United Nations Policy', p. 191.

54 Stultz, The Apartheid Issue at the General Assembly', p. 35.

55 Ibid., p. 190.

56 United Nations, *Official Records of the General Assembly – 35th Session, Plenary Meetings*, 9 November 1976.

57 United Nations, *Official Records of the General Assembly – 22nd Session, Plenary Meeting*, 22 September 1967.

58 United Nations, *Official Records of the General Assembly – 24th Session, Special Political Committee*, 30 October 1969.

59 United Nations, *Official Records of the General Assembly – 25th Session*, 4 November 1970.

60 United Nations, *Official Records of the General Assembly – 26th Session, Special Political Committee*, 3 November 1971.

61 United Nations, *Official Records of the General Assembly – 28th Session, Special Political Committee*, 1 November 1973.

62 United Nations, *Official Records of the General Assembly – Plenary Meetings*, 9 November 1976.

63 United Nations, *Official Records of the General Assembly – 36th Session, Plenary Meetings*, 30 November 1981.

64 United Nations, *Official Records of the General Assembly – 24th Session, Third Committee*, 24 November 1969.

65 United Nations, *Official Records of the General Assembly – 21st Session, Special Political Committee*, 539th meeting, 19 December 1966.

66 United Nations, *Official Records of the General Assembly – 24th Session, Third Committee*, 24 November 1969.

67 United Nations, *Official Records of the General Assembly – 26th Session, Special Political Committee*, 3 November 1971.

68 United Nations, *Official Records of the General Assembly – 29th Session, Special Political Committee*, 22 October 1974.

69 United Nations, *Official Records of the General Assembly – 32nd Session, Plenary Meetings*, 14 November 1977.

70 United Nations, *Official Records of the General Assembly – 32nd Session, Plenary Meetings*, 15 November 1977.

71 United Nations, *Official Records of the General Assembly – 35th Session, Plenary Meetings*, 11 November 1980.

72 United Nations, *Official Records of the General Assembly – 36th Session, Plenary Meetings*, 30 November 1981.

73 United Nations, *Official Records of the General Assembly – 37th Session, Plenary Meetings*, 9 December 1982.

74 Interview at UN Japan Mission Office, New York, 10 November 1989.

6   Japanese aid to Tanzania

An assessment of the political marketing of Japan in Africa*

In view of its performance at the UNGA on the question of South Africa's apartheid policy, Japan's popularity among the AA group of states remained, at best, low. In order not to exacerbate this situation while continuing to expand trade with the pariah state and depend on it for the strategic resources, it became diplomatically essential, if not strategically crucial, for Japan to cultivate good relations with the most politically significant OAU member state. This, as is argued in the following pages, was done by increasing economic assistance to Tanzania.

The possible application of aid[1] as a political instrument, with the result that the recipient country's foreign policy behavior towards the donor is constrained, is an issue that brings into perspective the dynamics of the relationship between weak states and strong states. The aid donor in this case is Japan, and the country on the receiving end of such aid is Tanzania. And although the subject of real interest here is the application of aid by Japan's policy makers as a political (diplomatic) instrument, it is important to note the general development of Japanese aid policy, and indeed how sub-Saharan Africa fits into it. Hence, whilst the focus of this study is essentially on aid to mainland Tanzania, the analysis can be located within what are referred to as the third and fourth phases of the development of Japanese aid policies (1974–1985 and 1985–1990), when Japan started to extend geographically the application of aid as a diplomatic instrument.

As this introduction suggests, Japanese aid to Tanzania, especially starting from the latter half of the 1970s to the end of the 1980s, was primarily determined by Tokyo's diplomatic interests in sub-Saharan Africa. This point is interesting in one particular respect: by extension, it questions the popular argument that Japanese aid was directly correlated to its economic interests in the recipient country. This is, however, not to say that these overtures towards Tanzania were devoid of an economic motive, since aid to Tanzania was, in a not too convoluted manner, influenced by

* This chapter is an updated version of my article in *African Affairs*, vol. 95, no. 378, January 1996.

Japan's economic interests in South Africa. At this stage, a passing reference to the theoretical 'refreshment' developed earlier in Chapter 1 should be of use here. Bruce Moon's theory of 'constrained consensus', which suggests that, without a prior and massive penetration of the system and functions of other states, the dominant state will not find it easy to violate and 'fine-tune' the foreign policies of those states, is indeed a good reminder of the complicated nature of the relations between nation-states. It is also worth reflecting on the argument concerning the dimensions of power, and the fact that weak states also find themselves in positions of power, even against dominant states.

More useful background information is that the independence of Tanganyika from Britain on 9 December 1961 was, according to Issa Shivji, merely symbolic. It was primarily a case of the colonial power handing over a country that was already integrated in the world capitalist system to African administrators, the petit bourgeoisie that Shivji identifies in his analyses of the socio-political crises in Tanzania.[2] Shivji seems to contend that the main contribution of this class to the post-independence development has been the perpetuation of the links between Tanzania and the capitalist states in the West.[3]

An important variant of this argument remains, therefore, that the foreign policy of Tanzania, like its economy, was programmed by its colonial rulers to serve the interests of the industrialized capitalist states. This argument reflects on the question of Tanzania's extensive dependence on the Western countries for economic assistance, for even as President Nyerere tried to check this trend by controlling the speed at which Tanzania was being further integrated into the world capitalist economy as a satellite state, donor assistance to the country rose steadily after the 1970s, contributing at least 40 percent to official development expenditure.[4] In 1980/81, 60 percent of Tanzania's development budget ($534 mn.), which was approximately the same as its export earnings for the same fiscal year, was externally generated. Thus, Tanzania, despite its self-reliance policy, became the largest recipient of development assistance in sub-Saharan Africa during the 1970s. It received $32 per capita in ODA in 1979, compared to Kenya's and Uganda's $23 and $3, respectively.[5] According to the indicators, it also received generous grants. By 1982 grants accounted for 92 percent of all assistance to Tanzania compared to 13 percent in 1970. This was because by then its major donors – the Scandinavian countries, Canada, the Netherlands, the USA, West Germany, the UK and Japan – had decided, based on the Development Assistance Committee (DAC) countries' decision to extend all new assistance to Tanzania on a grant basis. The Tanzanian economy, like many of the economies of the Third World, was seen to be too bankrupt to make loans to.

Nevertheless, Tanzania, on the whole, was the recipient of a phenomenal dose of economic assistance both on the bilateral and multilateral levels. Between 1970 and 1979 aid from the International Bank for Reconstruction and Development (IBRD) and the International Development Agency (IDA) rose from $11 mn. to $72 mn. Essentially, Tanzania followed a broad-based approach to courting foreign aid. The idea was to be less dependent on any one particular donor and, as much as possible, to reduce the influence of the big capitalist powers on Tanzania. The Scandinavian countries, as already noted, answered Tanzania's plea for assistance promptly, thus providing it with 30 percent of the country's aid resources from 1970 to 1979. Sweden emerged as Tanzania's leading donor in the 1970s, providing it with $548.4 mn. of which $498 mn., was in the form of grants.

THE INCEPTION AND EXPANSION OF JAPANESE AID

The development of Japanese aid can be divided into four phases, although these phases overlap a great deal. From 1954 to the latter 1960s constituted the first phase. The process started with the payment of war reparations, 'or as "economic cooperation" agreements in lieu of reparations'[6] to a number of Asian states who had been victims of Japanese imperialism before and during World War II. The second stage runs from the late 1960s to 1973 or 1974. By this time, Japan's aid had begun making inroads into other regions of the world, albeit in a small way.[7]

During the third phase (from 1974 to 1985), aid seemingly assumed a wider significance in terms of Japan's overall foreign policy objectives. The period coincides with the oil shocks of 1973/74 and 1979, when Japan's resource vulnerability was heightened by the application of oil as a political weapon by the Organization of Arab Petroleum Exporting Countries (OAPEC) against the USA and its allies, including Japan. The Arab–Israeli War and its concomitant oil crisis of 1973 therefore brought about a globalization of Japan's aid policy with the view, primarily, to arresting the energy and other resource problems haunting Japan. The next phase of Tokyo's foreign aid programs may be seen as starting from the second half of the 1980s. During this period, demands on Japan from the DAC member states included requests for it to increase its aid and to improve the quality of its assistance. This was followed by another phase (starting at the end of the 1980s) which dealt with questions relating to 'conditionality'; and pertained to attempts by the USA and some European donor states to force Japan to correlate its aid policies to the human rights record of the (potential) recipient. At issue, therefore, were the political institutions and democratic capabilities of the recipient country. During this period there were pressures on Japan's policy makers, for example, to withdraw aid from countries like China, and indeed Kenya, because of the poor human rights records of these countries.

The rate at which Japan's Official Development Assistance (ODA) has increased since the 1950s is overwhelming. Tokyo distributed $5.6 bn. in aid in 1986. The amount had risen to $9.1 bn. by 1988. In 1989 Japan's ODA allocation came to $10.95 bn., surpassing that of the USA. In 1993 it reached $11. 25 bn., compared to $9.01 bn. for the US. It is almost a truism, therefore, that since the 1980s aid has become one of Japan's most expanding enterprises, extending in its processes and consequences over the whole world. And it cannot be denied that Japan's own national security interests, couched in economic terms, were largely responsible for the expansion of Japanese aid. Thus, its aid was of necessity correlated to its commercial and overall economic interests.[8] Japan's economic assistance policy has also been influenced by the other DAC[9] members, and indeed by the World Bank,[10] both of which have pressurized it to make more aid available to the African states and other developing countries. It may be said that this indirectly assisted in the provision of more grant aid to Tanzania. The point being made here is that, if Japan was pressurized to provide more aid to sub-Saharan Africa, then it would, considering its interests in the region, give more aid to those countries in the region that were relevant to its interests, as most states would do in such a case.

Generally, Japan started making efforts to improve the quality of its aid from the early 1980s; providing more aid to the poorest nations and as a result sprucing up its ODA with more grants. The institutions (MOFA, MOF, MITI) and the two aid agencies (JICA and OECF) in charge of Japan's aid were all keen to make Japanese aid appear respectable. According to Dennis Yasutomo, by the early 1980s the government had 'begun to refer to "aid" (*enjo*) and "ODA" rather than "economic cooperation" (*keizai kyōryoku*), in an effort to separate the commercial and development uses of economic assistance'.[11]

The political and strategic uses of aid assumed more importance in the early 1980s, bringing into perspective the political foundations of Japan's aid in the 1960s. But 'the government down-played its importance because of domestic opposition to any political/strategic colouring of economic aid'.[12] It is also plausible to argue that the government downplayed the political significance of its aid because of its own obsession with the idea of keeping a low profile when it came to dealing with sensitive political issues in global politics. In that sense, the CNS strategy, as initiated by Prime Minister Ōhira Masayoshi, developed Japan's aid policies into a diplomatic instrument designed to articulate the country's political and strategic interests, without overdramatizing them.

According to William Brooks and Robert Orr, no other political region in Asia is as important to Japan as ASEAN, because it ensures political stability; and 'a stable political order in [Asia] is judged to be essential to Japan's policy interests'.[13] In short, the region is of major strategic interest to Japan. Thus, on average, Japan assigned about 35 percent of its bilateral ODA to the then six member states of ASEAN (Brunei, Indonesia, Malaysia, the Philippines, Singapore and Thailand). In 1986 and 1987, for example, $1.1 bn. and $1.8 bn. of its $3.8 bn. and $5.2 bn. bilateral ODA, respectively, went to the ASEAN states, compared to sub-Saharan Africa's share of $340 mn. and $526 mn. for the same period. Indeed, the combined Japanese ODA to Thailand and the Philippines at $693.7 mn. for the period 1986 to 1987 period was more than the whole of Japan's ODA to the 44 OAU sub-Saharan African states for the same period. What needs to be stressed here is that the CNS was designed to especially accommodate the strategic importance of ASEAN, albeit through a diplomatic initiative.

Japanese aid policy and the African states

Japanese governments in the 1980s, starting with the Ōhira and followed by the Suzuki Zenkō administrations, were intent on expanding Japan's role in the global aid enterprise. It entered the 1990s in the number one position as aid dispenser, and refurbished the quality of its aid by increasing the grant element of its aid to the African states. Although insignificant compared to Japan's performance in Asia, it is worth noting that Japan was the leading donor to five countries[14] in sub-Saharan Africa in 1986. And its economic assistance to the region increased immensely during the second half of the 1980s. From $252 mn. in 1985, Japan's ODA to the region increased by more than 100 percent to $516 mn. in 1987. By 1989 it had reached $1.04 bn., until it started climbing down. As part of this development, Tokyo provided a $500 mn. non-project grant aid package to eleven countries in sub-Saharan Africa in 1987. And in 1989 the government established a system to support the Structural Adjustment Program undertaken by the debtor nations of Asia and Africa. This plan was supported with a $600 mn. grant, which was further extended for three years beginning fiscal year 1990. The new system succeeded the 'non-project aid' program initiated in 1987. In 1993 Africa took 24.4 percent of Japan's grant aid.

In spite of these developments, Japanese policy makers, somewhat understandably, maintained that they lack an understanding for Africa's developmental problems. They attributed this to what they perceive as complex layers of cultural barriers between Japan and Africa. This perceived lack of familiarity with the continent apparently made Japan's aid policy makers choose the Crown Agents, the implementing Agency of the British Overseas Development Administration, to disburse a huge part of the $500 mn. grant aid mentioned above. The official reason given was that the Crown Agents 'have abundant experience and know-how on Africa, a region with which Japan has had little historical interaction'.[15] Orr, however, mentions a concern about corruption and inefficiency in Japan's involvement of the Crown Agents in the program, that is, to prevent its aid from being wasted. The real concern, therefore, was about the *dysfunctional* nature of corruption in the region.

Also, the Japanese find the region impenetrable because their business enterprises do not perceive the region as a viable economic entity. By implication, it is been suggested here that, had the Japanese business community found the region economically attractive, it would have expanded its investments in a manner that would have drawn the attention of the governments and public of Japan much closer to the African situation. The above argument may be supported by Orr's disclosure concerning bureaucratic politics in Japan and its influence on the country's aid policies. As he points out, 'MITI has frequently been an opponent of increasing aid to Africa since that assistance is earmarked for BHN [Basic Human Needs] projects or emergency food aid', neither of which hardly promote Japanese commercial interests.[16]

THE ANATOMY OF JAPANESE AID TO TANZANIA

It should be stressed that Japan's bilateral ODA to Tanzania (during the period examined) was very small compared to that of other donors, especially the Scandinavian states. Yet it grew very fast (although not smoothly) in the 1980s, as demonstrated in Table 6.1 and in the following figures. In 1986, for example, bilateral ODA from Sweden, Norway and The Netherlands was $107.40 mn., $71.82 mn. and $60.74 mn., respectively, compared to Japan's $35 mn. And in percentage terms, Japan's bilateral ODA to Tanzania was a mere 0.9 percent of its total bilateral aid. It was higher the previous year, at 1.1 percent (at the amount of $28.48 mn.).[17]

But as far as Japan's bilateral ODA to sub-Saharan Africa is concerned, aid to Tanzania was of considerable significance. Table 6.2 indicates where Tanzania fits in the picture of Japanese aid to the region. It shows that Tanzania was by far the largest recipient of grant aid from Japan among the African states; and only second to Kenya in terms of technical aid from Japan. The types and nature of aid that Tanzania received from Japan were mainly in the form of grant aid and technical assistance. The form of technical assistance that Dar es Salaam received from Tokyo consisted

Table 6.1 Share of DAC countries in total bilateral ODA received by Tanzania

1982 ($mn.)			1988 ($mn.)		
Sweden	73.84	15.3%	Sweden	100.18	12.8%
W. Germany	58.77	12.1%	Japan	96.70	12.4%
Holland	56.29	11.6%	Norway	79.05	10.1%
Norway	51.09	10.7%	Holland	78.88	10.1%
Japan	49.97	10.3%	Denmark	77.81	10.0%
UK	41.00	8.4%	Italy	76.93	9.8%
Denmark	39.08	8.2%	West Germany	68.07	8.7%
Canada	35.00	7.0%	Finland	67.22	8.6%
Others	77.31	16.0%	UK	59.14	7.6%
			Others	78.03	10.0%

Notes: *1982*: Total bilateral ODA received: $482.74. Total multilateral ODA received: $172
1988: Total bilateral ODA received $782.01. Total multilateral ODA received: $195.88

Table 6.2 Leading African states receiving Japanese ODA, cumulative to 1986
(¥ 100 mn.: exchange rate approx. 159.10 = $1)

Rank	Loans		Grants		Tech. assistance	
1	Kenya	549.17	Tanzania	283.40	Kenya	205.74
2	Zambia	495.50	Kenya	236.59	Tanzania	125.58
3	Nigeria	401.00	Zambia	193.74	Ghana	65.63
4	Tanzania	353.57	Senegal	171.39	Zambia	56.70
5	Zaire	344.96	Niger	159.90	Malawi	50.47
6	Madagascar	239.66	Ghana	149.61	Zaire	46.85
7	Malawi	146.69	Zaire	114.95	Nigeria	40.12
8	Ghana	118.00	Somalia	110.60	Ethiopia	36.46
9	Guinea	111.50	Madagascar	108.20	Senegal	30.36

Source: Gaimushō, *Wagakuni no seifu kaihatsuenjo*, 1989, p. 265

mainly of Japanese technical experts and technicians, and the training of Tanzanians in technical skills locally and in Japan under the Technical Assistance Scheme. The scheme also involved the application of the skills of volunteers from the Japan Overseas Cooperation Volunteers (JOCV) in Tanzania; and the provision of technical equipment for relevant projects.

Grants were the main feature of Japanese ODA to Tanzania, particularly in the period starting from the early 1980s. Japan's grant aid to Tanzania was primarily earmarked for basic human needs (BHN) projects and emergency food aid. As demonstrated in Table 6.3 the projects include agricultural and industrial development, road and bridge construction and improvement, public health projects (including the supply of medical

Table 6.3 Japanese grant aid/projects in Tanzania, 1973–1987

Year	Project	Amount: (¥ mn.)
1973	Rufiji River bridge – design	165
1977	Food aid: purchase of Thai rice	198
1978	Program to increase food production: purchase and supply of 60 Kubota tractors for Kilimanjaro Agriculture Development Center	400
	Debt relief	235
1979	Kilimanjaro Agricultural and Industrial Development Center (construction)	2,000
	Food aid: purchase of Japanese rice	342
	Program to increase food production: purchase and supply of fertilizer	500
	Purchase and supply of medical instruments and drugs	100
	Promotion of fishing industry – TAFICO: supply of fishing equipments	400
	Debt relief	226
1980	Construction of Selander Bridge	1,500
	Program to increase food production: purchase and supply of fertilizer, and agro-machinery: spare parts for Kubota tractors	500
	Social welfare program: purchase and supply of powdered milk	600
	Debt relief	218
	Supply of medical facilities, equipment	300
1981	Promotion of fishing industry: supply of trawler	500
	Food aid: purchase of Japanese rice	540
	Increase of food production: supply of fertilizer, agro-machinery: Kubota tractor spare parts	500
	Equipments for technical college	30
	Social welfare program: supply of textile products/milk	250
	Supply of medical equipment	300
1982	Food aid: Purchase of Japanese rice	812
	Fertilizer/agro-chemicals	600
	Supply of milk powder (social welfare)	200
	Equipment for Dar es Salaam Technical College	250
1983	Food aid: purchase and supply of Japanese rice	790
	Fertilizer	600
	Social welfare program	200
	Construction of two food grain storage houses in Tanga and Mbeya	900
1984	Morogoro road maintenance program	834
	Social welfare program	200
	Dar es Salaam water works program	889
	Dar es Salaam electrification program	597
	Promotion of fishing industry	1,140
	Food aid program	690
	Program to increase food production: supply of fertilizer	600

Table 6.3 Continued

Year	Project	Amount: (¥ mn.)
1985	Morogoro road maintenance program	944
	Social welfare program	200
	South Bank road construction program	474
	Public sanitation maintenance program	844
	Agriculture transportation build-up program	300
	Food aid program	750
	Program to increase food production: supply of fertilizer	800
	Supply of film equipment to the government's film production corporation	36
1986	Dar es Salaam electrification program	1,320
	Medium-wave radio broadcasting expansion program	864
	Social welfare program	200
	Agriculture transportation build-up program	400
	Malaria control program	500
	Program to increase food production: fertilizer supply	800
	Cultural aid to Zanzibar: sports and audio-visual equipment	650
1987	Ndungu agricultural village development program	781
	Dar es Salaam electrification program	1,145
	Medium-wave radio broadcasting expansion	715
	Kilimanjaro area: supply of management and harvest facilities	596
	Non-project grant aid	2,500
	Food aid	650
	Program to increase food production: supply of fertilizer	800
Grand Total		35,375

Note: Exchange rate value of the ¥ to the US$1: 1973–1976, ¥280.00 – ¥300.95; 1977–1979, ¥240.00–239.70; 1980–1985, ¥212.20 – ¥200.00; 1986, ¥159.10; 1987, ¥123.50.
Sources: Gaimushō, *Wagakuni no seifu kaihatsu enjo*, 1991; Ministry of Finance, Dar es Salaam, 1991.

instruments and drugs) and telecommunication projects, among others. The first Japanese grant to Tanzania, in 1973, was a sum of ¥165 mn. for the construction of a bridge over the Rufiji river. As part of Japan's grant allocations to the African states in the latter part of the 1980s, Tanzania received ¥4.5bn. in non-project grant aid from Japan between 1987 and 1990 (see Appendix 5). Between 1974 and March 1987 Tanzania received grants to the tune of ¥28.3 bn. from Japan, jumping to ¥35.5 bn. the following year.[18]

By the end of 1967, Japan had given Tanzania loan aid to the tune of 200 mn. However, Japan's first loan to Tanzania in 1966 was not followed by any more loans until the big loans in 1978. The first loan (in 1966), was used to finance the production of cashew nuts, a blanket factory and a radio cassette and battery manufacturing company, as shown in Table 6.4. By 1986 Tanzania had received a total of some ¥35.4bn. in loans from Japan.[19] However, Japan was less encouraged to give loan aid to Tanzania and the rest of the least-developed countries (LDCs) after 1981. A country that promised little or no economic benefits directly to the Japanese economy was less likely to get loans from Japan because of MITI's opposition to such forms of assistance. This is an indication that Tanzania was really of no economic importance to Japan. As was shown in Table 6.2, however, Kenya was by far the leading recipient of loans from Japan in sub-Saharan Africa. This suggests that, within the region, Kenya was seen by Japan's policy makers as economically more viable. The emphasis on grant and technical aid to Tanzania, as should be stressed, shows that Gaimushō was the primary initiator of Japan's economic assistance to Tanzania.

Table 6.4 Japanese firms with equity holdings in Tanzania, 1981

Name of company	Year established	Products (manufactured)	Initial investment	(%)
Cashew	1968	Cashew Nuts	$80,000	(50%)
Nissho Iwai	1965	Fabrics	T2.6 mn./-	(7.7%)
Hirata Boseki	1964	Fishing nets	T1.7 mn./-	(20%)
Matsushita Electric	1966	Radio, cassette batteries	T31 mn./-	(100%)
Maruzen Shoten	1961	Blankets	T19.5 mn./-	(50%)
Marubeni/Yamayo Blanket	1967	Blankets	T2.5 mn./-	(32%)
Yuasa Denchi	1978	Car batteries	T4.5 mn./-	(16.7%)

Note: % indicates percentage share of Japanese investor. From 1961 to 1974 the exchange rate for the (T) shilling remained at 7.14/= to $1. In 1978 it was T7.96/- to $1.
Source: Gaimushō, *Tanzania no kaizai shakai no genjō*, no. 4, 1983, p. 49

Major Japanese aid projects in Tanzania

Two main Japanese aid projects in Tanzania received wide publicity in the country. They were, first, the two developments under the Kilimanjaro Regional Integrated Development Plan (KRIDP) – the Kilimanjaro Industrial Development Center (KIDC) and the Kilimanjaro Agricultural Development Center (KADC). The second project that also received some publicity was the Malaria Control Project for the Dar es Salaam and Tanga area. There were (as indicated in Table 6.3) also less publicized projects undertaken by Japan. These included road construction and telecommunications. Almost all of Japan's aid projects were in the Kilimanjaro area and Dar es Salaam.[20]

The KRIDP was part of Tanzania's third five-year development plan from 1975 to 1985, during which period Tanzania launched its integrated development plans for each region to facilitate rural development. The plans were based on the initiatives of the respective regions and involved 45 projects which were estimated at the cost of (Tanzanian shillings) T1.8 bn./-. They were scheduled to be finished by 1995. The two major projects undertaken by Japan, out of six urgent project items selected by Tokyo,[21] were estimated at the cost of T60 mn./-,[22] of which the Japanese government provided ¥2 bn. as grant aid.[23] In effect, the KRIDP was a joint project involving the two governments. In tune with the terms of agreement between them, the main centers of the two projects were handed over to the Tanzanian government upon completion in 1981.[24] The actual agricultural and industrial projects started in 1982.

Japan's involvement in the project started in 1970 when it sent a Keidanren survey team (the Kōno mission), under the leadership of a Mr. Kōno.[25] This team was followed by several more missions to Tanzania to assess the potential for agricultural and small-scale industries in the region.[26] The Japanese government, however, did not make any commitments towards the projects until the host government had formally requested help from Japan, a standard administrative requirement known as *yōsei shugi*. In other words, unless Tanzania submitted a formal request for the extension of concessional loans or grant aid, as well as a report on the economic and technical viability of each project, Japan would not give it any assistance.[27] The objective here was to allay any potential fears on the part of the recipients that Japan was being aggressive, or 'imperialist'.[28] In other words, Japan did not want to be accused of being pushy and domineering.

On the whole, the Japanese government, through its aid agency, the Japan International Cooperation Agency (JICA), negotiated for, and got, sixteen of the fifty projects identified in the reports of the Japanese missions. The sixteen projects comprised the already mentioned six urgent project items, which included the development of 1,200 hectares of irrigated farm land and 1,100 hectares of paddy field in Moshi, with a loan of ¥3.3 bn. The agricultural project also entailed doing research on the use of underground water in the lower land areas of Kilimanjaro for irrigation purposes. It further involved a program to impart agricultural knowledge and the carrying out of research and extension services to farmers, and a vegetable production project. Agricultural seeds were provided to the peasants, who were also provided with tractors for tilling the land and paddy fields. All these come under the KADC. In addition, within the agricultural project the Ndugu area was selected for a village development plan with a grant of ¥800 mn. There was also the village electrification project, which was implemented with a 1981 loan of ¥1.6 bn.

The Industrial Development Center was set up to encourage the development of small-scale industries and to recruit technical personnel to manage these industries in the region, among other things. Its services were to include the development of metal for the production of farm implements, the fixing and repairs of industrial machines, the training of technicians, and research for the development of industrial technology.[29]

The next most important Japanese assistance to Tanzania was the malaria Control Project for the Dar es Salaam and Tanga municipality. The five-year project (starting in 1986) was initially financed with a grant of ¥500 mn. from the Japanese government.[30] The goal of the program was to reduce the dangers caused to people's health by malaria to as low a level as possible. The project involved the provision of insecticides, spraying machines, trucks, methods to improve the drainage system in the city, and other relevant research and educational materials. Under the agreement, the Sumitomo Corporation of Japan provided the greater part of the resources for the program while its subsidiary company, Sumitomo Chemicals Ltd., supplied most of the chemicals – sumithion 40 percent and emulsifiable concentrates.[31] The project was reviewed every year and Japan pledged to provide funding until completion of the end of the project.[32] A third phase of the project was signed in February 1991,[33] with Japan providing a T.456 mn./- grant towards it.

A last important area of Japanese involvement in the Tanzanian development program worth our mention was in the area of road construction. The most outstanding Japanese road construction projects include the Selander road works in Dar es Salaam (1980), completed with ¥1.5 bn. grant,[34] the Morogoro road improvement scheme and the Zanzibar road works. The Japanese construction company, Kajima Kensetsu was responsible for all of these projects,[35] including their maintenance.[36] It is important to mention that the performance of Kajima Kensetsu also helped turn Japan into a brand name in Tanzania. Needless to say, the company's performance was (in 1991) threatening the dominance of the Italian companies in the construction sector.

As one would expect, criticisms were raised from time to time of elements of the Japanese aid effort in Tanzania. Yoshida Masao points out that the Kilimanjaro projects did have some serious problems.[37] The agricultural projects, for example, suffered from water shortage regularly, as a result of which production lagged far behind the original target. He also notes that as a result of the water shortage not all the 1,100 hectares allocated for rice cultivation were used for the production of the crop.

According to Yoshida, work in the industrial centre was slow, because of lack of raw materials for the production of metal, for example. And because the industrial sector of the economy was hardly developed, the trained workers could not really apply their skills in any meaningful way. On the whole, however, the Kilimanjaro project is noted as successful, considering its size.[38]

Certain officials, on their part, viewed Japanese ODA as tied, since some of the projects, for example the malaria control project and the role of the Sumitomo Corporation in it, indicate. According to one Tanzanian official, it would be impossible to get an affirmative answer for a request for aid from the Japanese government if the project in question were designed for a company unrelated to Japan. However, this practice is not unique to Japan. In fact, most aid donors have that conditionality. Another criticism against Japan, as voiced by President Nyerere, was that Japan let its 'technical experts leave too quickly once a project has been built or established, and [the] volunteers leave . . . when their usefulness is at its height'.[39]

On the whole, however, Tanzanian officials appreciated what they saw as generous Japanese economic assistance to their country, and the official English language newspaper *Daily News* constantly made note of it. According to one news item, Tanzania 'if anything, has every reason to breath comfortably since an economically powerful friend is behind many of [its] current economic programs'. The article further states that, 'authorities in Dar es Salaam are comfortable that Japanese aid is not politically motivated.'[40]

President Nyerere himself commended the Japanese for their assistance to Tanzania, during the visit of Emperor (then Crown Prince) Akihito to Tanzania in August 1983. The President made particular reference to Japan's food aid to Tanzania during the drought period, and to the Selander bridge, 'the building of which so greatly impressed all of us by its speed and efficiency'.[41] And Mr. Evarist Mwanansau, during his term as Minister of Lands, Water, Housing and Urban Development, announced that Tanzania had gained a great deal of technical skill through Japanese assistance.[42]

In another article in which it compliments Japan, the *Daily News* states that Tokyo's 'grants . . . have enabled the Tanzanian government to execute fifty projects'. It points out that the JICA had sponsored 600 Tanzanians to attend training courses in Japan, in addition to about 200 Japanese experts and 450 volunteers who had extended their technical skills to Tanzania. On the basis of the above, the newspaper might be right to suggest that the Japanese were successful in fostering a (politically expedient) sense of gratitude within the Tanzanian polity.

Trade as a determinant of Japanese aid

The argument that Japanese ODA to Tanzania was hardly correlated to Japanese economic interests in Tanzania holds.[43] In order to make this proposition meaningful to the discussion, it is useful to look at Japanese economic interests in Tanzania, which remained rather paltry. The lack of a meaningful economic relationship between the two countries is demonstrated in the mostly frustrated attempts on the part of Tanzanian trade officials, especially since the country's economic liberalization program in 1986, to attract Japanese businesses to participate actively in the country's export economy.

At a seminar held in Dar es Salaam in July 1978 to promote trade between Tanzania and Japan, the Director General of the Board of External Trade complained that the trade imbalance between Japan and his country remained grossly unfavourable to Tanzania. As indicated in Table 6.5 trade between the two countries in 1978 brought an outstanding balance of $98.2 mn. in favour of Japan. Japanese exports to Tanzania in 1989 were $92 mn. compared to its $27 mn. imports from the latter in that year.[44] The Director General noted in his speech that the huge trade imbalance was due to the nature of the exchange between the two countries. Whereas Tanzania's imports from Japan consists of vehicles, machinery and equipment, Japanese imports from Dar es Salaam are raw materials like sisal, cotton, coffee, and sea foods.[45] At the seminar, the Minister of State of the Ministry of Foreign Affairs, Amina Salim Ali,

Table 6.5 Trade between Japan and Tanzania, 1977–1989 (US $mn.)

Year	Exports	Imports
1977	68.21	19.29
1978	109.95	11.73
1979	71.86	28.55
1980	113.33	23.25
1981	93.40	18.63
1982	90.60	18.02
1983	75.17	18.41
1984	78.29	17.07
1985	75.70	16.68
1986	99.56	22.95
1987	89.43	18.68
1988	94.17	26.54
1989	92.15	27.39

Source: Japanese Embassy, Dar es Salaam, 1991

urged Japanese companies to join their Tanzanian counterparts in utilizing Tanzania's raw materials with a view to creating export capacities for the country.[46]

Thus, at a workshop for the 'Promotion of Industrial and Commercial Cooperation Between Japan and Tanzania' held in Dar es Salaam in 1988, Dr. Nicas Mahinda, the Deputy Minister for Industries and Trade, urged Japanese companies to help create more export capacities for Tanzania. The workshop was organized by the (Tanzania) Board of External Trade and JETRO.[47] It concerned, on the whole, the question of Japanese investments in Tanzania, which were rather insignificant, as was indicated in Table 6.4.

In 1991, there were only seven Japanese companies, with about eighteen cases of investment, worth $5.5 mn. operating in the country. And there had been no new Japanese investments in Tanzania since 1978. The last one before that, in 1968, was for the production of cashew nuts.[48] As Table 6.4 has shown, all the Japanese companies in the country, except Yuasa Denchi, were established in the 1960s. According to a Japanese government publication, Tanzania's 'socialist policies and its bankrupt economy' were responsible for the few Japanese investments in the country.[49]

And while Japan was registered as Tanzania's third most important trading partner in 1991, Tanzania, on its part, was Japan's 101st trading partner.[50] This commercial insignificance of Tanzania to Japan was further confirmed by the Deputy Director of the JICA office in Tanzania, Mr. Tsutsui Noboru, who stressed that Tanzania was of no economic importance to Japan. This point, to put it in its proper context, was meant to show that Japanese aid to Tanzania was for humanitarian reasons, and not because it was bringing in any economic rewards to Japan.

THE POLITICAL IMPLICATIONS OF JAPANESE AID TO TANZANIA

Given the lack of any strong Japanese commercial interests in Tanzania, it is imperative to try and identify at least some of the determinants of Japanese aid to Tanzania. But, to dismiss Japanese aid to Tanzania as having no humanitarian element is tantamount to saying that the Japanese have no natural charitable impulse; an argument which seems to have neither an empirical nor a cultural basis.[51] Indeed, it would seem to represent too easy an alternative to a proper investigation of the possible motives behind Japanese aid. It is true, as Alan Rix points out, that Japan's aid policy makers point to differences in cultures between Japan and the other major aid donors as a determinant of the philosophical underpinnings of their differences in attitude to aid. But one wonders whether this is not simply an attempt on the part of Japan's aid policy makers to rationalize, if not justify, the strong correlation between Japan's aid and its economic interests.[52] It is also tempting to view this attempt to embrace such cultural determinism as an explanation for the differences in approaches to aid as yet another manifestation of Japan as a unique phenomenon in the international scheme of things, as epitomized in the *nihonjin-ron*, a body of literature and ideas exalting the 'uniqueness' of Japan.[53]

Needless to say, Tanzania was only one of the many LDCs in sub-Saharan Africa, and it was by no means the worst. It nevertheless received (for most of the 1980s) more grant aid from Japan than any other country in the region. It is, therefore, tempting to see such assistance to Tanzania as determined by something more simple and practical than a humanitarian reason. Indeed, one is inclined to ask, what was so special about Tanzania? In fact, Japan's global aid policy as a whole calls for a similar inquiry. The fact that more than 40 percent of Japanese aid went to North and South East Asia alone (in 1990), a region that was relatively well-off economically, while only 11 percent of its aid went to sub-Saharan Africa, a region traumatized by perennial economic disasters, calls the proclaimed humanitarian element in Japanese aid into question.

Be that as it may, one cannot completely rule out a humanitarian element in Japanese ODA. Yet nor is the argument paraded by some Japanese officials that Japan's aid to Tanzania was primarily determined by Japan's humanitarian instincts convincing.[54] The main preoccupation here, then, is to try to identify why Tanzania occupied such a favourable position in terms of Japanese aid to the region.

The following reasons are posited:

1 Tanzania's leading frontline position in the struggle against colonialism and minority rule in the Southern African region[55] from the 1960s into the 1980s. As Horace Campbell points out, 'the formation of the Frontline States . . . showed the ability of Tanzania to bring together states of differing ideological postures in the cause of liberation', a fact which contributed to the Japanese interest in Nyerere.[56]

2 Tanzania's popularity among the Third World states and in international politics, a fact related to the first point.

3 The centrality of Nyerere in all of the above. Interestingly, Japanese politics shares with 'African politics' the culture of placing importance on 'individuals'. This last point alludes to the Japanese obsession with identifying someone to depend on. That person has to be dependable.

Thus, a person with an active and long political career, and who also enjoys political stability and a certain amount of respect and popularity, would be the wisest choice. Nyerere fitted that position perfectly well in Africa. In this respect, it may be appropriate to note that the Japanese Foreign Ministry took note of Tanzania's political stability.[57]

The fourth reason is that Japan's aid to Tanzania may also have been influenced by a sharing of interests and perceptions, particularly with regard to solving the problem of minority rule in Southern Africa, between the elites in Tanzania and Japan. Nyerere was perceived as a man of peace (although he was not a pacifist), who fervently believed in negotiation rather than resorting to force.[58] The point that war as a means to solving the problem of minority rule in Southern Africa was seen as potentially risky to Japan's accessibility to the strategic resources in the region has been made several times before. Thus, Japan's diplomacy towards the Southern Africa problem revolved, categorically, around finding a peaceful solution to it and (as shown in Chapter 5), Japan abhorred the idea of 'armed struggle' as a means to tackling the problem. On the whole, Japanese policy makers saw Japan and Tanzania as being very closely related (*kinmitsu na kankei*), and placed much importance (*jūten*) on Tanzania in the context of Tokyo's diplomacy towards sub-Saharan Africa.[59]

Another factor that might have encouraged Japan to select Tanzania as an important recipient was the latter's popularity with the major aid donors at the time. It is common knowledge that, regarding Third World issues, Japan in many instances followed what the other OECD countries did.[60] But there was also much pressure on Japan, especially in the 1980s, from the other DAC members, and particularly from the World Bank, to increase its aid to the African states.[61] Japanese aid to Tanzania, finally, was influenced by the huge trade balance in its favour.

Essentially, Japan's attraction to Tanzania since the 1970s was primarily due to the latter's political importance. Given the political implications of trade with Pretoria and the diplomatic risks involved in it, Japan's policy makers saw it as diplomatically expedient to cultivate close relations with Tanzania. With a friend like that behind it, Tokyo hoped to nip in the bud any criticisms that might be levelled against it by the member states of the OAU, and by the Third World community as a whole for expanding trade with Pretoria. The idea, thus, was to have an influential insider who would manipulate any ill-feeling among the OAU states against Japan. And Japan might have succeeded in legitimizing the cross-cutting requirements of its relations with the conflicting political positions in Africa by having Tanzania as its 'spokesman'[62] within the Organization of African Unity. A Dahlain formulation of power, 'the ability to get others to do things they normally would not do', is not being suggested here. But it would soon be established that despite Tanzania's hardline position against apartheid and all countries that supposedly supported that system through trade, Japan's relations with South Africa were seemingly dealt with differently.

It must be noted, then, that when, in early November 1974, the Japanese Foreign Minister Mr. Kimura Toshio, visited Tanzania, his counterpart, Mr. John Malecela, assured him that 'being fully aware of Japan's reliance on external trading [Tanzania] has no intention of requesting the Japanese to call an immediate halt to normal trading with South Africa'. He then 'urged Japan to boost its economic aid to African states bordering South Africa and Rhodesia'.[63] Inevitably, Malecela's statement is suggestive of a transactional proposition. And Kimura's mission in Africa, as he himself poignantly put it, was to 'win over the critics of Japan one at a time [*kakko gekiha sakusen toshite*].'[64]

The two most burning issues that Kimura had to contend with during his visit to the four states in sub-Saharan Africa (Ghana, Nigeria, Zaire and Tanzania) were (1) Japan's relations with South Africa, and (2) Japanese economic assistance to the African states. Kimura's tour of Africa, the first of its kind by a Japanese Cabinet Minister, took place in the aftermath of the first oil crisis, when the Japanese awareness of the political connotations of economic issues had become heightened. The Foreign Minister's trip to Africa was, in essence, in response to the new developments in the international political economy, punctuated by threats from countries holding certain crucial resources. Incidentally, in May 1973, the African states, through their Ambassadors in Tokyo, had delivered a warning to Japan to the effect that the latter would be isolated from the AA group if it did not support the African states in their struggle against the minority regimes in Southern Africa. Indeed, they further threatened to refuse Japan access to the resources in Africa, if it continued expanding its economic relations with Pretoria.

With reference to Foreign Minister Malecela's comments above, however, it is also worth pointing out that Tanzania's response to the problem of Japan's relations with South Africa contradicted the position adopted by the other African states as expressed through the Ambassadors in Tokyo. With this particular Tanzanian behavior as a point of reference, it can be assumed that the issue of Japan's relations with South Africa did pose a problem of conflict of interests among the African states. Malecela's assurances to Japan can be seen as having defined a relationship between Tokyo and Dar es Salaam; and conceivably one that was different from what the OAU as a body might have adopted towards Japan.

Whether Tanzania's response to Japan's relations with South Africa was primarily defined by the need to solicit aid from Japan is, however, hard to say, because it is difficult to establish the counterfactual baseline. How, for example, Tanzania would have acted in the absence of economic assistance from Japan. But then one wonders whether the fact that Tanzania became one of the leading recipients of Japanese grant and technical aid to sub-Saharan Africa after those reassuring words from the Tanzania Foreign Minister is a mere coincidence. It seems obvious, though, that Tanzania was judged 'worthy' of aid primarily on the basis of political criteria. That is not, however, to say that the relationship was based on 'reward and compliance'. It might have been based on consensus. And it might have been 'a consensus that occurs within a relationship that imposes constraints' on the aid recipient.[65] Nyerere himself foresaw such constraints on a nation that depended on external assistance. 'He who pays the piper calls the tune', he said.[66]

Whether Tanzania, based on the arguments above, served Japan's interests at all is also difficult to ascertain. And it would be equally difficult to establish how it did it, if it did so at all. Suffice to say that Tanzania has been a bellwether of African public opinion, and Japan's policy makers saw it as such.

To reiterate the point, Tanzania's importance in the international community was primarily cultivated around the image of Nyerere and, of course, in response to certain situational imperatives like the Cold War. The Cold War, among other things, turned Nyerere into an outstanding spokesman for the Third World countries as represented by the Non-aligned Movement. Nyerere is, however, no longer the head of the Tanzanian political system, having vacated the presidency in 1985, and finally relinquished his last political post as chairman of the Chama Cha Mapinduzi (CCM) (the ruling, and at the time the only, political party in Tanzania) in 1989. His absence from Tanzanian politics undoubtedly deprived the country of its important role in regional and international politics. Subsequent developments in Eastern Europe, culminating in the end of the Cold War, made the non-aligned position in international politics even more redundant, and thus any leadership position, in that respect, rather superfluous.

Most important for this analysis is the fact that the political implications of trade with South Africa had started to lose their original importance and intensity by the latter of part of 1989, due to political developments in the country. Tokyo therefore saw no use in seeking help from any state to assuage African public opinion on the question of Japan's trade relations with South Africa. In other words, the importance of Tanzania to Japan in its foreign relations with sub-Saharan Africa became less crucial; and in 1991 Japanese officials were asking whether it was at all necessary to give Tanzania such a prominent place in Tokyo's aid policy towards sub-Saharan Africa.[67] In fact, Tanzania's ranking among Japan's grant aid recipients in sub-Saharan Africa started to decline from 1988. Tanzania was Japan's leading grant aid recipient in the region from 1985 to 1987. In 1988 and 1989, however, it was fourth and third, respectively. In both of these years Zaire and Zambia, respectively, assumed the leading position, as indicated in Appendix 2. Tanzania was further demoted to the fifth position in 1990, while Zambia remained the leading recipient of Japanese grant aid to the region.

In addition, for the first time since 1978,[68] Tanzania's ranking as the second recipient of technical aid from Japan (see Appendix 4) declined to the third position in 1989, and remained so in 1990 (see Appendix 3). Zambia replaced it as the second recipient of technical assistance in both years. Zambia's importance in this respect is captured more vividly in its share of the non-project grant aid that Japan gave to twenty-seven African states from 1987 to 1990. Over this four-year period Zambia, as the leading recipient of this aid, received $105 mn. compared to the $45 mn. that Tanzania received over the same period (Appendix 5). Nevertheless, Tanzania, in cumulative terms, remains the leading recipient of Japanese grant aid and the second leading recipient of Japanese technical assistance to the region (Appendices 2 and 3).

Zambia's importance to Japan may be attributable to the 'spokesman' role of President Kenneth Kaunda in African politics at the time. It is conceivable that Kaunda was seen by Japan's policy makers as a good substitute for Nyerere. He was also a veteran statesman. Moreover, he was, until 1991, a head of state, and commanded some respect in international politics. Like Nyerere, he was committed to a peaceful solution to the South(ern) Africa problem. And, incidentally, Zambia was also a frontline state.

CONCLUSION

Due to Tanzania's importance in Third World, and indeed African, politics, Japan's policy makers found it necessary to cultivate good diplomatic relations with the country. The idea was to get the bellwether of African public opinion and the moral voice in the region's politics to assuage African anxiety over Japan's expanding economic relations with South Africa. Despite Tanzania's committed position against imperialism, apartheid and the countries that supposedly supported the latter system through trade, there was hardly a critical finger raised in the face of Japan for its expanding economic relations with the pariah state as Ronald Dore tells us (in Chapter 1, p. 19). It has been shown that, instead, Foreign Minister Malecela gave Japan assurances that it was not expected to put an end to its trade with South Africa; and that the amount of economic assistance Tanzania received from Japan, compared to what went to the other African states, was determined by Tanzania's standing in African and indeed international politics.

Thus, as Tanzania lost its position as a moral voice in global affairs, aid allocated to it by Japan declined in importance, and indeed in value, relative to Japanese aid allocations to states in the region that previously received less aid from it. Conceivably, these states might have emerged in Japan's diplomatic perception as being more important. It is difficult, however, to corroborate the argument that Tanzania was successful in keeping the African states (as a unit) quiet over the question of Japan's relations with Pretoria. That Malecela's assurances to Mr. Kimura contradicted the position expressed in May 1973 by the African Ambassadors to Japan is, however, obvious from the arguments presented here.

One of the most essential points made in this discussion is that Japanese aid to Tanzania after the mid-1970s was not based on securing any economic interests in Tanzania itself. The allocation of few loans to the country support this argument. Instead, aid was used to win Tanzania's 'understanding' of Japan's so-called 'predicament' as a nation that survives on trade and therefore had to trade with South Africa. And evidently, Japan was extensively dependent on Pretoria for a range of strategic raw materials. These resources, needless to say, were essential for Japan's economic security. Trade with South Africa was therefore part of the grandiose formula for Japan's CNS. Tanzania, as shown here, became an adjunct of that equation. Yet, Tanzania's supposed silence on Japan's relations with Pretoria was not necessarily based on 'reward and compliance', because Tokyo lacked the prior and massive penetration of the Tanzanian political economy which it would have needed in order to fine-tune the latter's foreign policy. It was, presumably, as Bruce Moon might say a position reached through consensus between the two actors. Nevertheless, a consensus between Japan and Tanzania on the question of the former's relations with South Africa might have been one that imposed major constraints on Tanzania.

NOTES

1 Aid is strictly defined here as the transfer of money on concessional terms and technical assistance by the governments of rich countries to the governments of poor countries. This form of assistance shall be categorized as grant aid, technical assistance and yen loans. The above categorization may cause definitional problems, since the first two categories may overlap in meaning, at least as far as the grant element of aid is concerned. Grant aid includes aid for disaster relief (which may involve food aid), cultural activities, food production, and aid which is not tied to any specific project or training, but simply enables the recipient economy to import for the priority sectors of the economy – non-project grant aid. Grant aid imposes no obligation of

repayment on the recipient country. Technical assistance covers (1) assistance in education and training given to individuals of developing countries at home or abroad, and (2) the delivery of assistance by donor country personnel as teachers, administrators, technical experts, doctors and other professionals with skills in developmental projects. This second category, in the case of Japan at least, includes volunteers and the provision of certain types of technical equipment. Also in this instance, technical assistance as applied by Japan is nearly always in the form of grants. The recipients of yen loans, on the other hand, are expected to repay the loan with interest, although interest rates are pegged below commercial rates and are determined according to the level of economic development achieved by the recipient state.

2 Issa Shivji, *The Silent Class Struggle,* Dar es Salaam, 1973; Issa Shivji, *Class Struggles in Tanzania*, London, Heinemann Educational, 1976, pp. 48–50.

3 Shivji, *The Silent Class Struggle*, chapters 7 and 8.

4 World Bank, *Tanzania: Agricultural Sector Report, 1983*, Washington D.C., 1983, p. 4.

5 World Bank, *Accelerated Development in Sub-Saharan Africa, 1981*, Washington D.C., 1981, p. 164.

6 Dennis Yasutomo, 'Why Aid? Japan as an Aid Great Power', *Pacific Affairs*, vol. 62, no. 4, Winter, 1989/90, p. 419.

7 Japan's first aid to Africa was in 1966, when it gave financial assistance in the form of loans to Nigeria, Kenya, Tanzania and Uganda.

8 Alan Rix, *Japan's Economic Aid: Policymaking and Politics*, London, Croom Helm, 1980; Alan Rix, 'Japan's Comprehensive Security and Australia', *Australian Outlook: The Australian Journal of International Relations*, vol. 41, no. 2, August, 1987; Alan Rix, *Japan's Foreign Aid Challenge: Policy Reform and Aid Challenge*, London, Routledge, 1993; Aoki Kazuyoshi, 'Nihon to afurika: hyo na kankei kara mitsunaru kankei no kōchiku', in Oda Hideo (ed.), *Afurika no seiji to kokusai kankei*, Tokyo, Keisō shobō, 1991.

9 Robert Orr, *The Emergence of Japanese Foreign Aid Power*, New York, Columbia University Press, 1990, p. 130.

10 Edward V.K. Jaycox, 'Japan's Role in African Development: Challenges and Opportunities', keynote address to the African Symposium, Kaidanren kaikan, Tokyo, 27–28 October 1988.

11 Yasutomo, 'Why Aid?', p. 493.

12 Ibid., p. 494.

13 William Brooks and Robert Orr, 'Japan's Foreign Economic Assistance', *Asian Survey*, vol. xxv, no. 3, March, 1985, p. 329.

14 According to 1986 figures the countries are Zambia, Kenya, Ghana, Nigeria, and Sao Tome and Principe in that order of value of aid.

15 Ministry of Foreign Affairs, *Japan's ODA, Annual Report, 1988*, Tokyo, Association for the Promotion of International Cooperation, 1989, p. 58.

16 Orr, *The Emergence of Japanese Foreign Aid Power*, p. 37.

17 Ministry of Foreign Affairs, *Japan's ODA*, 1988, p. 202.

18 Gaimushō, *Wagakuni no seifu kaihatsu enjo gekan, vol. 2*, Tokyo, Kokusai kyōryoku suishin kyōkai, 1987, p. 265; Gaimushō, *Wagakuni no seifu kaihatsu enjo gekan, vol. 2*, Tokyo, Kokusai kyōryoku suishin kyōkai, 1988, p. 283. The exchange rate for the yen in 1973 was ¥271.22 to $1. From 1987 to 1989 the value of the yen oscillated between ¥146 and ¥142 to $1.

19 Gaimushō, *Wagakuni no seifu kaihatsu enjo gekan, vol. 2*, 1987, p. 283.

20 Kokusai kyōryoku jigyōdan kokusai kyōryoku sōgo kenshūjo, *Kaihatsu tōjō gijutsu jōhō dētā shiito tanzania (1/2), kaihatsu enjo koku gijitsu dēta*, Tokyo, Kokusai kyōryoku shuppankai, September, 1990.
21 Yoshida Masao, 'Nihon no keizai enjo ni okeru afurika', in Suzuki Nagatoshi (ed.), *Nihon no keizai kyōryoku no ashidori*, Tokyo, Ajia keizai shuppankai, 1989, p. 180. The other urgent project items were: (1) the introduction of agricultural machines – mainly tractors; (2) the construction of agricultural irrigation in Lower Moshi; (3) development work on the Nkomaji river; and (4) electrification of agricultural villages.
22 *Daily News*, 24 November 1980. The exchange rate in 1975 was T8.26/- = $1.
23 *Daily News*, 8 September 1978. The exchange rate in 1979 was ¥296.80 = $1.
24 *Daily News*, 22 June 1981.
25 Yoshida, 'Nihon no keizai enjo', p. 177.
26 Yoshida, 'Nihon no keizai enjo', p. 177; Dr. Okita Saburo (President, International Development Center of Japan), *The Development of Tanzania and Possibilities of Japanese Cooperation: With Special Reference to the Comprehensive Development of the Kilimanjaro Region'*, Tokyo, International Development Center of Japan, 1971.
27 Yoshida, 'Nihon no keizai enjo', p. 177.
28 Inada Juichi, 'Taigai enjo', in Uno Shigeaki, Kido Shigeru, Yamamoto Yoshinari, and Watanabe Akio, *Kōza kokusai seiji 4: Nihon no gaikō*, Tokyo, Tokyo daigaku shuppankai, 1981, p. 199; Orr Jr., *The Emergence of Japan's Foreign Aid Power*, p. 60.
29 Kokusai kyōryoku jigyōdan chiikaka, *Tanzania: keizai gijutsu kyōryoku*, Tokyo, Kokusai kyōryoku shuppankai, 1988, p. 29.
30 Ibid., p. 31.
31 'Anti-malaria Project Starts', *Sunday News*, 5 June 1988.
32 *Sunday News*, 22 May 1988.
33 *Daily News*, 12 February 1991.
34 Gaimushō kanshū afurika hen, *Tanzania no keizai shakai no genjō. No. 4*, Tokyo, Kokusai kyōryoku shuishin kyōkai, 1983, p. 51.
35 'Kajima Hails Tanzanian Workers', *Sunday News*, 24 November 1985.
36 Interview with Mr. R.H.T. Msoffe (Assistant Director, Japan International Cooperation Agency, Tanzania), 10 April 1991.
37 Yoshida, 'Nihon no keizai enjo', p. 83.
38 See also Katsuki Toshitaka (Ministry of Agriculture and Fisheries), 'Some Findings from Farm Economy Survey (KADP, Lower Moshi Area): Short-term Economic Survey', Tokyo, Japan International Cooperation Agency, 1991.
39 *Daily News*, 18 July 1983.
40 Charles Mmbaga, *Daily News*, 15 June 1989, p. 3.
41 *Daily News*, 18 March 1983.
42 *Daily News*, 6 November 1986.
43 Iwaki Gou's attempts to attribute the expansion of Japanese aid to Tanzania partly to the good trade relations between the two countries is unacceptable. See 'Tanzania ni taisuru nihon no ODA', in Kawabata Masahisa (ed.) *Afurika to nihon*, Tokyo, Keisō shobō, 1994, p. 229.
44 Gaimushō, *Wagakuni no seifu kaihatsu enjo, vol. 2*, Tokyo, Kokusai kyōryoku suishin kyōkai, 1990, p. 482.
45 Welcome address by the Director-General of the Board of External Trade at the

opening of the seminar on Promotion of Trade Between Tanzania and Japan, Kilmanjaro Hotel, Dar es Salaam, 23 July 1987.

46 *Daily News*, 24 July 1987

47 'Dar Wants Greater Trade Ties With Tokyo', *Daily News*, 5 February 1988.

48 Gaimushō, *Tanzania no keizai shakai no genjō no. 4*, p. 49; Gaimushō, *Wagakuni no seifu kaihatsu enjo, vol 2*, 1990, p. 482.

49 Gaimushō, *Tanzania no keizai shakai no genjō, no. 4*, p. 49.

50 Peter Mwanguo (Director of Exports, Promotion and Publicity, Board of Trade), 'Tanzania Exports to Japan', paper delivered in Dar es Salaam, 11 April 1991, p. 6.

51 Alan Rix, *Japan's Foreign Aid Challenge*, pp. 16, 18, 41–42.

52 By 1990 Japan had, remarkably, improved its performance in this matter so much that Japan ranked first among DAC donors for its level of untying of aid.

53 A body of books and articles written by Japanese authors about Japanese cultural identity, and stressing the perceived 'uniquely unique' aspects of Japanese culture.

54 Interview with Mr. Tsutsui Noboru (Deputy Director, Japan International Cooperation Agency, Director of Japan Overseas Cooperation Volunteers, Tanzania), 9 April 1991; Interview with Mr. Kania Seiichi (Director – Third Regional Division: Africa, Middle East, East Europe – Planning Department, Japan International Cooperation Agency, Africa Division, Tokyo), 23 September 1991.

55 Gaimushō, *Wagakuni no seifu kaihatsu enjo gekan*, vol. 2, 1990, p. 482.

56 Horace Campbell, 'Tanzania and the Liberation Process of Southern Africa', *The African Review*, vol. 14, nos. 1 and 2, 1987, pp. 15–16.

57 Gaimushō, *Wagakuni no seifu kaihatsu enjo gekan, vol. 2*, 1989, p. 481; 'Japan Will Aid Africa in Anticolonial Struggle', *The Japan Times*, 7 November 1974, p. 4.

58 Campbell, 'Tanzania and the Liberation Process of Southern Africa'.

59 Gaimushō, *Wagakuni no seifu kaihatsu enjo gekan, vol. 2*, 1990, p. 482.

60 Iwaki Gou, 'Tanzania ni taisuru nihon no ODA', seems to suggest that the expansion of aid to Tanzania by the world's leading capitalist countries, including Japan, was essentially dictated by these countries' determination to win Tanzania over to the Western camp (p. 226). In his assessment of Japanese aid to Tanzania, Iwaki also mentions some of the reasons I have given above as having influenced Japanese economic assistance to Tanzania, and mentions in particular Tanzania's importance in international politics (p. 229), and President Nyerere's criticisms against imperialist countries (p. 226); conceivably those countries including Japan who supported South Africa.

61 Orr, *The Emergence of Japanese Foreign Aid Power*, p. 150.

62 This 'spokesman' role could have simply amounted to Tanzania not saying anything critical of Japan's relations with South Africa. The point being made here is that, since Tanzania was an opinion leader within the OAU, if it had chosen to be publicly critical of Japan the latter's standing among the OAU member states may have become very bad indeed.

63 'Japan and Africa: Minister's African Tour Fruitful', *The Anglo-Japanese Economic Institute*, no. 104, 1974, p. 1.

64 *Asahi shimbun*, 8 November 1974, p. 4. The literal translation of the phrase *kakko gekiha* is: defeat (the opposite members) one by one; destroy (the enemy) one at a time. See also 'Japan Pledges Aid to Equalize Africa Trade', *The Japan Times*, 8 November 1974, p. 9.

65 Bruce E. Moon, 'Consensus or Compliance? Foreign-policy Change and External Dependence', *International Organization*, vol. 39, no. 2, Spring, 1985.
66 Julius Nyerere, *Freedom and Socialism: A Selection from Writings and Speeches, 1965–1967* , London, Oxford University Press, 1969, pp. 239–40.
67 Interview with Mr. Saitō Kōji (Economic Attaché, Embassy of Japan, Tanzania), 10 and 15 April 1991.
68 Gaimushō, *Wagakuni no seifu kaihatsu enjo gekan, vol. 2*, 1990, 1991.

7   Conclusion

Using the issue of the Japanese conception of security as a framework of analysis, and focusing in particular on the economic dimensions of Japan's CNS, this study has analyzed, empirically, the political, economic and diplomatic factors surrounding Japan's relations with sub-Saharan Africa during the period from 1974–1991. By examining Japan's relations with three African states, South Africa, Nigeria and Tanzania, the study shows that the key determinants of Japan's relations with each of these countries are rather different. In the case of Tanzania, Japanese aid was primarily motivated by the need for good relations with a significant 'frontline' state. With respect to Nigeria, Japanese involvement was concerned with the need to secure access to markets and constrained by the uncertainties of government policy and an erratic macro-economic environment. Japan's relations with South Africa were shaped by the need for certain strategic raw materials from that country. This need made it impossible for Japan's policy makers to take a firm and consistent stand against South Africa's apartheid policies – a fact that is confirmed, in this study, by the analysis of Japan's voting on apartheid-related issues at the UNGA. The central argument of the study is that Japan was faced with what Morikawa Jun refers to as *nigen kōzō*, a 'double preoccupation' of accommodating the interests of the minority regime in South Africa, on the one hand, and fulfilling certain diplomatic requirements pertinent to its relations with the other African states, on the other.

Whether the economic diplomacy employed in relation to sub-Saharan Africa by Japan succeeded in reconciling Tokyo's resource and other economic interests in South Africa, on the one hand, and its diplomatic efforts towards the OAU states, on the other, is a useful point of reference for the following discussion. The first point to make is that Japanese foreign policy was very ingenious and successful in dealing with these two conflicting interests. Thus, Japanese diplomacy towards sub-Saharan Africa was successful.

In light of this, it might be suggested that the dynamic aspects of Japanese foreign policy decision making are more articulate than the overall immobilist tendencies of its foreign policy pattern suggests. Japanese diplomacy towards the Middle East, especially in the 1970s, and its diplomacy towards sub-Saharan Africa during the period under review may be seen as good examples of a rather dynamic response to crisis situations, with the ultimate objective of meeting the state's economic interests; and the parallels between the two cases are eminently striking. The contradictions are also self-evident.

As has been pointed out, the oil crisis of 1973/74 jolted the sensibilities of Japan's policy makers into realizing and coming to terms with the political implications of international trade. In particular, it increased Japanese awareness of the politicization of economic issues, and accentuated the Japanese perception of the indivisibility of economic and security issues, especially in the realms of natural resources acquisition. In essence, the Arab states' oil embargo against the USA and its allies, including Japan, proved that the Japanese economy was potentially vulnerable to raw materials shortages.

Thus, central to this analysis are Japan's economic and raw materials interests and how these impinged on the question of national security. The analysis of the Japanese security problematic in Chapter 1, and the examination of Japan's trade relations with South Africa in Chapter 2 (where the extent of Tokyo's dependence on Pretoria for 'strategic raw materials' is demonstrated) underline the overall argument that Japan's foreign policy towards sub-Saharan Africa, at least after the 1970s, was replete with a cross-current of conflicting requirements. This was partly because Japan's relations with the OAU states, obviously as a result of its ever-expanding trade relations with South Africa, were influenced by a moral determination to appease the former on the question of South Africa's racial discrimination policy. It was this obfuscating nature of Japan's behavior towards the region that prompted Morikawa Jun to note that Japanese policy makers were faced with a 'double preoccupation'. His analysis was designed to expose the 'hypocritical' elements in Japan's foreign policy towards the region.

THE CENTRAL VARIABLES DETERMINING THE RELATIONSHIP

Japan's solidarity with the OAU states against South Africa's apartheid policy derived from an assortment of reasons and factors. Most importantly, Japan had to show in no uncertain terms that it was vehemently opposed to apartheid. Translated into bloc politics this meant that it had to show solidarity with the AA group. This manifested itself in its support for less, in most parts, sensitive UNGA resolutions on apartheid. Its support rate for cultural matters (as, for example, the ban on sports links with Pretoria) was relatively high, as has been demonstrated. And on resolutions banning investments to South Africa Japan tended to vote more with the majority position. This seemed to support the official Japanese position against investments in South Africa. It was also not an inconvenient policy approach at a time of Japan's increased awareness of its resource needs, and when an expansion of its economic relations with South Africa might have further jeopardized its standing with the AA member states – which included the Arab oil exporting countries.

On the other hand, it has also been revealed that Japan stood out as a deviant case within the AA bloc because of its propensity to oppose politically emotive resolutions, including resolutions that called for comprehensive sanctions against South Africa. It is shown in Chapter 5 that Japan's mean ZSA of 2.32 on sanctions was extreme, meaning that only a small number of Assembly members voted against the resolution and therefore supported the Japanese position on the issue. The overall assessment of Japan's voting behavior is therefore that it did not, on the whole, support the AA position on the apartheid debate where it mattered most. This was not so much because of racial distance from the problem, nor a conceptual inertia in relation to the nature of South Africa's racial policies, but conceivably because of the gap between Tokyo's level of economic development and that of the majority of the members of the group. As Jack Vincent argues, there is a causal relationship between a country's votes and the level of its economic development. Suffice to say, the extent of Japan's economic advancement, and the commitment towards sustaining and expanding what it had achieved, translated into a continuing dependence on South Africa for the 'strategic resources'. This effectively meant not voting in favor of resolutions that would jeopardize access to those resources. It was, quite simply, a case of protecting a crucial aspect of its national security.

In Chapter 6 the point is made clearly that Japanese ODA to Tanzania was not based on any economic gains to be had from that country itself. This argument is posed with the broader (established) question of the correlation between Japan's aid and its economic interests in the recipient country in mind. This case study does not sustain the argument that Japanese aid is necessarily tied to economic interests in the recipient country. It is argued, and an attempt is made to prove, that Japan's economic assistance to Tanzania was devised and implemented within the wider context of Japan's diplomatic and economic interests in sub-Saharan Africa. Aid to Tanzania, as suggested, was designed to legitimize Japanese commercial interests in South Africa. In effect, Tokyo used its economic assistance to the region to attract the moral voice of the frontline states and Tanzania's charismatic leader, Mr. Julius Nyerere, so that he could assuage African anxiety over Japan's expanding economic relations with South Africa. The argument is corroborated by the point that, despite Tanzania's virulent position against imperialism, apartheid and the countries that supposedly supported the latter through trade, there was hardly a criticism of Japan's relations with South Africa from the Tanzanian leadership, as the quotation from Dore in Chapter 1 shows.

Instead, Foreign Minister Malecela gave Japan assurances that it could carry on trade with South Africa. In the same breath, he requested Japanese economic assistance to the frontline African states. The above argument reinforces the notion that the value of Japanese economic assistance to Tanzania, compared to its aid to the other states in the region, was largely determined by Tanzania's standing in African and indeed in international politics. It reflects the wider theoretical point that geo-politics has its own dynamism, and reallocates the importance of states as determined by strategic location – a variable which includes diplomatic profile, the characteristics of immediate neighbours, and a plethora of economic factors.

Indeed, as Tanzania lost its position as a moral voice in global affairs, Japan's aid allocations to it declined in importance, as well as in value, within the context of its diplomatic priorities in the region. And Zambia rose in importance to replace Tanzania in this diplomatic shuffle. This was no coincidence: Zambia, then under Kenneth Kaunda, was a prominent frontline state and bellwether of African opinion – and a moderate one at that. In addition, Japanese aid in this respect was also designed to attract a peaceful solution to the problems in the region, because protracted political violence in the region was bound to disturb access to its natural resources. This was a scenario that Japan's policy makers, understandably, wanted to prevent.

As shown in Chapter 5 there is an inherently strong link between Japan's voting pattern at the UNGA on apartheid issues, and the application of its foreign aid as a diplomatic instrument. The convergent point for these variants of Japan's foreign policy is, at the expense of overstating the fact, its dependence on South Africa for certain strategic resources. By 1975 Japan was more dependent on South Africa's mineral exports (excluding gold) than any of the advanced Western industrialized states. It took 19.8 percent of such exports compared to 18.2 percent for Germany, 16.6 percent for the UK and 10.6 percent for the USA. In 1971 the comparative figures stood at 17.8 percent, 8.8 percent, and 26.5 percent and 9.2 percent, respectively. And by 1985/86, South Africa was supplying Japan with 63 percent of its chrome ore requirements, and 36 percent and 84 percent of its platinum and vanadium needs, respectively. These resources, among others, were crucial for Japan's industrial development and thus for sustainable economic growth. For example, both the automobile and electronic industries were dependent on the platinum group of metals for the production of durable and competitive goods. In view of this, Japan's consumption of platinum and palladium (one of the platinum metals) grew at the average rate of 10.1 percent per annum during the 1970s. It is also pointed out that Japan was dependent on South Africa for a large percentage of its uranium requirements. Despite the secrecy surrounding the production and export of this particular resource, Maull informs us that Japan was expected to take 43 percent of its uranium needs during the 1980s from South Africa alone.[1] Japan is, indeed, 100 percent import-dependent on uranium, a product which it has been developing as a resource for energy and thus as an alternative to oil.

Given South Africa's dominance in the production of some of these resources, Japanese dependence on it for such goods was inevitable. But Japan was simply following the dictates of market forces, attempting to take the liberal economic system to its most logical and fullest extent. Yet, as has been argued in this study, the apartheid policies of the Nationalist Party made it impossible for Japan to take full advantage of South Africa's resources. This is confirmed by the ban imposed by the Japanese government on Japanese companies with regard to investments in the country; a factor that conceivably made apartheid rather unpopular to Japanese business executives and potential investors. It must be noted, however, that some Japanese companies found ways to circumvent the ban on investments in South Africa.

The persistence of Japan in maintaining economic links with South Africa was indicative of two main things. The first was that it showed how important South Africa was to Japan. The second point is related to and reinforces the first one: there was no comparable country of such economic importance to Japan in the whole of sub-Saharan Africa. It is demonstrated in the analysis of Japan's investment profile in Nigeria that contrary to popular perception, the Japanese business community was not particularly attracted to the resources under the control of the OAU states. The point to emphasize here is that, if, in the wake of the oil crisis, the Japanese policy makers were concerned about widening the country's sources for resource procurement, the non-competitiveness of the raw materials in sub-Saharan Africa (outside South Africa) would soon have become evident. As noted in the case study on Japanese investments in Nigeria, the Keidanren rated Africa's resources very poorly. Indeed, as illustrated in Table 4.1 (p. 108), to Japanese raw materials prospectors Africa was the least attractive of the major regions for Japanese investment.

Although most theoretical explanations of FDI tend to stress the availability of resources (land, labor and capital) or micro-policies, such as trade barriers and taxes as determinants of FDI, this study does not fully support such explanations. Instead, it specifically reveals that Japanese FDI in Nigeria was not in fact attracted by the availability of raw materials in the country. Of the forty firms with Japanese equity that existed in Nigeria in 1986, only four (see Table 4.4, p. 126) mentioned resources (including cheap labor) as a motive for investing in the country. The 'push factors' for Japanese FDI in Nigeria were primarily 'good market prospects', Nigeria's corporate tax reductions and exemptions, import tax reductions for raw materials and machinery, and refunds for import taxes for infant and small firms. The data shows that ten firms saw the above categories as attractions, while twenty firms specifically mentioned the local market and third country sales as an incentive. Of the twenty firms, however, only one actually engaged in exports to a third-country market (Japan).

A variant of the above argument is that it questions Kojima Kiyoshi's trade-oriented theory concerning Japanese FDI. It also shows that macro-economic policy and performance of a country is a crucial determinant of how much investment the country receives and sustains. Of the ninety-three firms with Japanese equity that were established in Nigeria between 1951 and 1990, there were only twenty-four left by the end of 1992. On the whole, Nigeria, like the rest of the OAU sub-Saharan states, did not prove itself competitive enough to attract Japanese investments. This fact is essential to a constructive appraisal of Japanese foreign policy towards sub-Saharan Africa, given the centrality of resource acquisition and economic security to Japanese foreign policy goals.

This fact was not lost on Japanese policy makers when African ambassadors in Tokyo threatened Japan with removal of access to resources in Africa, indicating that their countries would not provide Japan with the resources it needed in the region if it did not terminate trade with South Africa. But Japanese policy makers were sufficiently well informed not to be too worried about it. The country's big firms continued to trade extensively with South Africa, in a way that (to go back to the comparison with Japanese diplomacy in the Middle East) some Japanese firms could not do with Israel, with the advent of the 1973 oil embargo against Japan. It could therefore be argued that if the resources in South Africa had been under the control of the OAU member states of sub-Saharan Africa – that is, if the position of the goalposts in the region had been reversed – it is conceivable, that from the very start, Japanese attitudes towards apartheid would have been markedly supportive of the OAU states.

A possible outcome of such a position would have been an early recognition of the ANC and other liberation movements in South Africa as legitimate political forces; and possibly the establishment of an ANC liaison office in Tokyo much sooner than it happened in 1988. Incidentally, the PLO set up its liaison office in Tokyo in 1976, having been given the permission by the Japanese government to do so in the aftermath of the oil crisis. This gesture, among others (including the first visit, in 1981, of Yasser Arafat, Chairman of the PLO, to Japan) from the Japanese government, was 'designed to make Japanese commitments', in a number of the oil exporting countries in the Middle East, 'economically viable'.[2] Conversely, Japan's refusal to recognize the ANC as a legitimate representative of the political process in South Africa until the late 1980s was designed not to offend Pretoria and to ensure a workable economic relationship with it. Incidentally, by the time Japan started making overtures towards the ANC, Tokyo was under enormous pressure from the international community, having emerged in 1987 as Pretoria's leading trade partner. By that time, a close economic relationship with Pretoria had become a diplomatically dangerous exercise.

THE DYNAMIC DIMENSIONS OF JAPAN'S IMMOBILIST DIPLOMACY TOWARDS SUB-SAHARAN AFRICA

What has been highlighted so far in this appraisal is what may be seen, essentially, as the economic determinants of Japanese foreign policy towards sub-Saharan Africa. These have been central to Japan's relations with the countries of the region, as indeed they are to its overall foreign policy. As has been argued in the analysis of Japan's strategies for a CNS policy (*sōgo anzen hoshō senryaku*), the structure of the state creates incentives for a definition of security favoring economic dimensions. Critics see this as static behavior in Japanese foreign policy. In this vein, Japanese foreign policy towards sub-Saharan Africa may represent the worst of all cases of its immobilist foreign policy. In the first place, a constructive foreign policy towards the region, if ever there were one,[3] is still in 'dress rehearsal stage', with Japan's materials still written on cue cards, as it were. None the less, a clear dynamism within the foreign policy operations of Japan towards the region has been identified in this study; and it is worth itemizing aspects of it in this concluding chapter.

It might be appropriate to point out that aspects of Japan's foreign aid initiatives concerning sub-Saharan Africa were characterized by an immobilist tendency. The argument concerning external influence on Japanese foreign aid decision making is a particular case in point. When Japan's ODA increased enormously from the mid-1980s onwards, for example, it was primarily in response to 'encouragement' from the other

OECD member states, and from the multilateral agencies. From $252 mn. in 1985, Japanese ODA increased to $1.04 bn. by 1989, but fell to $859 mn. by 1992. Indeed, the large amounts of non-project grant aid given to a number of countries in sub-Saharan Africa from 1987 represented an aspect of the above, even though such generosity was in itself a new development in Japanese economic diplomacy *vis-à-vis* the countries in the area.

This point notwithstanding (even before Japan increased its overall ODA in the manner described), Japan's policy makers had fashioned out an independent strategy, using ODA, to deal with its conflicting interests in sub-Saharan Africa. Indeed, based on the analysis in this study, the ingenuity of Japanese aid to Tanzania may be seen as a key example of this, and a glimpse of the dynamism within an immobilist foreign policy. As Tanzania's influence in international politics, and in African politics in particular, faded, so did the importance Japanese policy makers assigned to it. This would manifest itself in a reduction in Japanese aid to the country. In fact, there was a corresponding link between these developments and how things were evolving in South Africa's domestic politics. Thus, as the political implications of trade with South Africa began to lose their original political importance and intensity, Tokyo rightly saw no strategic importance in seeking help from any African state to pacify regional public opinion on the question of Japan's trade with Pretoria.

Yet another example of the dynamism within Japan's immobilist foreign policy was the particular agility with which Japanese policy makers responded to a changing South Africa in the latter part of the 1980s, when the system of apartheid began to show signs of disintegration. As a crucial symbolic gesture, the ANC was allowed to set up a liaison office in Tokyo in 1988. The Consul-General (Ohta Masatoshi) appointed to Pretoria two years later, in 1990, had served as Ambassador to Zambia (1984–1987) and had developed good relations with the ANC in that country, but not without the knowledge of the Japanese government. The Consul-General in Pretoria was upgraded to Ambassador in February 1992, re-establishing a mutually strong desire for diplomatic relations. Without doubt, these measures were long-range policy decisions in preparation for an ANC government in South Africa. If we stick by the argument concerning Japan's extensive dependence on South Africa for raw materials, we could further argue that these decisions were made on the basis of Japan's prescient natural resource diplomacy. And, as a case of foreign policy decision making, clearly this cannot be dismissed as unimaginative or insipid. Nor could it be safely said that Japan was simply being 'reactive'. If anything, these measures were revealing of Japan's dynamic response to changes in international politics and in Africa in particular.

The dynamism of Japanese diplomacy towards sub-Saharan Africa was once again demonstrated through the initiative Japanese policy makers took to organize Tokyo's first Conference on African Development, on 5–6 October 1993.[4] The meeting was expected to bring delegates of at least ministerial status from all over sub-Saharan Africa; and Japan agreed to bear the costs, including airfares, of two representatives of every government. By all indications, it was an important new development in Japan's relations with sub-Saharan Africa – one which suggested an attempt on the part of Japan to reappraise its attitude towards the region and to formulate more constructive policies towards the African states. It appeared, however, that this initiative was less based on motives determined by Japan's own economic interests than was often said to be the case. For example, it is difficult to see a connection between Japan's resource interests in Africa and the conference.The initiative was certainly attributable to a determination to play a more active role in the international political economy, commensurate with its economic importance in the international scheme of things. It could be regarded as an attempt to move at least a step away from its traditional (post-1945) immobilist pattern of foreign policy and to carve out a role for itself, at least, within the rapidly changing international political environment.

The above analysis, on the whole, has demonstrated the success of Japanese foreign policy towards sub-Saharan Africa. Unlike the other OECD countries, especially the USA and the UK, Japan was able to get away with being less positive in terms of political commitment towards African interests. Its solidarity with the Afro-Asian community against apartheid, for example, was expressed through minimal sanctions at no risk to its expanding dependence on South Africa for 'strategic' raw materials. One observer in 1984 noted that, 'the Japanese–South African axis is clearly a strong one' and proceeded to ask whether 'African policy makers [will] attack [Japan] as vigorously as they have sometimes attacked Europe and America for retaining links with [South Africa] ?'[5]

The fact remains that African policy makers did not; and there are many reasons to explain why. One is historical, as alluded to in Chapter 2: the perception of Japan as the successful 'non-white' nation that was to redeem Africans from white colonial rule and domination. Another was that Japan, of all the members of the Axis powers, was the one that became the victim of the atomic bomb. This event drew a significant amount of solidarity from radical and non-aligned African leaders, who saw the attack on Japan as yet another example of the 'white man's' desire to dominate and control the 'coloured races'. Japan, in this sense, became blameless in the minds of most African leaders because it emerged as a member of that collective past and its consequences. Being aware of this,

Japanese leaders cultivated the 'kinship' while redefining and trumpeting their country's request for the inclusion of the so-called 'racial equality clause' in the League of Nations' Covenant as a plea for universal human rights. In addition, Japan's economic successes were evocative enough to attract their own folklore, one replete with lessons that the African states would like to emulate. Factors such as these, among others, invested Japan with quasi-magical powers great enough to ensure that it could get away with a close economic relationship with Pretoria, where other economically powerful states, like the UK and the USA, could not. Japan, in short, became a 'cuddly mascot' – the sort that is happily made an exception, because it was perceived as the only successful member of the 'tribe'.

The role played by Japanese aid to Tanzania in the country's successful diplomacy within the region has been stressed in this analysis. This achievement, however, must be seen within the broader perspective of the success attained by Japan's post-1945 foreign policy as a whole. Ultimately, this was in itself primarily a result of the country's immaculately orchestrated 'low-posture' diplomacy; what Edwin Reischauer referred to as the 'artful dodging of meaningful debate on controversial foreign policies'.[6] With respect to sub-Saharan Africa, that, in many cases, meant not declaring which side of the political fence it (Japan) was on, especially in relation to the stalemate in South Africa. It amounted to giving the two contesting parties in the region something of what each of them wanted, but not everything of what they wanted – an act of 'satisficing'. This was possible, it should be recalled, only because the OAU states had neither a series of attractive raw materials nor the macro-economic environment the Japanese needed. Pretoria, on the other hand, had both. It was also desperate to make friends with states with viable economies, such as Japan – states which could support its economy and, invariably, its system. Needless to say, within this triangular discomfiture, more often than not, the dice were loaded in Japan's favor.

On the face of it, it would seem difficult for states to conduct a foreign policy based on security concerns that are inherently beset with conflicting objectives. In fact, that is not necessarily the case, as has been demonstrated in this book. But the fact that Japan managed to articulate its conflicting interests in sub-Saharan Africa so successfully was partly because the prominent states with which it had a relationship, namely, Tanzania and South Africa, allowed it to do so. In essence, the arena in which Japan played the 'game' was largely defined by those states, who were themselves locked up in profoundly ambivalent roles within the relationship. Ultimately, however, the success with which Japan performed in this setting would be determined by the skill with which it was able to manipulate the two pillars of diplomacy and economy within the context of its CNS policy. It depended, indeed, on the dynamic impulse and policy tools of an otherwise immobilist economic diplomacy.

NOTES

1 Hanns Maull, *Raw Materials, Energy and Western Security*, London, Macmillan, 1984.
2 Ikeda Akifumi, 'Japan's Relations with Israel', in Sugihara Kaoru and J. A. Allen (eds.) *Japan in the Contemporary Middle East*, London, Routledge, 1992.
3 Kawabata Masahisa, in 'Nihon no nanbu afurika seisaku' (in Kawabata Masahisa and Satō Makoto, *Shinsei minami afurika to nihon* , Tokyo, keisō shobō, 1994, pp. 186–187), argues that it was not until the beginning of the 1990s that the Japanese government formally submitted that it had a formal policy towards sub-Saharan Africa. The first real announcement was made in 1991. His point is that before this period Japan had no policy towards Africa, and that relations between Japan and the continent were orchestrated on *ad-hoc* basis. Oda Hideo, 'Nihon no afurika seisaku: sono ikkōsatsu' in Kawabata Masahisa (ed.), *Afurika to nihon*, Tokyo, keisō shobō, 1994, p. 93, confirms this. He says that in general Japan's Africa policy has been, at best, woolly.
4 *Asahi Shimbun*, 8 October 1993, p. 2; *Tokyo Declaration on African Development – Towards the First Century, Tokyo International Conference on African Development*, 5–6 October 1993.
5 'Keeping Apartheid Alive', *West Africa*, 6–12 March 1989, p. 354.
6 Edwin Reischauer, 'Their Special Strengths', *Foreign Policy*, no. 14, Spring, 1974, p. 151.

Appendices

APPENDIX 1

Methodology to determine Japan's voting behavior at the UNGA

Chai identifies two steps in developing the ZSA. The first step was to rank the members according to the degree of agreement with the main country under study, in this case Japan. A full agreement with Japan therefore obtained the highest rank, a higher rank was scored for a partial agreement (or a partial disagreement), in effect, an abstention, and a full disagreement gained the lowest rank. Thus, following Chai's explanation, on the vote on Resolution 3151(XXVIII) E (action by intergovernmental and non-governmental organizations against apartheid) of 14 December 1973, for example, Japan voted 'yes' with 117 other members, with 1 voting 'no', and 10 abstaining. Since Japan cast an affirmative vote, 'yes' votes get the highest rank. The higher rank goes to the abstain votes, while the 'no' vote gets the lowest rank. The rank assigned to the three categories of voting would be their average rank, which is 70.5,[1] 6.5 and 1, respectively.

The second stage was to transform these raw scores into standard scores, which have a mean of zero and a standard deviation of 1.0. This was done by subtracting these raw scores from the average score of the 128 voting members, which provided us with a total mean of 65, the product of which was then divided by the standard deviation (9.27). Thus, the ZSA for 'yes' was 0.59,[2] −6.31 for 'abstain' and −6.90 for 'no'.

When Japan voted 'no', negative votes, according to the procedure suggested above, get the highest rank and affirmative votes the lowest rank, with 'abstain' votes in between. What makes the ZSA attractive for this study is its rejection of the assumption that 'abstain' represents a middle position. Chai quotes Hayward R. Alker and Bruce M. Russet to assert that in reality 'there are no completely neutral countries. Those abstaining against the pressure of a sizeable majority come out closer to the scores of those who said "no" than they do to those in the affirmative'.[3] Thus, if Japan cast an 'abstain' vote, 'abstain' would receive a higher rank, and 'yes' and 'no' would both get a lower rank, since they were considered as having the same distance from 'abstain'.

By using the ZSA it can be seen that if a country were the only one that voted together with Japan, the ZSA for that country would be extremely high. On the other hand, when a great number of countries joined that country to vote Japan's way, the ZSA for the country would be much lower than that in the former case.

Hence, the ZSA is considered to contain more useful information and can measure more accurately the degree of agreement in voting between two countries on a roll call than, for example, Arend Lijphart's 'index of agreement' and a few other pairwise (dyadic) measures, all of which Chai considered in his article but rejects as inadequate.[4]

NOTES

1 This is calculated thus:

$$129 - 118 = 11 \ (12+13+14 \ldots +127+128+129): 12 + 129 = \frac{141}{2} = 70.5$$

2 The ZSA value for 'yes' votes was computed as follows:

$$\text{ZSA} = \frac{Xi - X}{0} = \frac{70.5 - 65}{9.27} = 0.59$$

3 Trong R. Chai, 'Chinese Policy toward the Third World and the Super-powers in the United Nations General Assembly, 1971–77: A Voting Analysis', *International Organization*, vol. 33, no. 3, Summer, p. 394.

4 The others are Richard Vengroff's 'average disagreement score (AD), and Steven J. Brams and Michael K. O'Leary's measure of 'relative agreement'. See Chai 'Chinese Policy toward the Third World and the Super-powers', p. 394–395.

APPENDIX 2

Table A.2 Japanese grant aid to sub-Saharan Africa, 1985–1990 (¥100 mn.)

Country	1985	1986	1987	1988	1989	1990	Grand total
Angola	–	–	–	–	1.04	2.05	1.04
Uganda	–	2.51	9.70	7.76	14.26	11.23	82.88
Ethiopia	14.71	14.60	15.49	14.38	24.72	21.90	120.83
Ghana	27.45	26.22	36.18	22.46	35.30	14.24	243.55
Cape Verde	2.30	5.58	6.33	1.00	1.87	5.60	35.05
Gabon	–	–	–	–	–	0.43	0.74
Cameroon	6.00	0.52	–	6.59	0.39	8.58	24.10
Gambia	3.50	6.80	2.80	1.50	7.34	5.00	42.71
Guinea	12.50	12.35	4.00	12.40	11.82	18.37	92.56
Guinea Bissau	2.50	3.00	2.50	1.50	5.00	4.05	28.83
Kenya	30.09	32.02	51.20	30.56	62.74	52.06	381.09
Comoros	4.00	0.88	5.90	2.25	7.24	3.00	35.90
Congo	0.40	–	–	–	–	4.94	?
Zaire	16.50	20.65	32.40	60.29	22.94	21.17	230.58
Sao Tome & Principe	5.63	0.80	0.80	3.53	–	1.00	14.30
Zambia	36.77	39.68	61.97	33.25	74.38	54.76	363.34
Sierra Leone	4.50	6.00	9.24	8.16	6.08	1.00	55.39
Djibouti	2.00	4.97	1.50	4.71	13.96	8.26	30.77
Zimbabwe	2.00	4.83	27.47	14.88	27.98	16.94	136.95
Swaziland	–	–	–	–	1.50	1.50	3.96
Seychelles	0.26	3.50	0.18	0.34	–	6.85	7.79
Equitorial Guinea	1.00	0.80	0.80	–	1.00	2.05	6.63
Senegal	26.50	27.45	35.61	46.58	46.94	47.05	300.52
Ivory Coast	7.12	7.42	22.89	10.16	24.66	3.07	89.91
Somalia	23.77	19.68	21.98	13.72	16.98	3.45	172.34
Tanzania	43.48	47.77	71.87	43.55	60.59	41.12	459.41
Chad	6.00	6.31	–	1.49	–	–	25.67
Central Africa	10.00	9.27	9.49	9.27	11.11	11.45	87.78
Togo	8.50	5.00	8.00	8.00	11.27	8.16	65.12
Nigeria	–	12.80	11.60	37.06	31.64	18.31	121.46
Namibia	–	–	–	–	–	5.50	5.50
Niger	27.66	29.49	34.41	20.52	34.49	23.30	273.22
Burkina Fasso	11.95	9.56	4.80	4.00	3.00	3.50	72.76
Burundi	11.00	8.89	10.00	4.00	11.27	7.09	85.41
Benin	4.50	7.30	8.22	7.34	11.00	12.00	67.04
Botswana	–	–	0.11	–	0.72	1.04	2.47
Madagascar	16.36	16.06	16.68	41.39	12.52	47.75	226.55

Table A.2 Continued

Country	1985	1986	1987	1988	1989	1990	Grand total
Malawi	10.75	4.88	18.65	10.37	18.01	13.43	101.65
Mali	12.82	11.58	10.32	11.60	15.18	9.93	129.62
South Africa	–	–	–	–	–	0.15	0.15
Mozambique	21.50	27.96	21.41	47.77	36.48	21.50	218.93
Mauritius	1.09	8.49	–	6.75	8.57	0.46	40.67
Mauritania	8.00	7.50	5.50	5.00	7.16	11.58	74.57
Liberia	8.50	11.05	8.92	9.47	5.88	2.00	71.37
Rwanda	13.40	11.41	13.64	16.57	18.58	8.33	144.60
Lesotho	1.00	3.00	1.50	0.75	1.00	1.00	11.59
Total	446.06	478.60	604.60	581.91	704.88	560.39	5,104.96

Note: Fiscal year base: amount based on official exchange rate, $1= 200.50 (1985); 159.10 (1986); 123.50 (1987); 125.85 (1988); 143.45 (1989); 134.40 (1990)

The 5 leading recipients of grant aid:
1985: (1)Tanzania   (2)Zambia   (3)Kenya   (4)Niger   (5)Ghana
1986: (1)Tanzania   (2)Zambia   (3)Kenya   (4)Niger   (5)Mozambique
1987: (1)Tanzania   (2)Zambia   (3)Kenya   (4)Ghana   (5)Senegal
1988: (1)Zaire   (2)Mozambique   (3)Senegal   (4)Tanzania   (5)Madagascar
1989: (1)Zambia   (2)Kenya   (3)Tanzania   (4)Senegal   (5)Mozambique
1990: (1)Zambia   (2)Kenya   (3)Madagascar   (4)Senegal   (5)Tanzania

Source: Gaimushō, *Wagakuni no seifu kaihatsu enjō*, 1990, 1991

APPENDIX 3

Table A.3 Japanese technical assistance to sub-Saharan Africa in ¥100 mn.

Country	1985	1986	1987	1988	1989	1990	Grand total
Angola	–	0.01	0.00	–	0.01	–	0.01
Uganda	0.36	0.12	0.26	0.47	0.5	0.87	14.63
Ethiopia	5.64	2.79	3.25	3.33	2.62	2.72	48.38
Ghana	6.53	6.07	7.39	7.69	8.49	9.13	89.20
Cape Verde	0.44	0.60	0.22	0.16	0.24	1.62	4.28
Gabon	0.65	0.43	0.10	0.55	0.09	0.18	4.39
Cameroon	2.38	0.94	0.32	0.42	0.43	1.49	7.01
Gambia	0.78	0.67	0.91	1.11	0.98	0.89	6.10
Guinea	0.46	1.11	0.47	0.79	1.50	1.48	23.08
Guinea Bissau	–	0.05	0.16	0.07	0.11	0.12	0.60
Kenya	22.54	25.44	25.70	28.40	31.31	38.20	329.34
Comoros	0.42	0.60	0.72	0.94	0.66	0.31	4.68
Congo	0.01	0.05	0.06	0.11	0.11	0.20	0.45
Zaire	3.24	4.08	5.18	3.36	4.13	2.80	62.32
Sao Tome & Principe	0.92	–	0.11	0.32	0.29	0.32	1.27
Zambia	12.62	12.13	14.43	14.90	21.43	23.64	131.11
Sierra Leone	0.57	0.54	0.34	0.49	0.75	0.22	7.43
Djibouti	–	0.12	0.03	0.11	0.34	0.52	1.16
Zimbabwe	0.93	3.00	2.64	3.30	3.63	3.46	21.11
Swaziland	1.53	0.47	0.21	0.04	0.10	0.16	13.30
Seychelles	0.15	0.50	0.32	0.42	0.63	0.59	3.06
Equitorial Guinea	–	–	0.11	0.17	0.04	0.08	0.44
Senegal	6.78	9.07	8.92	12.40	13.37	12.32	77.38
Ivory Coast	0.84	1.19	1.63	1.94	1.46	5.03	16.12
Somalia	1.22	0.70	1.24	0.86	0.38	0.21	8.54
Tanzania	12.84	14.55	19.70	15.61	20.94	18.21	200.04
Chad	0.01	–	0.09	–	0.05	–	0.23
Central Africa	0.52	0.48	1.10	0.90	1.17	1.01	6.73
Togo	0.62	0.39	0.18	0.22	0.33	0.34	2.71
Nigeria	3.32	5.63	7.14	8.19	7.58	6.44	69.74
Namibia	–	–	–	–	–	0.52	0.52
Niger	1.40	2.26	3.51	8.00	5.06	5.04	33.22
Burkina Fasso	0.11	0.68	0.21	0.30	0.35	0.24	3.54
Burundi	0.54	0.40	0.47	0.96	0.54	0.75	4.24
Benin	0.07	0.13	0.49	0.40	0.22	0.21	1.98
Botswana	0.09	0.03	–	0.12	0.05	0.07	5.73
Madagascar	1.73	1.49	1.23	1.76	4.91	6.35	32.18

Table A.3 Continued

Country	1985	1986	1987	1988	1989	1990	Grand total
Malawi	4.86	5.45	6.56	6.53	6.40	6.51	76.46
Mali	0.69	0.43	0.69	0.85	1.37	1.27	18.54
South Africa	–	–	–	–	–	–	–
Mozambique	0.18	0.28	0.17	0.64	0.17	0.79	2.57
Mauritius	0.88	0.46	1.95	3.02	3.30	6.00	20.63
Mauritania	0.30	–	0.03	0.02	0.01	0.01	4.92
Liberia	2.65	2.93	3.82	4.28	4.06	2.65	38.08
Rwanda	2.10	1.20	1.28	3.32	4.32	3.45	20.60
Lesotho	0.10	0.05	0.10	0.05	0.01	0.05	0.61
Total	101.12	107.55	123.45	137.68	154.90	166.78	1,429.57

Note: Fiscal year base: Amount based on official exchange rate, $1= 200.50 (1985); 159.10 (1986); 123.50 (1987); 125.85(1988); 143.45 (1989); 134.40 (1990)

The 5 leading recipients of Grants Aid:
1985: (1)Kenya	(2)Tanzania	(3)Zambia	(4)Senegal	(5)Ghana
1986: (1)Kenya	(2)Tanzania	(3)Zambia	(4)Senegal	(5)Ghana
1987: (1)Kenya	(2)Tanzania	(3)Zambia	(4)Senegal	(5)Ghana
1988: (1)Kenya	(2)Tanzania	(3)Zambia	(4)Senegal	(5)Nigeria
1989: (1)Kenya	(2)Zambia	(3)Tanzania	(4)Senegal	(5)Ghana
1990: (1)Kenya	(2)Zambia	(3)Tanzania	(4)Senegal	(5)Ghana

Source: Gaimushō, *Wagakuni no seifu kaihatsu enjō*, 1990, 1991

APPENDIX 4

Table A.4 Major recipients of Japanese aid

a: Major recipients of grant aid from Japan, 1978–1983 ($ mn.)

Country	1978	1979	1980	1981	1982	1983
Kenya	0.76	12.32	10.20	6.31	4.96	13.24
Tanzania	0.73	10.93	10.26	13.51	5.93	7.21
Ghana	5.94	3.88	0.62	2.51	2.58	3.78
Zambia	0.01	–	–	2.49	8.57	9.24
Madagascar	–	0.07	4.56	7.48	4.21	7.34
Zaire	–	4.56	5.73	6.44	2.81	0.57

b: Major recipients of technical aid from Japan, 1978–1983 ($ mn.)

Country	1978	1979	1980	1981	1982	1983
Kenya	3.51	4.27	6.89	9.41	8.35	11.39
Tanzania	2.43	2.90	3.08	3.99	4.99	5.35
Ghana	2.09	1.72	1.92	2.82	2.58	3.11
Zambia	1.41	1.20	1.38	1.66	1.61	2.13
Madagascar	0.62	0.81	0.73	1.11	0.85	1.00
Zaire	1.73	1.00	1.71	2.22	1.91	1.87

Source: compiled from Gaimushō, *Wagakuni no seifu kaihatsu enjō*, 1984

APPENDIX 5

Table A.5 Japanese non-project grant aid to sub-Saharan Africa ($ mn.)

Countries (27)	1987	1988	1989	1990	Total
Uganda	9	–	5	–	14
Ghana	20	–	15	–	35
Gambia	–	–	–	3	3
Guinea	–	5	–	5	10
Guinea Bissau	–	–	3	–	3
Kenya	35	–	30	30	95
Zaire	–	–	35	–	35
Zambia	35	–	35	35	105
Sierra Leone	–	3	–	–	3
Zimbabwe	25	–	15	–	40
Sudan	25	–	–	–	25
Senegal	–	25	–	25	50
Ivory Coast	–	20	17	–	37
Somalia	9	–	–	–	9
Tanzania	25	–	20	–	45
Central Africa	–	–	3	–	3
Togo	–	7	5	–	12
Nigeria	–	30	25	–	55
Niger	15	–	15	–	30
Burundi	–	–	3	–	3
Benin	–	–	7	9	16
Madagascar	–	35	–	35	70
Malawi	3	–	3	–	6
Mali	–	–	5	–	5
Mozambique	–	25	15	–	40
Mauritania	–	5	–	5	10
Luanda	–	–	5	–	5
Total	192	164	261	147	764

Source: Gaimushō, *Wagakuni no seifu kaihatsu enjō*, 1991, p.362

Bibliography

NEWSPAPERS AND SERIALS

Asahi shimbun (Japan), daily
Business Daily (South Africa), daily
Daily News (Tanzania), daily
Daily Sketch (Nigeria), daily
Financial Times (London), daily
Financial Mail (South Africa), weekly
Guardian (Nigeria), weekly
Japan Times (formerly *Nippon Times*), daily
The Japan Economic Journal, weekly
Mainichi Daily News (Japan), daily
Nihon keizai shimbun, daily
Official Records of the General Assembly, annual
Sunday Post (Nigeria), weekly
Sunday News (Tanzania) weekly
The Star (South Africa), daily
Weekly Cape Times and Farmers' Record (South Africa), weekly
West Africa (London), weekly
White Paper on International Trade (formerly *Foreign Trade of Japan*), annual
Yearbook of the United Nations, annual

BOOKS, PERIODICALS AND GOVERNMENT DOCUMENTS

Address of Mr. Takasaki Tatsunosuke, Principal Japanese Delegate, Before the Asian–African Conference, 19 April 1955 (Gaikō shiryōkan: Nihon seifu daihyo ni taisuru kunrei, B6.1.0.24–1.B–0049. Text in English).
'Afurika dokuritsu no nagare no naka de', *Sekai*, no. 177, September 1960, pp. 141–145.
'Afurika keizai seminā o kaisai', *Keidanren shūhō*, no. 1939, February, 1989.
Agbi, S.O, 'Africa – Japan's Continent-sized Blind Spot', *Japan Times*, 6 June 1982.
——, *Japanese Relations with Africa, 1868–1978*, Ibadan, Ibadan University Press, 1992.
'Agreement Between the Government of the Republic of South Africa and the

Government of Japan to Place Source Material Transferred from South Africa to Japan Under the Safeguards of the International Atomic Energy Agency', *Republic of South Africa, Treaty Series*, no. 4, 1962.

Akaha Tsuneo, 'Japan's Comprehensive Security Policy', *Asian Survey*, vol. xxxi, no.4, April, 1991, pp. 324–340.

Akindele, R. A., 'The Domestic Structure and National Resources Profile of Nigeria's External Trade', in R.A. Akindele and Ate E. Bassey (eds.), *Nigeria's Economic Relations with the Major Developed Market-economy Countries, 1960–1985*, Lagos, The Nigerian Institute of International Affairs, 1988, pp. 3–83.

——, 'Nigeria's External Economic Relations, 1960–1985', *Africa Spectrum*, vol. 1, 1986, pp. 54–83.

Akindele, R. A., and Bassey, Ate E. (eds.), *Nigeria's Economic Relations with the Major Developed Market-economy Countries, 1960–1985*, Lagos, The Nigerian Institute of International Affairs, 1988.

Ali, S.S. 'United Nations Struggle Against Apartheid', *Africa Quarterly*, vol.xxv, nos. 1–2, 1988, pp. 30–47.

Alker, Hayward A. Jr., 'Dimensions of Conflict in the General Assembly', *The American Political Science Review*, vol. lviii, no. 3, September, 1964, pp. 642–657.

Alker, Hayward A. Jr. and Bruce Russet, *World Politics in the General Assembly*, New Haven, Yale University Press, 1965.

Ampiah, Kweku, 'British Commercial Policies Against Japanese Expansionism in East and West Africa, 1932–1935', *The International Journal of African Historical Studies*, vol. 23, no. 4, 1990, pp. 619–641.

Aoki Kazuyoshi, 'Nihon to afurika: hyo na kankei kara mitsunaru kankei no kōchiku', in Oda Hideo (ed.), *Afurika no seiji to kokusai kankei*, Tokyo, Keisō shobō, 1991, pp. 310–337.

Armstrong, Adrienne, 'The Political Consequence of Economic Dependence,' *Journal of Conflict Resolution*, vol. 25, no. 3, 1981, pp. 401–428.

Barnett, Robert, *Beyond War: Japan's Concept of Comprehensive National Security*, Washington, D.C., Pergamon, Brassey's, 1984.

Benson, Mary, *The African Patriot*, London, Faber & Faber, 1963.

Birchenough, Henry, 'Some Effects of the War Upon British and German Trade in South Africa', *Journal of South African Society*, vol. xiv, no. lv, April, 1915, pp. 229–249.

Bloomfield, Lincoln, *The United Nations and United States Foreign Policy*, Boston, Little, Brown, 1961.

Bloomhill, Greta, 'The Japanese Trade Menace: The Story of how Japan Invaded the African Market', *African Observer*, vol. 4, no. 4, 1936, pp. 42–46.

Bogor Conference Final Joint Communique, 29 December 1954.

Brooks, William and Robert Orr, 'Japan's Foreign Economic Assistance', *Asian Survey*, vol. xxv, No.3, March, 1985, pp. 322–370.

Buckley, Peter J., 'A Critical View of Theories of the Multinational Enterprise', in Peter J. Buckley and M. Casson, *The Economic Theory of Multinational Enterprise*, London, Macmillan, 1985, pp. 1–19.

——, 'The Economic Analysis of the Multinational Enterprise: Reading Versus Japan?', *Hitotsubashi Journal of Economics*, vol.26, 1985, pp. 117–124.

——, 'Kojima's Theory of Japanese Foreign Direct Investment Revisited', *Hitosubashi Journal of Economics*, vol.32, 1991, pp. 103–109.

Buckley, Peter J. and M. Casson, *The Economic Theory of Multinational Enterprise*, London, Macmillan, 1985.

Buckley, Peter J. and J. Clegg (eds.), *Multinational Enterprises in Less Developed Countries*, London, Macmillan, 1991.

Bukarambe, Bukar, 'Nigeria's Economic Relations with Japan: The Direct and Indirect', in R.A. Akindele and Bassey, E. Ate (eds.), *Nigeria's Economic Relations with the Major Developed Market-economy Countries, 1960–1985*, Lagos, The Nigerian Institute of International Affairs, 1988, pp. 263–282.

Burea of Statistics (Office of the Prime Minister), *Japan Statistical Year Book [Nihon tōkei nenkan]*, Tokyo, October 1956.

Buzan, Barry, *People, States and Fear: An Agenda for International Securities Studies in the Post-Cold War Era*, London, Wheatsheaf, 1991.

——, *People, States and Fear: The National Security Problem in International Relations*, London, Wheatsheaf, 1983.

Calder, Kent E., 'Japanese Foreign Economic Policy Formation: Explaining the Reactive State', *World Politics*, vol. xl, no. 4, July, 1988, pp. 516–541.

Campbell, Horace, 'Tanzania and the Liberation Process of Southern Africa', *The African Review*, vol.14, nos. 1 & 2, 1987, pp. 13–26.

Cantwell, John, 'Foreign Multinationals and Industrial Development in Africa', in Peter J. Buckley and J. Clegg (eds.), *Multinational Enterprises in Less Developed Countries*, London, Macmillan, 1991, pp. 183–224.

Casely-Hayford, Joseph Ephraim, 'Yellow Peril' in Joseph Ephraim Casely-Hayford, *Ethiopia Unbound: Studies in Race Emancipation*, London, Francas, 1969, pp. 107–115.

Central Office of Information, *The Campaign in Burma*, London, HMSO, 1946.

Chai, Trong R., 'Chinese Policy toward the Third World and the Super-powers in the United Nations General Assembly, 1971–77: A Voting Analysis', *International Organization*, vol.33, No.3, Summer, 1979, pp. 391–403.

Chapman, J. W. M., R. Drifte and I. T. M. Gow, *Japan's Quest for Comprehensive Security: Defense-Diplomacy, Dependence*, London, Francis Pinter, 1983.

Claude, Inis L., Jr., *Power and International Relations*, New York, Random House, 1962.

Cohen, Sir Andrew, 'The New Africa and the United Nations', *International Affairs*, vol. 36, no.4, October, 1960, pp. 476–488.

Collier, Paul, 'Aid and Economic Performance in Tanzania', in Uma Lele and Ijaz Nabi (eds.), *Transition in Development: The Role of Aid and Commercial Flows*, California, International Center for Economic Growth, 1991, pp. 151–171, 491–492 (notes).

——, 'The Role of the African State in Building Agencies of Restraint', Mimeograph of the Centre for the Study of African Economies, Oxford, 1995.

Cooper, Richard N., 'Trade Policy is Foreign Policy', *Foreign Policy*, Winter, 1972/73, pp. 18–35.

Cortazzi, Sir Hugh, *British Influence in Japan Since the End of the Occupation, 1952–1984*, Nissan Occasional Paper Series, no. 13, 1990.

Crowder, Michael, *West Africa under Colonial Rule*, Evanston, Northwestern University Press, 1968.

Crowson, Phillip, *Minerals Handbook, 1987–88: Statistics and Analysis of the World's Mineral Industry*, Basingstoke, Macmillan, 1987.

——, *Minerals Handbook, 1988–89: Statistics and Analysis of the World's Mineral Industry*, Basingstoke, Macmillan, 1988.

Curtis, Gerald (ed.), *Japan's Foreign Policy After the Cold War: Coping with Change*, New York, M. E. Sharpe, 1993.

Deutsch, Karl, *Analysis of International Relations*, Englewood Cliffs, Prentice Hall, 1968.

Dokoritsu no shōchō, *Sekai*, June, 1955.

Dore, Ronald, 'Japan and the Third World: Coincidence or Divergence of Interests', in Robert Cassen (ed.), *Rich Country Interest and Third World Develpment*, London, Croom Helm, 1982.

Dower, J. W., *Empire and Aftermath: Yoshida Shigeru and the Japanese Experience, 1878–1954*, London, Harvard University Press, 1979.

Drifte, Reinhard, *Japan's Foreign Policy*, London, Royal Institute of International Affairs, 1990.

Drysdale, Peter, 'Foreword', in Okita Saburo, *Japan's Challenging Years: Reflecting on my Lifetime*, Canberra, George Allen & Unwin, 1985, pp. viii–ix.

El-Khawas, Mohammed, 'The Third-World Stance on Apartheid: The United Nations Record', *The Journal of Modern African Studies*, vol. 9, no. 3, October, 1971, pp. 443–452.

Farer, Tom J., 'The UN and Human Rights: More than a Whimper, Less than a Roar', in Adam Roberts and B. Kingsbury, *United Nations Divided World:The UN's Roles in International Relations*, Oxford, Clarendon Press, 1988, pp. 95–138.

Fasseur, C., 'Rulers and Ruled: Some Remarks on Dutch Colonial Ideology', *Journal of the Japan–Netherlands Institute*, vol. ii, 1990, pp. 11–30.

Federal Ministry of Industries (Federal Secretariat) *Industrial Policy of Nigeria: Policies, Incentives, Guidelines and Institutional Framework, 1988*, Lagos, 1989.

Federal Ministry of Information, 'Nigeria Reconciles with Japan', *News Release*, no.1145, Lagos, 8 October 1975.

Forrest, Tom, 'The Advance of African Capital: The Growth of Nigerian Private Enterprises', *Ld'A – QEH Development Studies Working Papers*, no. 24, 1990, pp. 1–57.

——, *Politics and Economic Development in Nigeria*, San Fransisco, Westview Press, 1993.

Foucault, Michel, *Power and Knowledge: Selected Interviews and other Writings, 1972–1977* (Colin Gordon, ed.), Brighton, Harvester Wheatsheaf, 1980.

'Furēza kokuren ichiji sanhin mondai senmon gurūpu iinchō to kondan', *Keidanren shūhō*, no. 1967, September, 1980.

Gaimushō, *Wagakuni gaikō no kinkyō, 1959*, Tokyo, 1960.

——, *Wagakuni gaikō no kinkyō, 1973*, Tokyo, 1974.

——, *Wagakuni no seifu kaihatsu enjo gekan, vol. 2*, Tokyo, kokusai kyōryoku suishin kyōkai, 1984.

——, *Wagakuni no seifu kaihatsu enjo gekan, vol. 2*, Tokyo, kokusai kyōryoku suishin kyōkai, 1987.

——, *Wagakuni no seifu kaihatsu enjo gekan, vol. 2*, Tokyo, kokusai kyōroku suishin kyōkai, 1988.

——, *Wagakuni no seifu kaihatsu enjo gekan, vol. 2*, Tokyo, kokusai kyōryoku suishin kyōkai, 1989.

——, *Wagakuni no seifu kaihatsu enjo gekan, vol. 2*, Tokyo, kokusai kyōryoku suishin kyōkai, 1990.

——, *Wagakuni no seifu kaihatsu enjo gekan, vol. 2*, Tokyo, kokusai kyōryoku suishin kyōkai, 1991.

Gaimushō kanshū afurika hen, *Tanzania, keizai shakai no genjō, No. 4*, Tokyo, kokusai kyōryoku suishin kyōkai, 1983.

George, Aurelia 'Japan's Participation in U.N. Peacekeeping Operations', *Asian Survey*, vol. xxxiii, No.6, June, 1993, pp. 560–575.

——, 'Japan and the United States: Dependent Ally or Equal Partner', in J.A.A. Stockwin et al. (eds.), *Dynamic and Immobilist Politics in Japan*, London, Macmillan, 1988, pp. 237–296.

Gilpin, Robert, 'Economic Interdependence and National Security in Historical Perspective', in Klauss Knorr and Frank N. Trager (eds.), *Economic Issues and National Security*, Kansas, University Press of Kansas, 1982, pp. 19–66.

Gluck, Carol, *Japan's Modern Myths: Ideology in the Late Meiji Period*, Princeton, Princeton University Press, 1985.

Haas, Ernst B., 'Regionalism, Functionalism and Universal International Organization', *World Politics*, vol.8, No.2, January, 1956, pp. 238–256.

Hartman, Frederick H., *The Relations of Nations*, New York, 1967.

Hayashi Kōji, 'A Half-hearted Anti-apartheid Policy', *Japan Quarterly*, July–September, 1989.

Hayashi Yōko, 'Hōgan hōdō kara dakkyaku o: nihon no minami afurika hōdō o furikaete', *Shimbun kenkyū*, no. 482, September, 1992, pp. 62–65.

Hellmann, Donald C., *Japanese Foreign Policy and Domestic Politics: The Peace Agreement with the Soviet Union*, Berkeley, University of California Press, 1969.

——, 'Japanese Security and Postwar Japanese Foreign Policy', in Robert Scalapino (ed.), *The Foreign Policy of Modern Japan*, Berkeley, University of California Press, 1977, pp. 321–340.

Hoshino Yasuo, 'Gana dokuritsu e no ayumi to sono shōrai', *Sekai*, No.137, May, 1957, pp. 199–204.

Hosoya Chihiro, 'Japan's Response to US Policy on the Japanese Peace Treaty: The Dulles–Yoshida Talks of January–February 1951', *Hitotusbashi Journal of Law and Politics*, vol. 10, December, 1981, pp. 15–27.

Hovet, Thomas Jr., *Bloc Politics in the United Nations*, Cambridge, Mass., Harvard University Press, 1960.

——, *Africa in the United Nations*, Evanson, Northwestern University Press, 1963.

Ikeda Akifumi, 'Japan's Relations with Israel', in Sugihara Kaoru and J.A. Allen (eds.), *Japan in the Contemporary Middle East*, London, Routledge, 1992, pp. 155–169.

Inada Juichi, 'Japan's Aid Diplomacy: Economic, Political or Strategic?', paper presented to the International Studies Association convention, London, 30 March 1989.

——, 'Taigai enjo', in Uno Shigeaki, Kido Shigeru, Yamamoto Yoshinori and Watanabe Akio, *Kōza kokusai seiji 4: Nihon no gaikō*, Tokyo, Tokyo daigaku shuppankai, pp. 183–209.

Inoguchi Takashi, 'Trade, Technology and Security: Implications for East Asia and the West', paper prepared for presentation at the 28th annual conference of the International Institute for Strategic Studies, Kyoto, Japan, 1986.

Inukai Ichirō, 'Why Aid and Why not? Japan and Sub-Saharan Africa', in Bruce Koppel and Robert M. Orr, Jr. (eds.), *Japan's Foreign Aid: Power and Policy in a New Era*, Boulder, Westview Press, 1993, pp. 252–274.

Irie Akira, *Nihon no gaikō: Meiji ishin kara gendai made*, Tokyo, Chuo kōronsha, 1966.

Iwaki Gou, 'Tanzania ni taisuru nihon no ODA', in Kawabata Masahisa (ed.) *Afurika to nihon*, Tokyo, Keiso shobō, 1994.

'Japan and Africa', *Bulletin of the Africa Institute of South Africa*, vol. viii, no. 7, August, 1970, pp. 305–317.

'Japan: ANC Office Opened', *Sechaba* (Official Organ of the ANC, South Africa), August, 1988.

Japanese Delegation (to the Bandung Conference), 'Proposal on Economic Cooperation', 18 April 1955.

Japan External Trade Organization, *1991 JETRO White Paper on FDI – Direct Foreign Investment Promoting Restructuring of Economy Worldwide – Summary*, Tokyo, 1992.

——, *Foreign Trade of Japan*, Tokyo, 1974.

——, *Sekai to nihon kaigai chokusetsu tōshi*, Tokyo, 1992.

Jaycox, Edward V.K., 'Japan's role in African Development: Challenges and Opportunities', keynote address to the African Symposium, Kaidanren kaikan, Tokyo, 27–28 October 1988.

Johnson, Chalmers, and E.B. Keehn, 'The Pentagon's Ossified Strategy', *Foreign Affairs*, vol. 74, 1995.

——, *MITI and the Japanese Miracle: The Growth of Industrial Policy, 1925–1975*, Stanford, California University Press, 1982.

Jones, Stuart and André Müller, *The South African Economy, 1910–1990*, Basingstoke, Macmillan, 1992.

Juster, Kenneth, 'Foreign Policymaking During the Oil Crisis', *The Japan Interpreter*, vol. xi, no. 3. Winter, 1977, pp. 293–312.

Katahara Eiichi, 'The Politics of Japanese Security Policy-making: A Case Study of Japan's Participation in UN Peace Keeping Operations', paper prepared for the Institute on Global Conflict and Cooperation Conference on Pacific Security Relations after the Cold War, Hong Kong, 15–18 June 1992.

Katakura Kunio, 'Narrow Options for a Pro-Arab Shift: Japan's Response to the Arab Oil Strategy in 1973', *Annals of Japan Association for Middle East Studies*, vol. 1., 1986, pp. 106–149.

Kataoka Tetsuya and Ramon Myers, *Defending an Economic Superpower: Reassessing the US–Japan Security Alliance*, London, Westview, 1989.

Katsuki Toshitaka, 'Some Findings from Farm Economy Survey (KADP, Lower Moshi Area): Short-term Economic Survey', Tokyo, Japan International Cooperation Agency, 1991, pp. 1–13.

Katzenstein, Peter and Nobuo Okawara, 'Japan's National Security: Structures, Norms and Policies', *International Security*, vol. 17, no. 4, 1993, pp. 84–118.

Kawabata Masahisa, 'Afurika no dokuritsu wa donoyōni nihon de tsutaeraretaka', *Ajia–Afurika kenkyū*, No.318, 1987, pp. 2–25.

——, (ed.), *Afurika to nihon*, Tokyo, Keisōshobō, 1994.

——, 'Nihon no nanbu afurika seisaka', in Kawabata Masahisa and Satō Makoto, *Shinsei minami afurika to nihon*, Tokyo, Keiso shōbō, 1994.

Kay, David, 'Instruments of Influence in the United Nations Political Process', in David Kay (ed.), *The United Nations Political System*, London, John Wiley & Sons, 1967, pp. 92–107.

Kedourie, Elie, 'A New International Disorder', in Hedley Bull and Adam Watson (eds.), *The Expansion of International Society*, Oxford, Clarendon Press, 1985, pp. 347–355.

Keiō Gijuku (ed.), 'Datsu a ron', *Fukuzawa Yukichi zenshū, vol. 10*, Tokyo, Iwanami shoten, 1960, pp. 238–240.

Kelly, T.H., 'South Africa's Foreign Trade, 1933–1953', *The South African Journal of Economics*, vol. 22, 1954, pp. 73–90.

Keohane, Robert, *After Hegemony: Cooperation and Discord in the World Political Economy*, Princeton, Princeton University Press, 1984.

Khan, Ali H., *The Political Economy of Apartheid*, London, Lynne Rienner, 1989.

Kibata Yōichi, 'Sekai no kiro to ichigonen sensō', in Rekishigaku kenkyūkai (ed.), *Nihonshi kenkyūkai, nihon rekishi kōza*, Tokyo, Tokyo University Press, vol. 12, kindai 4, 1985, pp. 1–37.

Kilby, Peter, *Industrialization in an Open Economy: Nigeria, 1945–1966*, London, Cambridge University Press, 1969.

Kindleberger, Charles, *The World Depression, 1929–1939*, Berkeley, University of California, 1973.

Kitagawa Katsuhiko, 'Senzenki nihon no ryōji hōkoku ni mirareru afurika keizai jijō chōsa no kenkyū – gaimushō tsūshōkyoku [tsūshō-kōhō] o chūshin toshite', *Afurika kenkyū*, vol. 35, 1989, pp. 47–63.

——, 'Japan's Economic Relations with Africa Between the Wars: A Study of Japanese Consular Reports', *African Studies Monographs*, vol.11, No.3, December, 1990, pp. 125–141.

Kitazawa Yōko, 'Aparutoheito e no nihon no katan – nihon, minami afurika keizai kankei chōsa hōkoku, *Ajia taiheiyō shiryō sentā*, 1975, pp. 1–941.

——, 'Japan Imports Namibian Natural Resources Illegally', *Pacific Asia Resource Centre*, 1976, pp. 1–9.

Kojima Kiyoshi, *Direct Foreign Investment: A Japanese Model of Multinational Business Operations*, London, Croom Helm, 1978.

——, 'International Trade and Foreign Investment: Substitutes or Complements', *Hitotsubashi Journal of Economics*, vol. 16, 1975, pp. 1–12.

——, 'Japanese-style Direct Foreign Investment', *Japanese Economic Studies*, vol. xiv, 1986, pp. 52–82.

——, 'Transfer of Technology to Developing Countries: Japanese Type versus American Type', *Hitotsubashi Journal of Economics*, vol. 17, 1972, pp. 1–14.

Kojima Kiyoshi and T. Ozawa, *Japan's Trading Companies: Merchants of Economic Development*, Paris, OECD, 1984.

Kokusai kyōryoku jigyōdan, *Tanzania no gairyaku*, Tanzania jimusho, January, 1991.

Kokusai kyōryoku jigyōdan chiīkika, *Tanzania: keizai gijutsu kyōryoku*, Tokyo, Kokusai kyōryoku shuppankai, 1988.

Kokusai kyōryoku jigyōdan kokusai kyōryoku sōgo kenshūjo, *Kaihatsu tōjō gijutsu jōhō dētā shoito tanzania(1/2), kaihatsu enjo gijitsu dēta*, Tokyo, Kokusai kyōryoku shuppankai, 1990.

Komiya Ryutarō and Itoh Motoshige, 'Japan's International Trade and Trade Policy, 1955–1984', in Inoguchi Takashi and D. Okimoto (eds.), *The Political Economy of Japan, vol. 2: The Changing International Context*, Stanford, Stanford University Press, 1988, pp. 174–224.

Krause, L.B. and J.S. Nye, 'Reflections on the Economics and Politics of International Economic Organizations', in C.F. Bergsten and L.B. Krause (eds.), *World Politics and International Economics*, Washington, DC., Brookings Institute, 1975, pp. 323–342.

Kuroda Yasumasa, 'The Oil Crisis and Japan's Middle East Policy, 1973', *Annals of Japan Association for Middle East Studies*, vol. 1, 1986, pp. 150–187.

Landgren, Singe, *Embargo Disimplemented: South Africa's Military Industry*, Oxford, Oxford University Press, 1989.

Lee, Chung H., 'Direct Foreign Investment, Structural Adjustment, and International Division of Labour: A Dynamic Macroeconomic Theory of Direct Foreign Investment', *Hitotsubashi Journal of Economics*, vol. 31, 1990, pp. 61–72.

Leffler, Mervin P., *A Preponderance of Power: National Security, the Truman Administration, and the Cold War*, Stanford, Stanford University Press, 1992.

Letter from Ambassador Okamoto Suemasa (The Hague) to Foreign Minister Shigemitsu Mamoru, 18 January 1955 (Gaikō shiryōkan: ajia–afurika kaigi e no nihon no sanka mondai, B6.1.0.24–1.B–0049. Letter in Japanese).

Letter from Consulate General Wajima Eiji (Jakarta) to Ambassador Shigemitsu Mamoru, 5 January 1955 (Gaikō shiryōkan: ajia–afurika kaigi e no nihon no sanka mondai, B6.1.0.24–1.B–0049. Letter in Japanese).

Letter from Foreign Minister Shigemitsu Mamoru to Ambassador Iguchi Sadao, 4 January 1955 (Gaikō shiryōkan: ajia–afurika kaigi e no nihon no sanka mondai, B6.1.0.24–1.B–0049. Letter in Japanese).

Letter from Foreign Minister Shigemitsu Mamoru to Ambassador Yamagata Kiyoshi, 17 December 1954 (Gaikō shiryōkan: ajia–afurika kaigi e no nihon no sanka mondai, B6.1.0.24–1.B–0049. Letter in Japanese).

Letter from Shigemitsu Mamoru to Takasaki Tatsunosuke, 15 April 1955 (Gaikō shiryōkan: nihon seifu daihyo ni taisuru kunrei, B6.1.0.24–1.B–0049. Letter in Japanese).

Lijphart, Arend, 'The Analysis of Bloc Voting in the General Assembly: A Critique and a Proposal', *The American Political Science Review*, vol. lvii, no.4, December, 1963, pp. 902–917.

Lipton, Merle, *Capitalism and Apartheid: South Africa, 1910–1986*, Aldershot, Wildwood House, 1986.

Liska, George, 'Alignments and Realignments', in G. Liska, *Nations in Alliance: The Limits of Interdependence*, Baltimore, The Johns Hopkins Press, 1962, pp. 12–60.

Louis, Roger, *Imperialism at Bay, 1941–1945: The United States and the Decolonization of the British Empire*, Oxford, Oxford University Press, 1977.

Luard, Evan, *A History of the United Nations: The Age of Decolonization, 1955–1965. Vol. 2*, London, Macmillan, 1989.

Marsden, Keith and Theresa Belot, *Private Enterprise in Africa: Creating a Better Environment, World Bank Discussion Paper, No. 17*, Washington, D.C., 1988.

Maruyama Masao, *Thought and Behaviour in Modern Japanese Politics*, London, Oxford University Press, 1963.

Mason, R. Hal, 'A Comment on Professor Kojima's "Japanese Type Versus American Type of Technology Transfer"', *Hitotsubashi Journal of Economics*, vol. 20, 1980, pp. 42–52.

Matsumoto Saburō, 'Japan's Voting in the United Nations', in Itoh Hiroshi (ed.), *Japanese Politics – An Inside View: Readings from Japan*, Ithaca and London, Cornell University Press, 1973, pp. 188–209.

Maull, Hanns, *Raw Materials, Energy and Western Security,* London, Macmillan, 1984.

——, 'South Africa's Minerals: The Achilles' Heel of Western Economic Security?', *International Affairs*, no. 4, Autumn, 1986, pp. 619–626.

Mazrui, Ali, *Africa's International Relations: The Diplomacy of Dependency and Change*, London, Heinemann, 1977.

——, 'The United Nations and Some African Political Attitudes', *International Organization*, vol. xviii, 1964, pp. 499–542.

Meltzer, Ronald, 'Contemporary Security Dimensions of International Trade Relations', in Klaus Knorr and Frank N. Trager (eds.), *Economic Issues and National Security*, Kansas, University Press of Kansas, 1982, pp. 200–230.

Meyers, Benjamin D., 'African Voting in the United Nations General Assembly', *The Journal of Modern African Studies*, vol. 4, no. 2, 1966, pp. 213–227.

'Minister's African Tour "Fruitful"', *Bulletin of The Anglo-Japanese Economic Institute*, no. 104, November, 1974.

Ministry of Finance, *Annual Report of International Affairs*, Tokyo, 1991.

Ministry of Foreign Affairs, *Foreign Ministry Blue Book*, Tokyo, 1959.

——, *Japan's ODA, Annual Report, 1988*, Tokyo, Association for the Promotion of International Cooperation, 1989.

——, (UN Bureau), *Statements Delivered by Delegates of Japan During the XIIth Regular Session of the General Assembly*, Tokyo, 1958.

Moon, Bruce E., 'Consensus or Compliance? Foreign-policy Change and External Dependence', *International Organization*, vol. 39, no. 2, Spring, 1985, pp. 297–329.

Morikawa Jun, in *Afurika kenkyu*, no. 47, September, 1995, pp. 64–66.

——, 'The Anatomy of Japan's South African Policies', *The Journal of Modern African Studies*, vol. 22, no. 1, 1984, pp. 133–141.

——, *Minami afurika to nihon: kankei no rekishi, kōzō, kadai*, Tokyo, Dōbunkan, 1988.

——, 'The Myth and Reality of Japan's Relations with Colonial Africa, 1885–1960', *Journal of African Studies*, vol. 11, no. 1, Spring, 1985, pp. 39–46.

Morrison, Godfrey, 'Japan's Year in Africa, 1973–74, in Colin Legum et al. (eds.), *Africa Contemporary Record, Annual Survey and Documents*, London, Rex Collings, 1974, pp. A65-A68.

Mortimer, Robert A., *The Third World Coalition in International Politics*, London, Westview Press, 1984.

Mosley, Paul, *Foreign Aid: Its Defense and Reform*, Lexington, University of Kentucky Press, 1987.

Moss, Joanna and John Ravenhill, *Emerging Japanese Economic Influence in Africa: Implications for the United States*, Berkeley, Institute of International Studies (University of California), 1985.

Murakami Hyōe, *Japan: The Year of Trial, 1919–1952*, Tokyo, Kodansha International Ltd., 1983.

Murray-Brown, Jeremy, *Kenyatta*, New York, George Allen & Unwin, 1972.

Mushi, Samuel and K. Mathews (eds.), *Foreign Policy of Tanzania, 1961–1981: A Reader*, Dar es Salaam, Tanzania Publishing House, 1981.

Mwanguo, Peter, 'Tanzania Exports to Japan', paper delivered in Dar es Salaam, 11 April 1991.

Mwansasu, Bismarck and Cranford Pratt, 'Tanzania's Strategy for Transition to Socialism', in Mwansasu and Pratt, *Towards Socialism in Tanzania*, Dar es Salaam, Tanzania Publishing House, 1979, pp. 3–15

Naikaku kanbō naikaku shingishitsu, *Kokusai kokka nihon no sōgō anzen hoshō seisaku*, (Heiwa mondai kenkyūkai hōkokusho), Tokyo, Ōkurasho insatsukyoku, 1985.

——, *Sōgō anzen hoshō senryaku*, (Ōhira sōri no seisaku kenkyukai hōkokusho – 5) Tokyo, Ōkurashō insatsukyoku (3rd edition), 1985.

Nester, William, *Japan's Growing Power over East Asia and the World Economy: Ends and Means*, London, Macmillan, 1990.

Nicol, D., 'Africa and the USA in the United Nations', *The Journal of Modern African Studies*, vol. 16, no. 3, 1978, pp. 365–395.

Nigeria–Japan Economic Newsletter, Lagos, January, 1970.

Nihon yushutsu-nyu ginkō, *Chokusetsu tōshi no kisō to keiei no gurobaruka: chokusetsu tōshi mondai kenkyū kai hōseisho*, Tokyo, Kaigai tōshi kenkyūjo, 1991.

Nigeria–Japan Association, Notes on the first meeting of members of Nigeria–Japan Association and a delegation of Japan–Nigeria Association, Lagos, 4 October 1990.

Noguchi Yuichiro, 'Sōgo anzen hoshō kōzō e no gimon', *Sekai*, no. 420, November, 1980, pp. 198–206.

Nyerere, Julius, *Freedom and Socialism: A Selection from Writings and Speeches, 1965–1967*, London, Oxford University Press, 1969.

——, *Ujamaa: Essays on Socialism*, London, Oxford University Press, 1966.

O'Brien, Conor C., *To Katanga and Back*, London, Hutchinson, 1966.

Oda Hideo, 'Nihon no afurika seisaku: sono kōsatsu', in Kawabata Masahisa (ed.), *Afurika to nihon*, Tokyo, Keisō shobō, 1994, pp. 80–96.

Oda Hideo and Aoki Kazuyoshi, 'Japan and Africa: Beyond the Fragile Partnership', in Robert Ozaki and Walter Arnold (eds.), *Japan's Foreign Relations: A Global Search for Economic Security*, London, Westview Press, 1985.

Ogata Sadaka, 'The Business Community and Japanese Foreign Policy: Normalization of Relations with the People's Republic of China', in Robert Scalapino (ed.), *The Foreign Policy of Japan*, Berkeley, University of California Press, 1977.

——, 'Japan's United Nations Policy in the 1980s', *Asian Survey*, vol. xxvii, no. 9, September, 1987, pp. 957–972.

——, 'The United Nations and Japanese Diplomacy', *Japan Review of International Affairs*, Fall/Winter, 1990, pp. 141–165.

Ogley, R., 'Voting and Politics in the General Assembly', *International Relations*, vol. 2, no. 3, April, 1961, pp. 156–167, and 183.

Ohata Tokushiro, 'Japanese-Chinese Relations after the Second World War: From the end of the Pacific War to Normalization of Japanese–Chinese Relations in 1972', *Waseda Bulletin of Comparative Law*, vol. 6. pp. 1–14.

Ōhira Masayoshi, 'Diplomacy for Peace: The Aims of Japanese Foreign Policy', *International Affairs*, vol. 40, no. 3 July, 1964, pp. 391–396.

Okita Saburo, *The Development of Tanzania and Possibilities of Japanese Cooperation: With Special Reference to the Comprehensive Development of the Kilimanjaro Region*, Tokyo, International Development Center of Japan, 1971.

Ohta Masatoshi, 'For a Smaller Indian Ocean: Japan–South Africa Relations, their Past, Present and Future', *The Round Table*, no. 336, October, 1995, pp. 413–431.

Olusanya, G.O. and R.A. Akindele (eds.), *Nigeria's External Relations: The First Twenty-Five Years*, Ibadan, Ibadan University Press Ltd, 1986.

Oman, Charles, *New Forms of Investment in Developing Country Industries: Mining, Petrochemicals, Automobiles, Textiles, Food*, Paris, OECD, 1989.

Orr, Robert, 'The Aid Factor in US–Japan Relations', *Asian Survey*, vol. xxvii, No.1, July, 1988, pp. 740–756.

——, *The Emergence of Japanese Foreign Aid Power*, New York, Columbia University Press, 1990.

Owoeye, Jide, *Japan's Policy in Africa*, New York, The Edwin Mellen Press, 1992.

Ozaki, Robert and Walter Arnold (eds.), *Japan's Foreign Relations: A Global Search for Economic Security*, London, Westview Press, 1985.

Panekal, M. K., 'Dokuritsu no shōchō', *Sekai*, No.114, June, 1955, pp. 71–73.

Passin, Herbert, 'Socio-cultural Factors in the Japanese Perception of International Order', Japan Institute of International Affairs, *Annual Review*, no. 5, 1969/70, pp. 51–75.

Payne, Richard, *The Non-superpowers' South Africa Policies: Interests and Strategies*, Princeton, Princeton University Press, 1990, pp. xv–27.

Pempel, T. J., 'From Trade to Technology: Japan's Reassessment of Military Policies', *The Jerusalem Journal of International Relations*, vol. 12, no. 4, 1990, pp. 1–27.

Pfaltzgraff, Robert Jr., *Energy Issues and Alliance Relationship: The United States, Western Europe and Japan*, Cambridge, Institute for Foreign Policy Analysis, 1980.

Pinto, Brian, 'Nigeria During and After the Oil Boom: A Policy Comparison with Indonesia', *The World Bank Economic Review*, vol. 1, 1987, pp. 419–445.

Rai, Kul B., 'Foreign Policy and Voting in the UNGA', *International Organization*, vol. 26, no. 3. Summer, 1982, pp. 589–594.

——, 'UN Voting Data', *Journal of Conflict Resolution*, vol. 26, no. 1. March, 1982, pp. 188–192.

Reischauer, Edwin, 'The Broken Dialogue with Japan', *Foreign Affairs*, no. 1, October, 1960, pp. 11–26.

——, 'Their Special Strengths', *Foreign Policy*, no. 14, Spring, 1974, pp. 242–253.

Richardson, Neil, *Foreign Policy and Economic Dependence*, Austin, University of Texas Press, 1978.

——, 'Political Compliance and US Trade Dominance', *The American Political Science Review*, vol. 70, no. 4, December, 1976, pp. 1098–1109.

Rix, Alan, 'Dynamism, Foreign Policy and Trade Policy', in J. A. A. Stockwin et al. (eds.), *Dynamic and Immobilist Politics in Japan*, London, Macmillan, 1988, pp. 297–324.

——, 'Japan's Aid Foreign Policy: A Capacity for Leadership?', *Pacific Economic Papers*, no. 186, August, 1990, pp. 1–19.

——, 'Japan's Comprehensive Security and Australia', *Australian Outlook: The Australian Journal of International Relations*, vol. 41, no. 2, August, 1987, pp. 79–86.

——, *Japan's Economic Aid: Policymaking and Politics*, London, Croom Helm, 1980.

——, *Japan's Foreign Aid Challenge: Policy Reform and Aid Challenge*, London, Routledge, 1993.

Roberts, Adam and B. Kingsbury, *United Nations Divided World:The UN's Roles in International Relations*, Oxford, Clarendon Press, 1988.

Rogers, Barbara and Brian Bolton, *Sanctions Against South Africa: Exploding The Myths*, Manchester, Manchester Free Press, 1981.

Rosecrance, Richard, *The Rise of the Trading State: Commerce and Conquest in the Modern World*, New York, Basic Books, 1986.

Rosecrance, Richard and Jennifer Taw, 'Japan and the Theory of International Leadership', *World Politics*, vol. xlii, no. 2 January, 1990, pp. 184–209.

Roux, Edward, *Time Longer than Rope: A History of the Black Man's Struggle for Freedom in South Africa*, London, 1948.

Russell, John, 'Race and Reflexivity: The Black Other in Contemporary Japanese Mass Culture', *Cultural Anthropology*, vol. 6, no. 1, 1991, pp. 3–25.

Russell, Bruce, 'Dimensions of Resource Dependence: Some Elements of Rigor in Concept and Policy Analysis', *International Organization*, vol. 38, no. 3, Summer, 1984, pp. 481–499.

——, 'Security and the Resources Scramble: Will 1984 Be Like 1914?', *International Affairs*, Winter, 1981/82, pp. 42–58.

St. Jorre, J. de, 'The African Group: A New Political Realism', *Africa Report*, March–April, 1985, pp. 76–79.

Saitō Shizuo, 'The Evolution of Japan's United Nations Policy', *Japan Review of International Affairs*, Fall/Winter, 1989, pp. 186–206.

Samuels, Richard J., 'Consuming for Production: Japanese National Security, Nuclear-free Procurement, and the Domestic Economy', *International Organization*, vol. 43, no. 4 Autumn, 1989, pp. 625–646.

——,*The Business of the Japanese State: Energy Markets in Comparative and Historical Perspective*, Ithaca, Cornell University Press, 1987.

Satake Takanori, *Trends in Japan's Direct Investment Abroad in Fiscal Year 1988*, Tokyo, Research Institute of Overseas Investment, 1991, pp. 2–31.

——, 'Options for Japan's Security Policy and their Implications for US–Japan Relations', paper prepared for the International Conference on Japan and the US in the Emerging Pacific Basin Era, Tokyo, 27–28 October 1987.

Satō Seizaburō, 'The Foundations of Modern Japanese Foreign Policy', in Robert Scalapino (ed.), *The Foreign Policy of Modern Japan*, London, University of California Press, 1977, pp. 367–390.

Satō Yukio, *The Evolution of Japanese Security Policy*, London, The International Institute for Strategic Studies, 1982.

Satō Yurie and Ishizaki Eriko, 'Afurika to nihon', *Afurika repōto*, Tokyo, Ajia keizai kenkyūjo. no. 12, 1991, pp. 14–17.

Saxonhouse, Gary R., 'Comparative Advantage, Structural Adaptation, and Japanese Performance', in Inoguchi Takashi and D. Okimoto (eds.), *The Political Economy of Japan, vol. 2: The Changing International Context*, Stanford, Stanford University Press, 1986, pp. 225–248.

Shamuyarira, Nathan, *Liberation Movements in Southern Africa, The Eighth Annual Hans Wolff Memorial Lecture, 14 April, 1977*, Bloomington, Africa Studies Program, Indiana University Press, 1978.

Shibusawa Masahide, *Japan and the Asian Pacific Region*, London, Croom Helm, 1984.

Shimazu Naoko, 'The Japanese Attempt to Secure Racial Equality in 1919', *Japan Forum*, no. 1, April, 1989, pp. 93–100.

Shivji, Issa, *Class Struggles in Tanzania*, London, Heinemann Educational, 1976.

——, *The Silent Class Struggle*, Dar es Salaam, 1973.

Shū On Rai, 'Ware ware no unmei wa ware ware no te de, *Sekai*, no. 114, June, 1955, pp. 57–65.

Shūgiin kaigi roku, *Kampō*, no. 9, 23 February 1961.

Shultz, Charles, 'The Economic Content of National Security Policy', *Foreign Affairs*, vol. 53. no. 4, 1973, pp. 522–540.

Skocpol, Theda, *States and Social Revolution*, Cambridge, Cambridge University Press, 1979.

Soukup, James R., 'Japanese–African Relations: Problems and Prospects', *Asian Survey*, vol. 5, no. 7, July, 1965, pp. 333–340.

Steering Committee of the fifth Shimoda conference, 'The Present State of US–Japan Relations', Shimoda conference, 1981.

Stockwin, J.A.A., 'Dynamic and Immobilist Aspects of Japanese Politics', in J. A. A. Stockwin et al. (eds.), *Dynamic and Immobilist Politics in Japan*, London, Macmillan Press, 1988, pp. 1–21.

——, *Japan: Divided Politics in a Growth Economy*, London, Weidenfeld & Nicolson, 1982.

Stoessinger, John, *The Might of Nations*, New York, 1961.

Stultz, N.M., 'The Apartheid Issue at the General Assembly: Stalemate or Gathering Storm?' *African Affairs*, vol. 86, no. 342, January, 1987, pp. 25–45.

Taira Kōji, 'Colonialism in Foreign Subsidiaries: Lessons from Japanese Investment in Thailand', *Asian Survey*, vol. xx, 1980, pp. 373–396.

Talabi, James, 'On Japan and Nigeria', *Daily Times*, 11 August 1979, p. 3.

Tikhomirov, V.B., 'Quantitative Analysis of Voting Behaviour in the General Assembly: Who Voted With Whom Within the United Nations', project of the UNITAR Research Dept., Policy and Efficacy Studies, no. 2. New York, 1981.

Tomlin, B.W., 'Measurement Validation: Lessons from the Use and Misuse of the UN General Assembly Roll Call Votes', *International Organization*, vol. 39, no. 1. Winter, pp. 189–206, 1985.

Tōyō keizai, *Kaigai shinshutsu kigyō sōran*, Tokyo, Shinpōsha, 1980.

——, *Kaigai shinshutsu kigyō sōran*, Tokyo, Shinpōsha, 1982.

——, *Kaigai shinshutsu kigyō sōran*, Tokyo, Shinpōsha, 1986.

——, *Kaigai shinshutsu kigyō sōran*, Tokyo, Shinpōsha, 1991.

——, *Kaigai shinshutsu kigyō sōran*, Tokyo, Shinpōsha, 1992.

——, *Kaigai shinshutsu kigyo sōran*, Tokyo, Shinpōsha, 1993.

Tsūshō Sangyosho, *Tsūshō hakushō*, Tokyo, 1977.

Turner, L.C.F., 'The Crisis of Japanese Strategy, January–June 1942', *R.M.C Historical Journal*, vol. 1, March, 1972, pp. 3–14.

Twitchet, Kenneth J., 'Strategies for Security: Some Theoretical Considerations', in Kenneth J. Twitchet (ed.), *International Security: Reflections on Survival and Stability*, London, Oxford University Press, 1971, pp. 1–47.

Umemoto Tetsuya, 'Comprehensive Security and the Evolution of the Japanese Security Posture', in Robert A. Scalapino et al. (eds.), *Asian Security Issues: Regional and Global*, Berkeley, University of California Press, 1988, pp. 28–49.

United Nations, *Official Records of the General Assembly, 44th Session, Supplement No. 44(A/44/44)*, 31 October 1989.

United Nations Centre Against Apartheid, *Special Issue: Resolutions Adopted by the United Nations General Assembly on the Question of Apartheid, 1962–1986*, New York, United Nations, 1987.

Urano Tatsuo, *Kokusai shakai no henyō to kokuren tōhyō kōdō, 1946–85*, Tokyo, Kokusai chīki shiryo sentā, 1989.

Van Rensburg, W.C.J and D.A. Pretorius, *South Africa's Strategic Minerals: Pieces on a Continental Chess Board* (Helen Glen ed.), Johannesburg, Valiant, 1977.

Vernon, Raymond, *Two Hungry Giants: The United States and Japan in the Quest for Oil and Ores*, Cambridge, Harvard University Press, 1983.

Vernon, Raymond and Brian Levy, 'State-owned Enterprises in the World Economy: The Case of Iron Ore', in Leroy P. Jones et al. (eds.), *Public Enterprise in Less-developed Countries*, Cambridge, Cambridge University Press, 1982, pp. 169–216.

Vincent, Jack E., 'An Application of Attribute Theory to General Assembly Voting Patterns, and Some Implications', *International Organization*, vol. 26, no. 3, 1972, pp. 551–582.

——, 'Predicting Voting Patterns in the General Assembly', *The American Political Science Review*, vol. lxv, no. 2, June, 1971, pp. 471–498.

Waltz, Kenneth, *Theory of World Politics*, Reading, Mass., Addison-Wesley, 1979.

——, *Man, the State, and War*, New York, Columbia University Press, 1989.

Watanabe Akio, 'Japanese Public Opinion and Foreign Affairs, 1964–1973', in Scalapino, Robert (ed.), *The Foreign Policy of Modern Japan*, Berkeley, University of California Press, 1977, pp. 105–146.

Watanabe Osamu, *Kigyō shihai to kokka*, Tokyo, Aoki shoten, 1991.

——, *Sengo seijishi no naka no tennōsei*, Tokyo, Aoki shoten, 1990.

——, 'The Sociology of Jishuku and Kichō: The Death of the Shōwa Tennō as a Reflection of the Structure of Contemporary Japanese Society', *Japan Forum*, vol. 1 no. 2, October, 1989, pp. 275–289.

'Welcome Address' by the Director General of the Board of External Trade at the opening of the seminar on Promotion of Trade Between Tanzania and Japan, Kilimanjaro Hotel, 23 July 1987.

Welfield, John, *An Empire in Eclipse: Japan in the Postwar American Alliance System*, London, Athlone Press, 1988.

Williams, Gavin, 'The World Bank in Rural Nigeria, Revisited: A Review of the World Bank's Nigeria: Agricultural Sector Review 1987', *Review of African Political Economy*, no. 43, 1988, pp. 42–67.

Wolfe-Phillips, Leslie, 'Why Third World?', *Third World Quarterly*, vol. 1, no. 1. January, 1979, pp. 105–116.

Wolfers, Arnold, 'National Security as an Ambiguous Symbol', *Discord and Collaboration*, Baltimore, Johns Hopkins University Press, 1962, pp. 147–165.

World Bank, *Accelerated Development in sub-Saharan Africa, 1981*, Washington, DC., 1981.

——, *Nigeria: Industrial Sector Report. Restructuring Policies for Competitiveness and Export Growth, vol. II, Main Report*, Washington, DC., 13 July 1990.

——, *Tanzania. Agricultural Sector Report*, Washington, DC., 1983.

Worsley, Peter, 'How Many Worlds?', *Third World Quarterly*, vol. 1, no. 2, April, 1979, pp. 100–108.

Yanaihara Katsu, 'Japanese Overseas Enterprises in Developing Countries Under Indigenization Policy: The African Case', *Japanese Economic Studies*, vol. 4, no. 1, 1975, pp. 23–51.

Yasutomo, Dennis, 'Why Aid? Japan as an Aid Great Power', *Pacific Affairs*, vol. 62, no. 4, Winter, 1989/90, pp. 490–503.

Yergin, Daniel, *Shattered Peace: The Origins of the Cold War and the National Security State*, Boston, Houghton Mifflin, 1977.

Yoshida Masao, 'Minami afurika kyōwakoku kara no tōmorokoshi yunyū no mondai', *Afurika repōto*, No.8, March, 1989, pp. 46–48.

Yoshida Masao, 'Nihon no keizai enjo ni okeru afurika', in Suzuki Nagatoshi (ed.), *Nihon no keizai kyōryoku no ashidori*, Tokyo, Ajia keizai shuppankai, 1989, pp. 162–184.

Yoshida Shigeru, 'Japan and the Crisis in Asia', *Foreign Affairs*, vol. 29, no. 2, 1951, pp. 171–181.

Yoshitsu, Michael, *Caught in the Middle East: Japan's Diplomacy in Transition*, Toronto, Lexington Books, 1984.

——, *Japan and the San Francisco Peace Settlement*, New York, Columbia University Press, 1983.

INTERVIEWS

Amissah, James L. M. (Ghanaian Ambassador to Japan), interview, 25 September 1991.

Ayoola, M.B. (Director) Japan External Trade Organization, Lagos office, interview, 21 August 1991.

Chikano, A. (The President's Office, Tanzania) Civil Service, Foreign Recruitment Section, interview, 16 April 1991.

Hidaka T. (Managing Director) JGC Nigeria Ltd., interview, 22 August 1991.

Iida Yōsuke (Senior Staff, Energy and Chemical Project Department) Marubeni Corporation, interview, August 1991.

Ishihara Kenichi (Director/General Manager) Chiyoda Nigeria Ltd, interview, 20 August 1991.

Kanai Seiichi (Director, Third Regional Division: Africa, Middle East, East Europe – Planning Department, Japan International Cooperation Agency [JICA]), interview, 3 November 1991.

Lungu, Luchibhikiye, L. (Senior Finance Officer, Ministry of Finance, Tanzania), interview, 8, 12 and 16 April 1991.

Matsila, Jerry (Africa National Congress [ANC] Chief Representative to Japan) interview, 23 September 1991.

Msoffe, R.H.T. (Assistant Director, Japan International Cooperation Agency [JICA], Tanzania), interview, 10 April 1991.

Mwandanji, K. K. (Ministry of Foreign Affairs [Asia Division]; (on a posting to Japan from 1984 to 1990), interview, 10 April 1991.

Osanai Takashi (First Secretary to the United Nations Japan Mission, New York), interview, 10 November 1989.

Saitō Kōji (Economic Attaché, Embassy of Japan, Tanzania) interview, 10 and 15 April 1991.

Takaoka Masato (Deputy Director, Second Africa Divison [Middle Eastern and African Affairs Bureau] Ministry of Foreign Affairs) interview, 30 September 1991.

Tsutsui Noboru (Deputy Director of Japan International Cooperation Agency; Director of Japan Overseas Cooperation Volunteers, Tanzania), interview, 9 April 1991.

Yamamoto Yoshimichi (Managing Director [Mitusi & Co. Division] MBK Nigeria Ltd.), interview, 20 August 1991.

Yoshino Kyoji (Second Secretary, Economic Attaché) Embassy of Japan, South Africa, interview, 23 January 1995.

Zulu, Boniface S. (Zambian Ambassador to Japan), interview, 24 September 1991.

Index